Contents

KV-198-560

One

The financial reporting framework

Syllabus

This chapter relates to syllabus Section 1: The Financial Reporting Framework. It focuses on the objectives of financial statements, the user groups who are intended to benefit from such statements, and the major concepts and principles underpinning such statements.

Objectives

After studying this chapter you should be able to:

♦ describe the objectives of financial statements;
♦ identify user groups and their information needs;
♦ explain accounting policies and their origins;
♦ describe the need for a conceptual framework and the IASB's *Framework for the Preparation and Presentation of Financial Statements*
♦ understand the principles behind the recognition of assets and liabilities;
♦ distinguish between alternative valuation bases (historic cost, current cost, market value and present value); and
♦ explain concepts of capital maintenance and the unit of measurement chosen.

1.1   The financial reporting framework

Financial statements

Financial statements are the 'accounts' of an organization – its balance sheet, profit and loss account, and so on. They show the financial position of the organization at a particular time, and give a financial picture of its activities over a period of time.

(a) All businesses, even sole traders, need to prepare accounts regularly, even if only to comply with tax law.

(b) Limited companies are required by law to prepare and publish financial statements annually. In the UK this is a requirement of the Companies Act 1985 (CA 1985).

The rules are more stringent for limited companies because such organizations are owned by shareholders who are typically not involved in the actual management of the company. The managers are therefore required to 'account' for how they have used the money provided by shareholders.

'Publish' simply means that the financial statements must be sent to all shareholders and must also (in the UK, for example) be submitted to Companies House, which makes them available to any other member of the public who wants to look at them, such as people who are considering investing in shares in a company. Most major companies go further and produce a glossy brochure that includes large amounts of both statutory and non-statutory information about their activities.

A complete set of financial statements consists of some items that will be familiar from your earlier studies and some that may not.

(a) Balance Sheet

(b) Income Statement (ie the Profit and Loss Account)

(c) Statement of Changes in Equity (in the UK presently called the Statement of Total Recognized Gains and Losses)

(d) Cash Flow Statement

(e) Notes explaining all the above in more detail, as appropriate

Basic format of accounts: the Companies Act 1985

In the UK the Companies Act 1985 (CA 1985), together with the Companies Act 1989 (CA 1989), specifies the basic form that company accounts and group accounts must take and what their content must include. Both of these Acts implement European Directives on the format for the published accounts of limited companies, and therefore the basic format is standardized by law throughout the EU.

The Companies Act includes some, but by no means comprehensive, detailed accounting requirements. For example, it gives a detailed format for the balance sheet and profit and loss account but gives no guidance on the cash flow statement, which both UK and international accounting standards (see below) declare to be one of the key components of a complete set of financial statements.

Where accounting requirements in the Companies Act conflict with those of an accounting standard, the **accounting standard** takes precedence. This is because the overriding requirement of the Companies Act is to give a 'true and fair view' and it is held that compliance with the standards will give a true and fair view unless the circumstances are exceptional.

It has been suggested that it is not appropriate for company law to contain specific accounting requirements – that it is more appropriate for them to be covered by accounting standards. On the other hand recent regulations issued under the Companies Act 1985 include detailed disclosure rules for directors' remuneration (2002) and at the time of writing (mid-2004) there are draft regulations requiring companies to present an 'Operating and Financial Review', again with very specific requirements for disclosures. Both of these measures are responses to concerns that have arisen in recent years (following well-publicized accounting 'scandals' such as that involving Enron) over corporate governance.

Listed companies and the Listing Rules

A company whose shares are traded on a market such as the London Stock Exchange is known as a 'quoted' or a 'listed' company. Shares traded on the main London market must be included in an 'Official List' of securities. Shares are accepted onto the Official List by a department of the Financial Services Authority, called the UK Listing Authority (UKLA). Almost all of the companies that you hear about in the news from day to day (Marks and Spencer, British Telecom, and so on) are listed companies, although there are one or two notable exceptions such as Virgin.

To obtain and maintain a listing for its securities, a company must comply with regulations contained in the Listing Rules issued by the UK Listing Authority. These include requirements concerning the disclosure of accounting information which are more extensive than the disclosure requirements of the Companies Acts. For example, listed companies must produce and publish half-yearly accounts as well as annual accounts. The Listing Rules also require a listed company to include with its financial statements explanations of various matters relating to corporate governance.

Accounting standards

As mentioned above CA 1985 also requires all companies (listed or otherwise) to comply with accounting standards that are issued by a regulatory body for the accounting profession. Accounting standards set out in detail how certain items in the financial statements are to be calculated and presented.

The body issuing regulatory standards in the UK is the Accounting Standards Board, or ASB, and since 1990 this body has issued its own financial Reporting Standards (FRSs) and administered the previous regime of standards (Statements of Standard Accounting Practice or SSAPs).

In March 2002, however, the European Council of Ministers agreed that the 9,000 or so listed European companies must adopt the standards of the International Accounting Standards Board (IASB). These include the IASB's own standards, which are called International Financial Reporting Standards (IFRSs), and also the standards issued by its predecessor up to 2001, known as International Accounting Standards (IASs). This applies for financial years starting on or after 1 January 2005.

In August 2002, the UK Department of Trade and Industry (DTI) set in motion processes to extend the use of International Financial Reporting Standards in the UK beyond listed companies. The ASB is therefore conducting a phased replacement of existing UK standards with new UK standards that have been aligned with the international version. Recent examples in 2004 are FRS 20 *Share-based payment*, which is identical to IFRS 2, and FRS 21 *Events after the balance sheet date*, which implements IAS 10.

At the time of publication of this book (Autumn 2004), therefore, the financial reporting framework for all UK companies, and particularly listed companies, is in a significant state of change.

Framework for the Preparation and Presentation of Financial Statements

The IASB's *Framework for the Preparation and Presentation of Financial Statements* describes the basic concepts according to which financial statements are prepared and it is the subject of most of the rest of this chapter. The Framework was most recently revised in December 2003.

After an introduction covering users of accounts, the framework has the following sections:

- the objective of financial statements;
- underlying assumptions;
- qualitative characteristics of financial statements;
- the elements of financial statements;
- recognition of the elements of financial statements;

- measurement of the elements of financial statements;
- concepts of capital and capital maintenance.

1.2 Users and their information needs

According to your syllabus 'the underpinning conceptual framework' for the Financial Reporting and Analysis (FRAA) module is that of 'decision usefulness'. In other words: 'the primary purpose of … financial reporting is that of providing useful economic related information to the stakeholders of enterprises.'

Therefore we need to be clear as to who these 'stakeholders' or 'users' are and what 'economic-related information' they might need.

These matters are addressed right at the start of the IASB's Framework. Users are identified as follows:

- investors (existing and potential shareholders);
- employees;
- lenders;
- suppliers and other trade creditors;
- customers;
- the government;
- the public.

Shareholders and potential shareholders need information in order to decide whether they should risk buying or selling the company's shares and how to vote at the company's annual general meeting. In order to make these decisions they need information on the company's performance and on its dividend policy.

Employees require information on the security of their employment and on their likely future wage levels, retirement benefits and so on.

Lenders will be concerned with the safety of their interest payments and the future repayment of their capital. They will therefore need to know the company's recent cash flows and the likely future cash flows.

Suppliers need to know that they will be paid and perhaps that the company will be a reliable long-term customer.

Customers need to know that their supplies will continue and that the company will not cease to trade.

The government, in addition to possibly being a customer or supplier of the company, takes an interest in:

(a) the current and prospective contribution of the company to the economic well-being and employment in the area/country;

(b) the ability of the company to pay taxes;

(c)   the company's compliance with company and tax law.

The public may have wide and varied requirements: some will be interested in the contribution that the organization makes to the local economy; others will have environmental or social concerns, and so on.

The Framework acknowledges that although the information needs of all users cannot be met there are needs that are common for all users. These needs will usually be met if the financial statements meet the needs of the providers of risk capital to the enterprise.

1.3   The objective of financial statements

The Framework states that:

'The objective of financial statements is to provide information about the financial position, performance and changes in financial position of an entity that is useful to a wide range of users in making economic decisions.'

It then goes on to emphasize the ways financial statements provide information about the financial position and performance of an enterprise. The main elements that affect the position and performance of a company are:

(a)   the economic resources it controls;

(b)   its financial structure;

(c)   its liquidity and solvency;

(d)   its ability to adapt to changes in its environment.

The importance of these elements and their disclosure is stressed and the point is made that the component parts of the financial statements (balance sheet, income statement, statement of changes in equity and cash flow statement) are interrelated because they reflect different aspects of the same transactions.

1.4   Underlying assumptions

This section of the IASB Framework deals with two concepts that should be familiar from your earlier studies. These both also appear in the Companies Act 1985, where they are referred to as fundamental 'accounting principles'.

Accrual basis

Financial statements are prepared on the accrual basis: the effects of transactions and other events are recognized when they occur, rather than when cash or its equivalent is received or paid, and they are reported in the financial statements of the periods to which they relate.

This means that users are aware not only of what has happened in the past but also what cash obligations the company has and what cash resources are receivable in the future.

Going concern

The going concern concept assumes that the entity will continue in operational existence for the foreseeable future. In other words it assumes that the company has no intention of ceasing or curtailing its operations, and does not have any need to do so.

The point here is that if the entity were not intending to carry on operating, or was not able to for some reason, that would have a significant impact on the values that should be stated in the financial statements. It might have to sell all its inventory for much less then it could have sold it otherwise; it would probably have to find the money to compensate its redundant employees. These are expenses and liabilities that do not need to be recognized if it is assumed that the company is a going concern.

Only two?

You may be aware from past studies that the Companies Act 1985 also identifies 'prudence' and 'consistency' as fundamental accounting principles. This was in line with the accounting standards that were current back in 1985.

As we shall see in a moment, in the IASB Framework prudence is regarded as one of several aspects of 'reliability', and consistency as an aspect of 'comparability'.

1.5 Qualitative characteristics of financial statements

As already noted users need useful information, and 'qualitative characteristics' are the attributes of economic-related information that make it useful.

The Framework identifies four main attributes:

♦ understandability;
♦ relevance;

♦ reliability;
♦ comparability.

Understandability

The information should be readily understandable, given that users are assumed to have 'reasonable' knowledge of business and accounting and to be willing to study the information with 'reasonable diligence'.

Relevance

Information in financial statements is relevant when it influences the economic decisions of users. It may do this by helping them to evaluate past, present, or future events or by confirming or correcting past evaluations they may have made.

Materiality is a component of relevance. Information is material if its omission or misstatement could influence the economic decisions of users.

♦ If the financial statements contained a large amount of small inconsequential items these could easily conceal the larger more significant items. Therefore only items of significance need to be highlighted or disclosed separately.

♦ Although materiality is usually taken to refer to the quantitative measure – ie how big the amount is – it should also encompass the qualitative measure of what kind of transaction is involved. For example, if a company were fined for restrictive trade practices, the fine should probably be disclosed separately because of the nature of the event, even if the amount would not normally meet the size criterion applied for materiality.

Timeliness is identified as a possible constraint on relevance. To be useful, information must be provided to users within the time period in which it is most likely to bear on their decisions.

Reliability

Users must have confidence that the figures and information are accurate and complete, and that they are neutral – in other words, free from bias.

Sometimes information that is relevant cannot be recognized in the accounts reliably. For example, if a company were disputing a legal claim against it for damages it would be inappropriate to recognize the amount in its accounts (this could be construed as admitting liability). The usual procedure in these circumstances is to disclose the full amount of the claim and explain the circumstances. Remember that users are expected to be 'reasonably diligent' when studying the financial statements.

Substance over form requires that the economic substance of a transaction be reported as opposed to its legal form. For example, under a hire purchase agreement, the legal title to the asset does not pass until the final payment is made; the economic reality is not that the asset was hired until the last payment was made, but that the asset was purchased using loan finance. The transaction is therefore reported in the financial statements as such with the asset being included in the balance sheet and depreciated. The loan is shown as a liability and the implicit rate of interest is charged to the profit and loss account.

Reliability is affected by the use of estimates and by uncertainties associated with items recognized and measured in financial statements. For example the company cannot know for sure in advance that all its debts will be paid, or precisely what the useful life of its machinery will be. These uncertainties are dealt with, in part, by disclosure and, in part, by being 'prudent' when preparing financial statements. **Prudence** means that a degree of caution should be exercised when making the estimates required, so that assets or income are not overstated and liabilities or expenses are not understated, bearing in mind the need for neutrality.

Comparability

Users must be able to compare the financial statements of a company over time so that they can identify trends in its financial position and performance. Users must also be able to compare the financial statements of different companies. There must therefore be **consistency** of accounting treatment of like items within each accounting period and from one period to the next. Disclosure of accounting policies is essential for comparability.

Truth and fairness

The Companies Act 1985 requires that, above all, a company's financial statements should give 'a true and fair view' of the company's state of affairs. The IASB Framework also refers to this phrase, although it does not attempt to deal directly with the concepts of truth and fairness.

In UK company law there is no precise definition of what 'true and fair' means. This is quite deliberate since it is felt that, once defined, some companies would attempt to comply with the letter of the definition rather than the spirit of the concepts.

For practical purposes, though, a company's financial statements give a true and fair view when:

(a)   the requirements of company law are complied with;

(b)   all applicable accounting standards have been complied with;

(c)   if no accounting standard is available, accepted industry accounting principles are followed;

(d)   all material items have been adequately disclosed; and

(e)   the presentation of the accounts is appropriate with regard to the information needed by the users of those accounts.

Since presenting a true and fair view is the most important requirement in the Companies Act 1985, it is permitted in law, on the very rare occasions where circumstances demand it, to ignore other, more specific, requirements of the Companies Act or accounting standards. If a company does this, however, it must still disclose the full circumstances.

1.6   The elements of financial statements

The IASB identifies five 'elements' of financial statements:

- ♦ elements related to financial position (balance sheet):
  - – assets;
  - – liabilities;
  - – equity;
- ♦ elements related to performance (income statement):
  - – income;
  - – expenses.

This covers all the elements in the complete financial statements because the cash flow statement and the statement of changes in equity reflect both income statement elements and changes in balance sheet elements.

All of these elements will be explored in much greater depth in later chapters, so we shall just give the basic explanations and some simple examples here.

Asset

An asset is a resource controlled by the enterprise as a result of past events and from which future economic benefits are expected to flow to the enterprise.

Trade debtors are the obvious example: they result from sales that have been made in the past. Economic benefits will flow to the enterprise in the future, when the debtors pay up. A machine in a factory is another example: the company bought it in the past and expects to use it in the future to make things that can then be sold.

Liability

A liability is a present obligation of the enterprise arising from past events, the settlement of which is expected to result in an outflow from the enterprise of resources embodying economic benefits.

Trade creditors are the obvious example here.

Equity

Equity is the residual interest in the assets of the enterprise after deducting all its liabilities.

This is what is due to the owners of the company: at its simplest that means the share capital plus any retained earnings.

Income

Income is increases in economic benefits during the accounting period in the form of inflows or enhancements of assets or decreases of liabilities that result in increases in equity, other than those relating to contributions from equity participants.

Income includes both revenue and gains. Revenue is referred to by a variety of different names depending on the type of business such as sales, fees, interest, dividends, royalties, rent, and so on. An example of a gain might be an increase in the value of an asset such as a building.

Expense

Expenses are decreases in economic benefits during the accounting period in the form of outflows or depletions of assets or liabilities incurred that result in decreases in equity, other than those relating to distributions to equity participants.

Expenses include both expenses that arise in the course of the ordinary activities of the organization such as the purchase of items for resale or wages expenses, and losses that arise, perhaps, as a result of a decline in value of an asset.

1.7 Recognition of the elements of financial statements

Recognition of an element means that a value is included for that element in the balance sheet or income statement.

The IASB Framework explains when this should be done.

An element should only be recognized when:

- ◆ it is probable that any future economic benefit associated with the item will flow to or from the enterprise;
  AND
- ◆ the item's cost or value can be measured with reliability.

Trade debtors again provide a good and simple example. It is probable that most of them will pay up and it is known reliably how much they will pay. There will probably be a few who do not pay the full amount or do not pay at all. Through no fault of its own the company cannot be sure, at the time of preparation of the financial statements, exactly who will and who will not pay up, nor what the extent of non-payment will be. The company is likely, however, to be able to make a reasonable estimate based on past experience.

The financial statements should therefore recognize the full amount due from trade debtors in the income element (eg $100m) but they will also include (as an expense element) any change needed in the provision for bad debts (eg $10m). The trade debtors part of the asset element will be reduced by the amount of the probable shortfall so only the net amount will be recognized (in this case $(100 − 10)m = $90m).

In other words recognition follows the accruals concept.

- ◆ Recognition of income should occur simultaneously with the recognition of increases in assets or decreases in liabilities.
- ◆ Recognition of expenses should occur simultaneously with the recognition of an increase in liabilities or a decrease in assets.

Again, we are just scratching the surface of this topic for the time being: later chapters will go into much more detail and more complex cases.

1.8 Measurement of the elements of financial statements

Measurement is the process of assigning the monetary amounts at which the elements of the financial statements are recognized and reported in the financial statements.

The Framework acknowledges that a variety of measurement bases are used today to different degrees and in varying combinations in financial statements, including the following.

- *Historical cost*: assets or liabilities are recorded at the transaction cost – the amount of cash or cash equivalents paid at the time of the transaction.
- *Current cost*: assets or liabilities are recorded at the amount of cash or cash equivalents that would have to be paid if they were acquired or settled now.
- *Realizable (settlement) value*: assets are recorded at the amount of cash or cash equivalents that could be obtained by selling them now (which may not be the same as current cost). Likewise would have to be paid if they were acquired or settled now.
- *Present value*: assets and liabilities are recorded at the present discounted value of the future net cash inflows or outflows that will be received or paid.

Historical cost is the measurement basis most commonly used today, but it is usually combined with other measurement bases for certain items. For instance inventories are usually recorded at the lower of cost and net realizable value. If the company invests some of its cash in a portfolio of shares (not so many shares that it actually controls the companies it owns shares in) then these would be recorded at their market value at the date of the financial statements, not at the date when they were bought. Pension liabilities are recorded at their present value.

1.9   Concepts of capital and capital maintenance

Accounts are usually prepared on a historic cost basis, but in times of rising prices the accruals concept means that yesterday's costs are deducted from today's revenues. The profit is therefore overstated in times of inflation, and if it is distributed by way of dividend payments this would deplete the capital of the business in 'real' terms.

The Framework concludes with a discussion of capital and capital maintenance. It observes that most entities adopt a 'financial' concept of capital under which capital is synonymous with the net assets or equity of the business.

An alternative is a 'physical' concept of capital. Under this concept a profit is earned only if the 'physical productive capacity' (in other words the ability of the business to operate) at the end of the period is greater than at the beginning, after excluding any distributions to or contributions from the owners during the period.

An example will make this clear. Say a trader sets up in business selling caravans. He has $10,000 initial capital and uses it to purchase his first caravan, which he sells three months later for $15,000. At the time of the sale it would cost the trader $11,000 to buy another caravan for resale.

It would appear that the trader has made $5,000 profit. If, however, he were to withdraw this amount from the business he would be unable to continue trading as there would be insufficient funds available to purchase a further caravan for resale.

The trader has made a 'holding gain' by owning the caravan while its price rose. We can draw up a trading account identifying the profit that can safely be distributed as follows:

	$	$
Sale proceeds		15,000
Historic cost		10,000
Historic cost profit		5,000
Less holding gain:		
Replacement cost	11,000	
Historic cost	(10,000)	
		(1,000)
Operating gain		4,000

The operating gain can be withdrawn from the business without impairing its operating capacity.

In current cost accounting the holding gain of $1,000 would normally be transferred to a capital maintenance reserve.

Historic cost maintains a business's capital only in nominal pounds and this fails to protect the business's operating capacity in times of rising prices. Modified historic cost accounts, where fixed assets such as buildings are revalued, are widely used and give useful information but they make no adjustment to profit in respect of holding gains.

Adjusted historic cost accounts (also known as current purchasing power or CPP accounts) recognize the change in the level of prices. The historic cost accounts are adjusted to reflect the change in the general level of prices. The financial statements are restated in terms of the value of money as at the business's year end.

The capital at the start of the year is maintained in terms of 'real' pounds. For example, assume that Alpha Ltd made a historic cost profit of $20,000 and that its opening capital was $100,000. During the year the general level of prices rose 5%. In order to maintain the company's capital $100,000 x 5% must be transferred to the capital maintenance reserve, increasing the non-distributable capital to $105,000.

The adjusted historic cost profit would be:

	$
Historic cost profit	20,000
Less: transfer to capital maintenance reserve	5,000
	15,000

Although adjusted historic cost accounts have the virtue of relative simplicity and are objectively based on historic cost accounts they do not necessarily lead to the business maintaining its operating capacity. The assets the business uses and goods it trades may be increasing in price at a rate different from the general increase in prices.

Replacement cost accounting is an attempt to overcome this drawback. The business's assets are valued at their replacement cost. Thus the holding gains on individual assets are recognized and retained in the business. Often specific price indices are used for groups of assets to reduce the work involved in obtaining the relevant replacement costs.

The use of replacement costs does have the following disadvantages:

- ◆ the replacement costs can be subjective;
- ◆ technological change may mean that the asset is obsolete;
- ◆ the business may not intend to replace the asset;
- ◆ replacement cost accounts are difficult for users to understand.

An alternative is to measure the business' capital using the net realizable value (NRV), or exit value, of its assets. The net realizable value of an asset is the cash that would be obtained if an asset were sold, ie the sale proceeds less the costs incurred in making the sale.

Current cost accounts using exit values recognize holding gains on the assets in the same way as entry values. The use of exit values has practical problems due to the difficulty of obtaining realizable values. Consequently it can be highly subjective, and on a theoretical basis it would seem to be contrary to the going concern concept.

It does have the following advantages, however:

- ◆ it recognizes the opportunity cost of holding the assets;
- ◆ the asset values are realistic and easy to understand;
- ◆ exit values are currently applied in practice to some extent (monetary assets, inventory, land and buildings).

Valuing assets using the net present value of the receipts they will generate is theoretically the most accurate method of measuring capital; the difficulty in estimating these future cash flows makes it impractical in most instances.

Adjusted historic cost accounts maintain the owner's purchasing power and this is known as the proprietary concept. The maintenance of the business's purchasing power, or operating capacity, is known as the entity concept.

In the UK the first standard dealing with changing prices proposed a system of adjusted historic cost accounts (*Current Purchasing Power*). This was widely criticized and was open to the theoretical objection that it failed to maintain a company's operating capacity.

A second standard, SSAP16, was issued requiring the use of current costs. This was very complicated, widely ignored, and subsequently abandoned.

International standards have had a similar fate. IAS 6 *Accounting Responses to Changing Prices* issued in 1977 was the first attempt but in 1981 it was replaced by IAS 15 *Information Reflecting the Effects of Changing Prices*. This became optional in 1989, and in December 2003 the IASB announced that IAS 15 was to be withdrawn with effect from 1 January 2005.

At the time when these standards were issued inflation levels were considerably higher than they are today. Low and stable rates of inflation in most developed economies mean that the issue has gone away for the time being. On the other hand technological change and diversification by businesses in recent years has again focused attention on adjusted historic cost accounts in some quarters. Specific price increases have less relevance because assets currently in use no longer have equivalent replacements available. It is also possible to compare one year with another using adjusted historic cost accounts, whereas this is not possible with current cost accounts.

We have dealt with this topic at some length here, not because it is especially important relative to other topics in this chapter but because it is the one topic in this chapter that we shall not mention again in the remainder of this book.

1.10 Standard-setting and the IASB

Standards are needed for a number of reasons, and new standards or revisions to existing standards are also a necessity.

- ♦ There are often many different ways of accounting for transactions. Even after considering all the principles outlined in this chapter the preparer of accounts may still be left with a number of choices. In the absence of standards the preparer of accounts is likely to choose the method that gives the most favourable view of the transaction in question, and this may mislead users.
- ♦ The world is constantly changing. For instance a few years ago nobody would have dreamt that there would be a need for accounting rules on how to account for transactions relating to an (arguable) asset such as a company's website if it should be regarded as an asset after all.
- ♦ The world of finance in particular has been prolific in recent years in inventing new ways of managing the financial affairs of large companies and handling financial risk – interest rate swaps, swaptions and so on are examples of brand-new financial instruments that were not even envisaged when many current standards were drawn up, but may now represent massive figures in the accounts of many large companies.

As we have seen, the objective of financial statements is to provide information that is useful to users in making economic decisions, and those decisions will often involve a comparison of one company with others – and the others may be anywhere in the world.

If there were no standards, comparison would be impossible because there would be no way for users to know whether they were comparing like with like.

The IASB organization

The International Accounting Standards Board was formed in 2001, and that makes it a relative newcomer to the standards-setting world, but really it has a much longer history. It replaced a body known as the International Accounting Standards Committee. This was originally founded in 1973 as a result of an agreement by accountancy bodies in countries such as the UK, the USA, France, Germany and Japan.

National standard-setting bodies sprang up at about the same time. During the 1960s there were a number of scandals as apparently healthy companies collapsed. This led to a call for a tighter accounting regime where company accounts would be properly comparable and the choice of accounting treatments would be less subjective.

What we are calling the IASB is made up of a number of bodies.

The International Accounting Standards Committee Foundation (IASCF)

The IASB organization as a whole is ultimately governed by an organization called the International Accounting Standards Committee Foundation (IASCF). This body appoints the members of the IASB, the International Financial Reporting Interpretations Committee and the Standards Advisory Council. Its functions include conducting an annual review of the strategy of IASB and its effectiveness, approving budgets, and so on, but it does not set standards.

The International Accounting Standards Board (IASB)

The International Accounting Standards Board is based in London and is currently chaired by Sir David Tweedie, former chairman of the UK standard-setting body, the Accounting Standards Board (ASB). It has the responsibility for setting new 'International Financial Reporting Standards' (IFRSs) and for amending the existing International Accounting Standards (IASs) if it is deemed necessary. There are 14 Board Members representing 'the best available combination of technical skills and background experience of relevant international business and market conditions'.

The IASB has a number of ongoing projects at any one time. New standards and amendments to existing standards first appear in the form of Exposure Drafts

(EDs). These are sent out to interested parties who are invited to comment. Full standards are issued once public views have been taken into account.

The Standards Advisory Council (SAC)

The Standards Advisory Council (SAC) has approximately 45 members from all over the world and provides a forum for organizations and individuals with an interest in international financial reporting to participate in the standard-setting process.

The SAC normally meets the IASB at least three times a year and the Board is required to consult the SAC in advance of decisions on major projects. It gives advice to the IASB on agenda decisions and priorities in the Board's work and informs the Board of the views of the organizations and individuals on the Council on major standard-setting projects.

The International Financial Reporting Interpretations Committee (IFRIC)

The International Financial Reporting Interpretations Committee (IFRIC) reviews accounting issues that are likely to receive divergent or unacceptable treatment in the absence of authoritative guidance, and tries to reach consensus as to the appropriate accounting treatment. In developing interpretations, the IFRIC works closely with similar national committees such as the Urgent Issues Task Force (UITF) in the UK.

The IFRIC addresses issues of reasonably widespread importance, and not issues of concern to only a small set of enterprises. The interpretations cover newly identified financial reporting issues not specifically addressed in IFRSs; and issues where unsatisfactory or conflicting interpretations have developed, or seem likely to develop in the absence of authoritative guidance.

The IFRIC issues 'Draft Interpretations' initially, and following public consultation and approval by the IASB it issues documents called 'Interpretations' – somewhat oddly abbreviated as SICs, Standing Interpretations Committee. For example SIC-32 concerns *Intangible Assets – Web Site Costs*.

In time SICs are either superseded by revisions to existing accounting standards or developed into new standards.

Standards in issue

In addition to the *Framework for the Preparation and Presentation of Financial Statements,* which we have looked at in this chapter, the IASC issued a total of 41 standards (IASs) in its lifetime. Ten of these have since been withdrawn, usually because they have been replaced by a new standard. For instance IAS 22 has recently been replaced by IFRS 3, and IAS 35 by IFRS 5.

To date the IASB has added five standards of its own. These are known as International Financial Reporting Standards (IFRSs) and that term should be taken to include IASs too.

For reference, and to give you an idea of the scope of international standards, the full list (as at the date of publication of this book) is shown below. Do not be alarmed by the length of this: for the purposes of this course you are expected to know only about the ones shown in **bold**.

IAS 1 **Presentation of Financial Statements**

IAS 2 **Inventories**

IAS 7 **Cash Flow Statements**

IAS 8 **Accounting Policies, Changes in Accounting Estimates and Errors**

IAS 10 *Events After the Balance Sheet Date*

IAS 11 **Construction Contracts**

IAS 12 *Income Taxes*

IAS 14 **Segment Reporting**

IAS 16 **Property, Plant and Equipment**

IAS 17 **Leases**

IAS 18 **Revenue**

IAS 19 *Employee Benefits*

IAS 20 *Accounting for Government Grants and Disclosure of Government Assistance*

IAS 21 *The Effects of Changes in Foreign Exchange Rates*

IAS 23 *Borrowing Costs*

IAS 24 *Related Party Disclosures*

IAS 26 *Accounting and Reporting by Retirement Benefit Plans*

IAS 27 **Consolidated and Separate Financial Statements**

IAS 28   *Investments in Associates*

IAS 29   *Financial Reporting in Hyperinflationary Economies*

IAS 30   *Disclosures in the Financial Statements of Banks and Similar Financial Institutions*

IAS 31   *Interests in Joint Ventures*

IAS 32   *Financial Instruments: Disclosure and Presentation*

IAS 33   *Earnings per Share*

IAS 34   *Interim Financial Reporting*

IAS 36   *Impairment of Assets*

IAS 37   *Provisions, Contingent Liabilities and Contingent Assets*

IAS 38   *Intangible Assets*

IAS 39   *Financial Instruments: Recognition and Measurement*

IAS 40   *Investment Property*

IAS 41   *Agriculture*

IFRS 1   *First-time Adoption of International Financial Reporting Standards*

IFRS 2   *Share-based Payment*

IFRS 3   *Business Combinations (supersedes IAS 22)*

IFRS 4   *Insurance Contracts*

IFRS 5   *Non-current Assets Held for Sale and Discontinued Operations (supersedes IAS 35)*

National standards and international standards

As mentioned earlier the EU is making international standards the norm for listed companies. In the UK the ASB is conducting a phased replacement of existing UK standards with new UK standards that have been aligned with the international version.

Similar moves are afoot in other major economies – in particular the EU countries, obviously. National standard-setters in the USA (the FASB) and Japan (the ASBJ) are also working in close coordination with the IASB.

FRSs and international standards

If you have previously learned about UK standards and you would like to map how they correspond to international standards, you will find that there is rarely an exact match – IAS 1, for example, would have to be mapped to FRS 3, FRS 18 and UITF Abstract 4, and there would still be significant gaps – and therefore we take the view that a map would be more of a hindrance than a help for a learner.

That said, if you have learned a little about UK standards already you have a considerable advantage. You will find many familiar ideas in the remainder of this book.

Summary

Now that you have completed this chapter you should be able to:

- ♦ **describe the objectives of financial statements;**
- ♦ **identify user groups and their information needs;**
- ♦ **explain accounting policies and their origins;**
- ♦ **describe the need for a conceptual framework and the IASB's** *Framework for the Preparation and Presentation of Financial Statements;*
- ♦ **understand the principles behind the recognition of assets and liabilities;**
- ♦ **distinguish between alternative valuation bases (historic cost, current cost, market value and present value); and**
- ♦ **explain concepts of capital maintenance and the unit of measurement chosen.**

Two

The balance sheet and the profit and loss account

Syllabus

This chapter is the first of three relating to syllabus Section 2: The primary financial statements. Particular attention is paid to the various components of these statements and to the interrelationships between them.

Objectives

After studying this chapter you should be able to:

- ♦ explain the purpose, components and format of the balance sheet;
- ♦ explain the purpose and format of the profit and loss account and explain its link with the balance sheet; and
- ♦ demonstrate knowledge and understanding of the following accounting standard:
  IAS 1 *Presentation of Financial Statements.*

2.1   The Companies Act accounting requirements

Principles and policies

In the UK the Companies Act 1985 requires that what it calls the 'fundamental accounting principles' of going concern, accruals, consistency and prudence be followed. All of these were discussed in Chapter 1.

It also requires the following.

(a)   Accounting policies should be applied consistently from one financial period to the next.

(b)   If accounts are prepared on the basis of assumptions that differ in material respects from any of the generally accepted fundamental accounting concepts the details, reasons for and effect of the departure from the fundamental concepts must be given in a note to the accounts.

(c)   The accounting policies adopted by a company in determining the amounts to be included in the balance sheet and in determining the profit or loss for the year must be stated in a note to the accounts.

Accounting policies are also the subject of IAS 18 which we shall look at in Chapter 4.

Annual accounts

The Companies Act requires that companies prepare annual accounts and lay them before its members in general meeting. The accounts must be filed with the Registrar of Companies either within seven months of the year end (for public companies) or within ten months (for private companies).

Accounting records

The term accounting records means the company's 'books'. These days the books will actually be maintained by means of computerized accounting systems, except in the case of the very tiniest companies.

Section 221 of the Companies Act requires that every company's accounting records must:

(a)   be sufficient to show and explain a company's transactions;

(b)   disclose with reasonable accuracy at any time the financial position of the company at that time;

(c)   enable the directors to ensure that any profit and loss account or balance sheet gives a true and fair view of the company's financial position.

The section also requires that the accounting records should contain:

(a)   day-to-day entries for money received and paid, with an explanation of why the receipts and payments occurred (the nature of the transactions);

(b)   a record of the company's assets and liabilities;

(c)   where the company deals in goods:

    (i)   statements of stocks at the financial year end;

    (ii)   statements of stock-taking on which the figures in (c)(i) are based;

    (iii) with the exception of retail sales, statements of all goods bought and sold, identifying the suppliers or customers for each item.

Incidentally, stock is called 'inventory' in international standards.

2.2   The balance sheet

Purpose

The balance sheet presents a snapshot of a company's financial position at a particular point in time, enabling users to see the value and nature of company's assets and liabilities and how those assets and liabilities were financed.

Do not forget to match this up with the overall objective of financial statements: the purpose of the balance sheet is to help users to make the sort of decisions that they might make in the light of information about assets, liabilities and financing.

Components and format

The way the balance sheet is presented is governed by company law and – for listed companies – by the provisions of various international accounting standards, especially IAS 1 *Presentation of Financial Statements* (revised December 2003). There has never been an equivalent UK standard that deals with the balance sheet in overall terms.

Some components of the balance sheet must be disclosed on the 'face' of the balance sheet, in other words as a line or lines in the balance sheet itself. For many items additional detail must be disclosed in the notes to the financial statements, for example an analysis of the make-up of fixed assets. We shall deal with some of these disclosures in more detail in later chapters, as required by the sections of the syllabus.

IAS I does not prescribe the format of the balance sheet – in other words it does not specify the exact order in which items should be presented – and this means that the different conventions that are popular in different countries can continue to be used, so long as the items required by IAS I are included.

Companies Act format

The Companies Act sets out two balance sheet formats, one horizontal and the other vertical. (Two formats were included because this section of the Companies Act was originally based on the 4th EU accounting directive which included the two formats to accommodate practice throughout the EU.)

In the UK the vertical format is almost invariably used and that is the one illustrated here.

Each item in the balance sheet is referenced by letters and roman and arabic numerals. The Companies Act requires that:

(a)   any item preceded by letters or roman numerals must be shown on the face of the balance sheet, unless it has a nil value for both the current and previous year;

(b)   items preceded by arabic numbers (1, 2, 3, etc) may be amalgamated:

  (i)   if their individual amounts are not material; or

  (ii)   if amalgamation facilitates the assessment of the company's state of affairs (but then the individual items must be disclosed in a note);

(c)   items preceded by arabic numerals may be:

  (i)   adapted (ie the titles can be altered); or

  (ii)   rearranged (their position altered);

  where the special nature of the company's business requires such an alteration.

Any item required to be shown may be shown in greater detail than required by the prescribed format.

A company's balance sheet or profit and loss account may include an item not otherwise covered by any of the items listed, except that the following must not be treated as assets in the company's balance sheet:

(a)   preliminary expenses;

(b)   expenses of and commission on any issue of shares or debentures;

(c)   research costs.

Assets and liabilities may not be set off against each other.

The vertical balance sheet is shown on the following pages. (Note that there is a choice over the display of certain items – they are not shown twice! The numbers are purely for illustration so that you can see how it all adds up.)

Proforma balance sheet (vertical format)

				€	€	€
A	CALLED-UP SHARE CAPITAL NOT PAID					
	(may be shown as item C(II)(5))					
B	FIXED ASSETS					
	I	Intangible assets				
		1	Development costs	5		
		2	Concessions, patents, licences, trade marks and similar rights and assets	5		
		3	Goodwill	5		
		4	Payments on account	5		
					20	
					20	
	II	Tangible assets				
		1	Land and buildings	5		
		2	Plant and machinery	5		
		3	Fixtures, fittings, tools and equipment	5		
		4	Payments on account and assets in course of construction	5		
					20	
	III	Investments				
		1	Shares in group undertakings	5		
		2	Loans to group undertakings	5		
		3	Participating interests	5		
		4	Loans to undertakings in which the company has a participating interest	5		
		5	Other investments other than loans	5		
		6	Other loans	5		
		7	Own shares	5		
					35	
						75

Brought forward

C   CURRENT ASSETS

   I   Stocks

I	Raw materials	5	
2	Work in progress	5	
3	Finished goods and goods for resale	5	
4	Payments on account	5	

                                                  20

   II   Debtors

I	Trade debtors	5
2	Amounts owed by group undertakings	5
3	Amounts owed by undertakings in which the company has a participating interest	5
4	Other debtors	5
5	Called-up share capital not paid *(may be shown as item A)*	5
6	Prepayments and accrued income *(may be shown as item D)*	5

                                                  30

   III Investments

I	Shares in group undertakings	5
2	Own shares	5
3	Other investments	5

                                                15

   IV Cash at bank and in hand   5

                                                  70

D   PREPAYMENTS AND ACCRUED INCOME *(may be shown as item C(II)(6))*   –

                                                  70

E   CREDITORS: AMOUNTS FALLING DUE WITHIN ONE YEAR

I	Debenture loans	I
2	Bank loans and overdrafts	I
3	Payments received on account	I
4	Trade creditors	I
5	Bills of exchange payable	I
6	Amounts owed to group undertakings	I
7	Amounts owed to undertakings in which the company has a participating interest	I
8	Other creditors including taxation and social security	I
9	Accruals and deferred income *(may be shown as item H(9) or J)*	I

                                                (9)

F   NET CURRENT ASSETS (LIABILITIES)   61

G   TOTAL ASSETS LESS CURRENT LIABILITIES   136

	Brought forward		136
H	CREDITORS: AMOUNTS FALLING DUE AFTER MORE THAN ONE YEAR		
	1 Debenture loans	I	
	2 Bank loans and overdrafts	I	
	3 Payments received on account	I	
	4 Trade creditors	I	
	5 Bills of exchange payable	I	
	6 Amounts owed to group undertakings	I	
	7 Amounts owed to undertakings in which the company has a participating interest	I	
	8 Other creditors including taxation and social security	I	
	9 Accruals and deferred income *(may be shown as item E(9) or J)*	I	
			(9)
I	PROVISIONS FOR LIABILITIES AND CHARGES		
	1 Pensions and similar obligations	I	
	2 Taxation, including deferred taxation	I	
	3 Other provisions	I	
			(3)
J	ACCRUALS AND DEFERRED INCOME *(may be shown as item E(9) or H(9))*		(12)
			124
K	CAPITAL AND RESERVES		
	I Called-up share capital		100
	II Share premium account		2
	III Revaluation reserve		2
	IV Other reserves		
	1 Capital redemption reserve	4	
	2 Reserve for own shares	4	
	3 Reserves provided for by the articles of association	4	
	4 Other reserves	4	
			16
	V Profit and loss account		4
			124

IAS I requirements

The basic requirement of IAS I is that entities should present a balance sheet that separates current and non-current assets and liabilities. We shall be looking at assets and liabilities in much more detail in later chapters, but the basic difference is that current assets and liabilities are those that are expected to be realized or settled within 12 months after the balance sheet date.

IAS 1 sets out the minimum items – 16 of them – that should be disclosed on the face of the balance sheet. Check for yourself to see whether there are any items in addition to those included in the Companies Act format. This will be a good way of getting familiar with the items:

(a)   property, plant and equipment;

(b)   investment property;

(c)   intangible assets;

(d)   financial assets (excluding amounts shown under (e), (h) and (i));

(e)   investments accounted for using the equity method;

(f)   biological assets;

(g)   inventories;

(h)   trade and other receivables;

(i)   cash and cash equivalents;

(j)   trade and other payables;

(k)   provisions;

(l)   financial liabilities (excluding amounts shown under (j) and (k));

(m)   liabilities and assets for current tax, as defined in IAS 12;

(n)   deferred tax liabilities and deferred tax assets, as defined in IAS 12;

(o)   minority interest, presented within equity; and

(p)   issued capital and reserves attributable to equity holders of the parent.

In fact the only additional item is 'biological assets' (these are defined in IAS 41 as 'living animals or plants', for example a herd of cattle, an orchard, a vineyard) which are clearly only relevant to certain types of business. ('Plant' in the Companies Act format means factories and the like.)

You may have identified other additional items if you were not sure of some of the terminology ('equity method', 'minority interest', 'participating interest' and so on). Do not worry about these for now: they are terms connected with group accounts and we shall cover them in later chapters.

IAS 1 says that additional lines, headings and sub-totals should be presented on the face of the balance sheet if this would make it easier for a user to understand the entity's financial position. Additional disclosures are required on the face of the balance sheet if IFRS 5 *Non-current Assets Held for Sale and Discontinued Operations* applies (we shall tackle this in a later chapter).

2.3 The Profit and Loss Account (Income Statement)

Purpose

The Profit and Loss Account (or Income Statement, in the terminology of international standards) shows the company's performance during the period covered by the financial statements.

Its purpose is to help users to make the sort of decisions that they might make in the light of information about income and expenses.

Format

Again IAS 1 does not prescribe the format of an income statement.

The Companies Act gives four profit and loss account formats, two vertical and two horizontal. Once again the reason for this is that different countries in the EU had different traditions. The vertical format is the norm in the UK. Two formats are given because each fits a different type of business. The first is probably the more common. The formats are identical from 'Income from shares in group undertakings' onwards.

Note that turnover is defined by the Companies Act as:

> 'the amounts derived from the provision of goods and services, falling within the company's ordinary activities, after deduction of:
>
> (a) trade discounts;
>
> (b) value added tax;
>
> (c) any other taxes based on the amounts so derived.'

Neither cost of sales nor distribution costs nor administrative expenses are defined. The allocation of costs to the three categories is based on accepted practice and must be applied consistently from one year to the next.

In addition every profit and loss account must show:

(a) the company's profit or loss on ordinary activities before taxation, no matter what format is used or how much it might be amended to suit the circumstances of a particular case;

(b) amounts to be transferred to or from reserves;

(c) the amount of dividends paid and (if applicable) proposed.

Amounts representing income may not be set off against items representing expenditure.

Corresponding amounts for the previous financial year must be given for every item shown in a company's balance sheet or profit and loss account. Where a corresponding amount for the previous year is not properly comparable with an amount disclosed for the current year, the previous year's amount should be adjusted and details of the adjustment given in a note.

Regarding dividends, a 'final dividend' is usually paid after the end of the financial year. The final ordinary dividend is usually proposed to shareholders at the annual general meeting (AGM) of the company, which takes place some months after the end of the financial year.

In such a case the final proposed dividend must be disclosed in the notes to the annual accounts of the company but it is not recognized as an expense and a liability in the financial statements unless it is declared on or before the balance sheet date.

This is a change to the original treatment of proposed dividends in the Companies Act 1985 in line with the issue of FRS 21 *Events after the Balance Sheet Date*. FRS 21 is a case in point of the ASB approach: it is a revision of an earlier standard to bring it into line with international standards.

Proforma profit and loss account: Format 1

		€	€
1	Turnover		X
2	Cost of sales *		(X)
3	Gross profit or loss		X
4	Distribution costs*	X	
5	Administration expenses*	X	
			(X)
			X
6	Other operating income		X
			X
7	Income from shares in group undertakings	X	
8	Income from shares in undertakings in which the company has a participating interest	X	
9	Income from other fixed asset investments	X	
10	Other interest receivable and similar income	X	
			X
11	Amounts written off investments	(X)	
12	Interest payable and similar charges	(X)	
			(X)
	Profit or loss on ordinary activities before taxation		X
13	Tax on profit or loss on ordinary activities		(X)
14	Profit or loss on ordinary activities after taxation		X
15	Extraordinary income	X	
16	Extraordinary charges	(X)	
17	Extraordinary profit or loss	X	
18	Tax on extraordinary profit or loss	(X)	
			X
			X
19	Other taxes not shown under the above items		(X)
20	Profit or loss for the financial year		X

*These figures will all include depreciation

Proforma profit and loss account: Format 2

		€	€	€
1	Turnover			X
2	Change in stocks of finished goods and work in progress			(X)/X
3	Own work capitalized			X
4	Other operating income			X
5	(a) Raw materials and consumables	(X)		
	(b) Other external charges	(X)		
			(X)	
6	Staff costs:			
	(a) wages and salaries	(X)		
	(b) social security costs	(X)		
	(c) other pension costs	(X)		
			(X)	
7	(a) Depreciation and other amounts written off tangible and intangible fixed assets**	(X)		
	(b) Exceptional amounts written off current assets	(X)		
			(X)	
8	Other operating charges		(X)	
				(X)
				X
9	Income from shares in group undertakings		X	
10	Income from shares in undertakings in which the company has a participating interest		X	
11	Income from other fixed asset investments		X	
12	Other interest receivable and similar income		X	
				X
13	Amounts written off investments		(X)	
14	Interest payable and similar charges		(X)	
				(X)
	Profit or loss on ordinary activities before taxation			X
15	Tax on profit or loss on ordinary activities			(X)
16	Profit or loss on ordinary activities after taxation			X
17	Extraordinary income		X	
18	Extraordinary charges		(X)	
19	Extraordinary profit or loss		X	
20	Tax on extraordinary profit or loss		(X)	
				X
				X
21	Other taxes not shown under the above items			(X)
22	Profit or loss for the financial year			X

**In Format 1 this figure will be disclosed by way of a note.

IAS I requirements

The basic requirement of IAS I is that all items of income and expense recognized in a period should be included in profit or loss unless another accounting standard requires otherwise.

IAS I sets out the minimum items that should be disclosed on the face of the income statement, but it acknowledges that additional line items may be needed to fairly present the enterprise's results of operations. Again, check for yourself to see whether there are any differences between these requirements and those of the Companies Act formats. This will be a good way of getting familiar with the items:

(a)   revenue;

(b)   finance costs;

(c)   share of the profit or loss of associates and joint ventures accounted for using the equity method;

(d)   pre-tax gain or loss recognized on the disposal of assets or settlement of liabilities attributable to discontinuing operations;

(e)   tax expense

(f)   profit or loss

The following items must also be disclosed on the face of the income statement as allocations of profit or loss for the period:

(a)   profit or loss attributable to minority interest; and

(b)   profit or loss attributable to equity holders of the parent.

No items may be presented on the face of the income statement or in the notes as 'extraordinary items'.

An analysis of expenses should be presented either on the face of the income statement or in the notes to the accounts. This should be done using either the 'nature of expense method', which corresponds to Companies Act Format 2, or the 'function of expense' (or 'cost of sales') method, which corresponds to CA 1985 Format 1.

Dividends must be disclosed either on the face of the income statement or in the notes.

If you have done your comparison one difference is the reference to items relating to discontinuing operations: we shall cover this in a later chapter.

The most striking point, however, is that the IAS forbids 'extraordinary' items. In fact this has been the case under both UK and international standards for some time. Extraordinary items were outlawed because the practice had developed of interpreting the definition of extraordinary items very loosely. The reason for this is that extraordinary items appeared after 'profit after tax' and therefore did not need to be included in the calculation of any of the key financial ratios that users use to assess performance.

Link with the balance sheet

As we have said, the balance sheet shows the financial position of the entity at the year end while the profit and loss account shows the performance of the organization during the year. Both statements are essential to get a proper view of the organization's finances.

Many items are intimately linked – in other words a change to one either directly or indirectly affects others. For example:

(a)   fixed assets (B/S) are stated net of depreciation brought forward (B/S) and the depreciation charge for the year (P&L);

(b)   revenue (P&L) includes amounts sold to trade debtors (B/S) but not yet paid for, but trade debtors are stated net of changes in the provision for bad debts (P&L).

To put it another way, a balance sheet as at, say, 31 December 2005 shows the entity's financial position at that point and also – because comparatives must be shown – the financial position at 31 December 2004. The profit and loss account for the year ended 31 December 2005 shows how the entity got from the 2004 position to the 2005 position.

On the other hand, suppose you saw this in a balance sheet:

	2005 €000	2004 €000
FIXED ASSETS		
Plant & machinery	488	512

You might then look at the (Format 2) profit and loss account expecting to see a depreciation charge of €(512,000 – 488,000) = €24,000. Instead, let us suppose you find the following:

	€000
Depreciation written off fixed assets	54

The charge is €30,000 more than you expected!

The reason for the apparent discrepancy in this example might be as set out below:

	€000
NBV of plant and machinery brought forward	512
Disposals	(37)
Additions	67
	542
Depreciation	(54)
NBV of plant and machinery carried forward	488

So, rather than just letting its existing assets get older, as you first thought, you now know that the company has actually invested in a fairly considerable amount of new machinery, and that probably bodes well for its productiveness in the future.

The point here is that, although they are intimately linked, the standard format balance sheet and profit and loss account are not sufficient on their own to provide all the information you need to make decisions. Much essential information is contained in notes to the accounts. To get a full picture we also need a further primary statement, the cash flow statement, as we shall see in the next chapter.

2.4   Notes to the accounts

Companies Act requirements

The Companies Act requires that the accounts be accompanied by notes on the following areas. You will see that they are very detailed in some areas, while not touching on others at all. Some, but not all, of the notes are also required by accounting standards:

(a)   particulars of turnover;

(b)   particulars of staff;

(c)   directors' emoluments (remuneration);

(d)   charges that must be disclosed;

(e)   income from listed investments;

(f)   rents receivable from land after deducting outgoings;

(g)   taxation;

(h)   extraordinary and exceptional items and prior year adjustments;

(i)   redemption of shares and loans;

(j)   earnings per share (listed companies only);

(k)   statement showing movement on reserves.

Particulars of turnover

Turnover must be analysed in terms of:

(a)   each class of business;

(b)   geographical markets.

Much more detailed requirements on segment reporting are contained in accounting standards such as IAS 14. We shall look at this in a later chapter.

Particulars of staff

The following facts must be disclosed:

(a)   average number employed by the company (or by the group in consolidated accounts), divided between categories of workers, eg between manufacturing and administration;

(b)   staff costs:

    (i)   wages and salaries paid to staff;

    (ii)   social security costs of staff;

    (iii)   other pension costs for employers.

Directors' remuneration

It has always been a requirement to disclose certain details of what were called 'directors' emoluments' but for listed companies the rules were expanded in 2002 under the Directors' Remuneration Report Regulations 2002. This was directly due to widespread public concern over so-called 'fat-cat' salaries – for example some directors were paying themselves enormous bonuses in spite of the fact that their companies were performing poorly.

The regulations require UK listed companies to prepare a detailed directors' remuneration report and seek shareholder approval for it via an ordinary resolution at the general meeting at which the annual accounts are presented (usually the AGM).

Items NOT subject to audit

The following items are not subject to audit — in other words they must be included but the auditors do not have to express an opinion on them. Items should be disclosed for each director, in tabular form:

(a)   the names of the remuneration committee;

(b)   details of anyone who has advised the committee, and how they were appointed if they are external consultants;

(c)   details of any performance conditions attaching to share options or awards under long-term incentive schemes including why the conditions were chosen. If a director's entitlement is not subject to performance conditions an explanation should be given;

(d)   a summary of the methods used to assess performance and why these methods were chosen;

(e)   details of any external factors used to assess performance;

(f)   details of any significant amendment that is proposed to be made to share option entitlements or awards under long-term incentive schemes;

(g)   an explanation of the relative importance of remuneration elements that are and are not performance-related;

(h)   an explanation of the company's policy on directors' service contracts, notice periods and termination payments. For each director the date, the unexpired term and details of the notice period must be given, together with any provisions for compensation payable on early termination, and details of any compensation payments made during the year;

(i)   a line graph providing details of the company's performance for the last five financial years by reference to the company's total shareholder return, plus details of the index chosen and why. Total shareholder return is explained at the end of this chapter.

Items subject to audit

The following items are subject to audit and must be disclosed for each director. Auditors have to state whether these parts of the report have been properly prepared in accordance with the regulations:

(a)   total salary and fees paid or payable;

(b)   total bonuses paid or payable;

(c)   total expense allowances;

(d)   total amount of any compensation for loss of office paid or payable;

(e) the estimated value of benefits received other than in cash (eg share options or awards under long-term incentive schemes);

(f) the total of the above items and the total for the preceding year;

(g) the number of shares under option and the interests in long-term incentive schemes at the beginning and end of the year;

(h) options that have been exercised, have lapsed or have been varied in the year. Similar information for interests in long-term incentive schemes;

(i) for outstanding options, details of any price paid on grant, the exercise price and lapse dates. Similar information for interests in long-term incentive schemes;

(j) any amendment made to options or long-term incentive schemes in the year;

(k) any performance targets attaching to options or long-term incentive schemes;

(l) for options exercised the market value of shares at the time. Similar information for interests in long-term incentive schemes;

(m) for options outstanding the market value of shares at the year end and the high and low values during the year;

(n) details of pensions and retirement benefits;

(o) details of any significant award made in the year to any person who was not a director of the company at the time the award was made but had previously been a director of the company, including (in particular) compensation in respect of loss of office and pensions. This is excluding any amount disclosed elsewhere in the report;

(p) sums paid to third parties in respect of a director's services.

Charges

The charges that must be disclosed are:

(a) auditors' remuneration including expenses;

(b) hire of plant and machinery;

(c) interest payable on:

   (i) bank loans, overdrafts and other loans repayable by instalments or otherwise within five years;

   (ii) loans of any other kind;

(d) depreciation:

    (i)   amounts of provisions for both tangible and intangible assets;

    (ii)   the effect on depreciation of a change in depreciation method;

    (iii) the effect on depreciation of a revaluation of assets.

Taxation

Taxation should be split between:

(a)   UK corporation tax, showing the basis of computation;

(b)   UK income tax, showing the basis of computation;

(c)   irrecoverable VAT.

If relevant the taxation should be split between that attributable to ordinary activities and that attributable to extraordinary activities. The charge for deferred tax should be shown as a component of the total tax charge. Any other special circumstances affecting the tax charge should also be disclosed.

Redemption of loans and shares

The amounts set aside for these purposes must be disclosed.

See for yourself ...

The above requirements probably seem pretty grim, but that is partly because we are explaining them in abstract terms. It will greatly assist your studies if you obtain some copies of the annual reports issued by quoted companies and see for yourself what they contain.

You can view many UK annual reports online or have them posted to you **free** using the *Financial Times* Annual Reports Service (http://ftcom.ar.wilink.com) or you can get an even wider variety (Europe and USA) from **WILink plc** themselves (http://www.wilink.com). If a company that you are interested in is not included you may well be able to obtain the latest report from the company's own website.

Bear in mind that EU companies are required to adopt international standards for financial years **starting** on or after 1 January 2005. In theory that means that the first reports that must follow international standards will not be available until **early 2006** but many companies are likely to adopt international standards earlier than this.

Exercise

It is high time you did some accounting work yourself, so now we would like you to prepare a Balance Sheet and Profit and Loss Account (Income Statement), following the formats and disclosure rules that you have read about so far in this chapter.

Christmas Plc's trial balance as at 31 December 20X0 was as follows:

	Dr €000	Cr €000
Administrative expenses	420	
€1 Ordinary shares – fully paid		1,075
10% Debentures repayable 20Y5		1,000
Debtors	940	
Cash at bank	80	
Distribution costs	840	
Fixed asset investments	1,170	
Dividend received		150
Plant and machinery:		
At cost	1,500	
Accumulated depreciation (at 31 December 20X0)		440
Profit and Loss Account		365
Purchases	1,920	
Inventory (at 1 January 20X0)	280	
Trade creditors		520
Revenue		3,900
Dividend paid	200	
Interest paid	100	
	7,450	7,450

Additional information

1   Inventory at 31 December 20X0 was valued at €300,000.

2   The following items are included in the above balances:

	Distribution costs €000	Administrative expenses €000
Depreciation for the year	57	10
Hire of plant and machinery	40	30
Auditors remuneration	–	60
Directors' emoluments	–	90

3   The following rates of taxation are applicable:

	%
Corporation tax	30

4   The corporation tax charge in the profit and loss account is made up as follows:

	€000
Corporation tax	104

5   There was no proposed dividend.

6   The corporation tax creditor as at 31 December 20X0 is €104,000.

7   50% of Revenue was in the UK and 50% in the rest of the EU.

Revenue was split as to 30% relating to retailing and 70% relating to the manufacture of car parts.

8   There were no additions or disposals of fixed assets during the year.

9   The fixed asset investments were in unquoted shares and none of the companies invested in were group companies.

Required

Prepare the company's published profit and loss account for the year ended 31 December 20X0 and balance sheet as at that date in accordance with the Companies Act. Provide the accompanying notes to the accounts insofar as the information permits.

Solution

CHRISTMAS PLC
PROFIT AND LOSS ACCOUNT FOR THE YEAR ENDED 31 DECEMBER 20X0

	Notes	€000	€000
Revenue	1		3,900
Cost of sales			1,900
Gross profit			2,000
Distribution costs		840	
Administration expenses		420	
			1,260
	2		740
Income from fixed asset investments			150
			890
Interest payable	3		100
Profit or loss on ordinary activities before taxation			790
Tax on profit or loss on ordinary activities	4		104
Profit or loss on ordinary activities after taxation			686
Interim dividend paid			200
Retained profit for the year			486
Retained profit brought forward			365
Retained profit carried forward			851

CHRISTMAS PLC
BALANCE SHEET AS AT 31 DECEMBER 20X0

	Notes	€000	€000	€000
FIXED ASSETS				
Tangible assets	5			1,060
Investments	6			1,170
				2,230
CURRENT ASSETS				
Inventorys			300	
Debtors			940	
Cash at bank and in hand			80	
			1,320	
CREDITORS: AMOUNTS FALLING DUE WITHIN ONE YEAR				
Trade creditors		520		
Corporation tax		104		
			624	
NET CURRENT ASSETS				696
TOTAL ASSETS LESS CURRENT LIABILITIES				2,926
CREDITORS: AMOUNTS FALLING DUE AFTER MORE THAN ONE YEAR				
10 % Debenture loans			1,000	
				1,000
				1,926

				€000
CAPITAL AND RESERVES				
€1 Ordinary shares – fully paid				1,075
Profit and loss account				851
				1,926

CHRISTMAS PLC
NOTES TO THE ACCOUNTS

1. **Revenue**
   Revenue represents amounts derived from the provision
   of goods and services falling within the company's
   ordinary activities net of value added tax:

	€000
Principle activities	
Retailing	1,170
Manufacture of car parts	2,730
	3,900
Geographical analysis	
UK	1,950
Rest of EC	1,950
	3,900

2. **Operating profit**
   Operating profit is stated after charging:

	€000
Depreciation	67
Hire of plant and machinery	70
Auditors' remuneration	60
Directors' emoluments	90

3. **Interest payable**

	€000
Interest payable on debenture loans	100

4. **Tax on profits on ordinary activities**

	€000
UK corporation tax (at 30%)	104
	104

5. **Tangible fixed assets**

Plant and machinery	€000
Cost as at 1 January 200X and 31 December 200X	1,500
Depreciation	
At 1 January 200X	373
Charge for the year	67
At 31 December 200X	440
Net book value 31 December 200X	1,060
Net book value 31 December 20W9	1,127

6. **Fixed assets investments**

	Investments other than loans in non-group companies €000
At 1 January 20X0 and 31 December 20X0	1,170
Unlisted	1,170

2.5   Directors' report

The Companies Act also requires that a Directors' Report is included with the accounts. The purpose of the report is to assist the users in obtaining a clearer picture of the company's state of affairs. At present the Companies Act does not give a formal layout but requires the report to include the following items. It is extremely common for the topics to be mentioned as headings but rather than repeat detail given elsewhere in a note to the accounts, a cross-reference is given to, for example, the note to the balance sheet on fixed assets.

(a) A fair review of the development of the business of the company (and its subsidiaries) during the financial year and of the position at the end of the year.

(b) The proposed dividends and transfers to reserves.

(c) The principal activities of the company and any changes that have occurred.

(d) Post-balance sheet events, ie significant events affecting the company between the end of the year and the date of signing of the accounts.

(e) Likely future developments of the business.

(f) An indication of the research and development undertaken by the company.

(g) Significant changes in fixed assets and, where significant, an estimate of the difference between the book value of land held as fixed assets and its realistic market value.

(h) Political and charitable contributions; if, taken together, these exceed £200 there must be shown:

   (i)   separate totals for each classification; and

   (ii) where political contributions exceeding £200 have been made, the names of recipients and amounts.

(i) Details of own shares purchased.

(j) With regard to employees:

   (i)   a statement concerning health, safety and welfare at work of the company's employees;

   (ii) for companies with an average workforce exceeding 250, details of employment policy relating to disabled people.

(k) With regard to the directors:

   (i)   the names of all persons who had been directors during any part of the financial year;

   (ii) their financial interests in contracts;

(iii)   for each director, his or her name and:

- ♦   the number of shares held at the start of the year;

- ♦   the number of shares held at the end of the year;

- ♦   for each director elected in the year, the shares held when elected;

- ♦   all the above should be shown as nil where appropriate.

Operating and Financial Review and Directors' Report Regulations 2004

At the time of publication of this book a new set of regulations under the Companies Act 1985 had been issued and were subject to public consultation. They will become law at some time during the lifetime of this book, but the new requirements are quite onerous and it is likely that there will be changes in the regulations before they are finalized.

Business review

The draft regulations *(The Companies Act 1985 (Operating and Financial Review and Directors' Report) Regulations 2004)* say that the business review (fair review) in the directors' report should be 'a balanced and comprehensive analysis of:

(a)   the development and performance of the business of the company and its subsidiary undertakings during the financial year;

(b)   the position of the company and its subsidiary undertakings.'

The fair review should include certain specific items, namely:

(a)   analysis using financial key performance indicators;

(b)   where appropriate, analysis using other key performance indicators, including information relating to environmental matters and employee matters.

Operating and Financial Review (OFR)

For accounting periods beginning on or after 1 January 2005 listed companies will also be required to publish an Operating and Financial Review (OFR) which provides information about the company's performance and future prospects.

The DTI's Draft Regulations explain that 'The OFR is a narrative report by quoted companies that will be made annually to shareholders, setting out the principal drivers of a company's performance both in the past and in the future. It will cover the issues traditionally seen as key to a company's performance – an account of its business, objectives and strategy, a review of developments over the past year, and a description of the main risks. But it will also cover prospects for the future and, where necessary, information about the environment, employees, customers or social and community issues where that information is important for an assessment of the company.'

The draft regulations were still subject to consultation at the time of publication of this text, so you should watch the press for further details, probably some time in Autumn 2004. The draft schedule specifying the contents is included as an appendix in this book.

Some time ago the UK Accounting Standards Board issued a Statement called 'Operating and Financial Review', giving specifications for the contents. In view of the forthcoming legislation the ASB is currently developing a full accounting standard on the OFR. There is no equivalent international standard at present.

The ASB's January 2003 revision of its Statement lists the essential features of the OFR and goes on to detail some of the specific sections of the OFR to which these general principles should be applied. These headings are:

(a)   the business, its objectives and strategy;

(b)   operating review:

    (i)   performance in the period;

    (ii)   returns to shareholders;

    (iii)   dynamics of the business;

    (iv)   investment for the future;

(c)   financial review:

    (i)   capital and treasury policy;

    (ii)   cash flows;

    (iii)   current liquidity;

    (iv)   going concern;

(d)   statement of compliance.

The OFR should be of benefit to less sophisticated users of accounts, because it should provide an objective analysis of a company's performance on the user's behalf. It should highlight the important items in the current year's annual report, as well as drawing out 'those aspects of the year under review that are relevant to an assessment of future prospects'.

2.7   Distributable profits

Section 263 of the Companies Act defines distributable profits as accumulated realized profits, so far as they have not been distributed or capitalized, less accumulated realized losses, so far as they have not been previously written off in a reduction or reorganization of capital.

Section 262(3) states:

> 'references to realized profits and realized losses, in relation to a company's accounts, are to such profits or losses of the company that fall to be treated as realized in accordance with principles generally accepted, at the time when the accounts are prepared, with respect to the determination for accounting purposes of realized profits or losses.'

What this means in practice is that, broadly, the profits that have arisen by passing through the profit and loss account are realized and therefore distributable. It is generally the case that the profit and loss reserve should equate to distributable profits.

The rules are more stringent for public companies. A public company cannot make a distribution if at the time:

(a)   the amount of its net assets is less than the combined total of its called-up share capital plus its undistributable reserves; or

(b)   the distribution will reduce the amount of its net assets to below the combined total of its called-up share capital plus its undistributable reserves.

Undistributable reserves are:

(a)   the share premium account;

(b)   the capital redemption reserve;

(c)   any accumulated surplus of unrealized profits over unrealized losses; and

(d)   any other reserve that cannot be distributed, whether by statute, or by the company's memorandum and articles of association. This would include the revaluation reserve to the extent that the asset revalued has not yet been depreciated or sold.

Summary

Now that you have completed this chapter you should be able to:

- explain the purpose, components and format of the balance sheet;
- explain the purpose and format of the profit and loss account and explain its link with the balance sheet; and
- demonstrate knowledge and understanding of the following accounting standards:
  IAS 1 *Presentation of Financial Statements.*

Three

Cash flow
statements

Syllabus

This chapter is the second of three relating to syllabus Section 2: The primary financial statements. Particular attention is paid to the various components of these statements and to the interrelationships between them.

Objectives

After studying this chapter you should be able to:

- ◆ explain the purpose and structure of the cash flow statement, using either the direct or the indirect approach; and
- ◆ demonstrate knowledge and understanding of the following accounting standards:
  IAS 1 *Presentation of Financial Statements*
  IAS 7 *Cash Flow Statements.*

3.1 Cash flow statements

The importance of cash

Cash flow statements are not a requirement of the Companies Acts 1985 and 1989, unlike the profit and loss account and balance sheet.

It is a very basic lesson of business, however, that no matter what 'profit' is shown in the profit and loss account, it is the cash generated by a business that actually pays the bills. For this reason the accruals-based profit and loss account and balance sheet need to be complemented by a statement that focuses on cash generation and use.

Early attempts at such a statement such as the 'Source and application of funds' that was required in UK financial statements from the mid-1970s did not fully fit the bill, due to problematic definitions of 'funds'. The very first act of the ASB in the early 1990s was to issue FRS 1 requiring a more informative 'Cash Flow Statement' instead.

International standards followed suit. Consequently IAS 1 *Presentation of Financial Statements* identifies the cash flow statement as one of the primary financial statements. It does not include any requirements of its own for such a statement because these are covered by IAS 7 *Cash Flow Statements.*

The need for cash flow reporting

It is important to understand the need for cash flow reporting.

- ♦ Firstly, historical cash flow information may assist users of financial statements in making judgements on the amount, timing and degree of certainty of future flows of cash, and the ability of the organization to adapt to changing circumstances. Can it service its loans? Is there enough cash to pay dividends? Can it invest in new resources?
- ♦ Second, the information helps users to assess the quality of the profits earned by a business by identifying how readily they are converted into cash.
- ♦ It makes it easier to compare the operating performance of different companies because it removes the effect of differences in accounting policies and treatments.
- ♦ It helps the user to check the accuracy of past assessments of future cash flows and to examine the relationship between profitability and cash flow and the impact of changing prices.

3.2   IAS 7 Cash Flow Statements

Objective

The objective of IAS 7 is to require the presentation of information about the historical changes in cash and cash equivalents of an enterprise by means of a cash flow statement which classifies cash flows during the period according to:

♦   operating activities;
♦   investing activities;
♦   financing activities.

Definitions

Before giving an example it will help to explain the key terms included in the above objective.

♦   'Cash' means cash on hand and money that is placed on deposit but can be converted into cash on hand immediately, on demand ('demand deposits').
♦   'Cash equivalents' are short-term, highly liquid investments that are readily convertible to a known amount of cash, and that are subject to an insignificant risk of changes in value.
♦   'Operating activities' are the main revenue-producing activities of the enterprise that are not investing or financing activities.
♦   'Investing activities' are the acquisition and disposal of long-term assets and other investments that are not considered to be cash equivalents.
♦   'Financing activities' are activities that alter the equity capital and borrowing structure of the enterprise.

The principal difference between IAS 7 and the UK version, FRS 1, is that IAS 7 defines cash flows as movements in cash and cash equivalents, whereas under the (more stringent) FRS 1 cash flows relating to cash equivalents are included in a separate section called 'management of liquid resources'.

FRS 1 also requires additional reconciliations to figures in the other primary statements.

Format: the direct method

Here is a typical statement, slightly adjusted from the example given in Appendix A of IAS 7. Operating activities are shown using the 'direct method' – we shall explain what this means in a moment.

CASH FLOW STATEMENT

	$000	$000
Cash flows from operating activities		
Cash receipts from customers	30,150	
Cash paid to suppliers and employees	(27,600)	
Cash generated from operations	2,550	
Interest paid	(270)	
Taxation paid	(900)	
Net cash from operating activities		1,380
Cash flows from investing activities		
Acquisition of subsidiary X	(550)	
Purchase of property, plant and equipment	(350)	
Proceeds from sale of equipment	20	
Interest received	200	
Dividends received	200	
Net cash used in investing activities		(480)
Cash flows from financing activities		
Proceeds from issue of share capital	250	
Proceeds from long-term borrowings	250	
Payment of finance lease liabilities	(90)	
Dividends paid	(1,200)	
Net cash used in financing activities		(790)
Net increase in cash and cash equivalents		110
Cash and cash equivalents at beginning of period		120
Cash and cash equivalents at end of period		230

Under the direct method the section on operating activities discloses major classes of cash receipts and cash payments.

This is the preferred method in IAS 7 because it gives additional information that is not available at a glance from other financial statements.

The figures can be arrived at either from the accounting records of the entity (although these would not be available to you in an exam question, of course!) or by making adjustments to sales, cost of sales and so on in the other financial statements (in an exam you would need to be given sufficient information to make the necessary adjustments).

Format: the indirect method

Only the section on operating activities is different using this method, under which the 'Cash generated from operations' figure is arrived at by adjusting the entity's profit or loss for the effects of transactions of a non-cash nature, for any deferrals or accruals of past or future operating cash receipts or payments, and items of income or expense associated with investing or financing cash flows.

	$000	$000
Cash flows from operating activities		
Profit before taxation	3,350	
Adjustments for:		
Depreciation	450	
Foreign exchange loss	40	
Investment income	(500)	
Interest expense	400	
	3,740	
Increase in trade and other receivables	(500)	
Decrease in inventories	1,050	
Decrease in trade payables	(1,740)	
Cash generated from operations	2,550	
Interest paid	(270)	
Income taxes paid	(900)	
Net cash from operating activities		1,380

This may look more complex than the direct method but the extra figures can usually be quickly derived from the other financial statements. For example to work out the 'Decrease in inventories' you simply look at the balance sheet and work out the difference between last year's closing inventory (shown as a comparative figure) and this year's.

Exercise 3.1

The following information is available for Helena Ltd for the year ended 31 December 20X0.

	£000
Cash paid to/on behalf of employees	(56,000)
Cash payments to suppliers	(110,000)
Cash received from customers	195,000
Corporation tax	(7,300)
Depreciation charges	3,150
Increase in creditors	10,950
Increase in debtors	3,750
Increase in inventories	1,500
Interest	(5,350)
Profit before interest and taxation	20,200
Profit on sale of machine	50

Required:

So far as you can with the information available prepare the 'Operating activities' section of Helena Ltd's cash flow statement using:

(a)   the direct method;

(b)   the indirect method.

Solution

(a)   **Direct method**

HELENA LTD
CASH FLOW STATEMENT FOR THE YEAR ENDED 31 DECEMBER 20X0

	$000	$000
Cash flows from operating activities		
Cash receipts from customers	195,000	
Cash paid to suppliers and employees	(166,000)	
Cash generated from operations	29,000	
Interest paid	(5,350)	
Taxation paid	(7,300)	
Net cash from operating activities	16,350	16,350

(b) Indirect method

HELENA LTD
CASH FLOW STATEMENT FOR THE YEAR ENDED 31 DECEMBER 20X0

	$000	$000
Cash flows from operating activities		
Profit before interest and taxation	20,200	
Adjustments for:		
Depreciation	3,150	
Profit on disposal	(50)	
Increase in trade and other receivables	(3,750)	
Increase in inventories	(1,500)	
Increase in trade payables	10,950	
Cash generated from operations	29,000	
Interest paid	(5,350)	
Taxation paid	(7,300)	
Net cash from operating activities	16,350	16,350

If you did not get the same figures in both versions for 'Cash generated from operations' and 'Net cash from operating activities' then you made a mistake.

It is worth spending a few minutes getting to grips with the indirect method. We are trying to adjust the profit, which is prepared on the accruals basis, to a cash basis.

- ◆ Depreciation charges must be removed by adding them back because they are purely a way of matching the cost of fixed assets to the benefit derived from them – depreciation does not give rise to any cash outflow.
- ◆ Similarly profit on the sale of the machine will have been included in the profit before tax but needs to be taken out because it is an accounting figure – it does not relate to an actual cash inflow because it is affected by depreciation. The actual cash received will be included under proceeds in the investing activities part of the statement.
- ◆ Any increase in the amount of inventory held or debtors outstanding will increase the amount of cash tied up in working capital, ie an effective reduction in cash available.
- ◆ On the other hand an increase in creditors means payments will be made later and more cash is available in the meantime.

The main advantage of the direct method is that it shows operating cash receipts and payments. Information about specific sources of cash receipts and the purposes for which cash payments were made in past periods may be useful in assessing future cash flows. These disclosures, other than the reconciliation of operating profit to operating cash flow, are optional, however, and are therefore only rarely provided.

3.3 Detailed requirements

Operating activities

These are the main revenue-producing activities of the enterprise that are not investing or financing activities.

IAS 7 gives examples of the cash flows that should be regarded as deriving from operating activities. Here are the main ones that you are likely to encounter.

(a) Cash receipts from the sale of goods, the provision of services, and from royalties, fees, commissions and other revenue.

(b) Cash payments to suppliers for goods and services, and payments made to and on behalf of employees. (For example, under the UK PAYE system companies pay income tax and national insurance on behalf of employees.)

(c) Cash payments or refunds of what the IAS calls 'income taxes' unless they can be specifically identified with financing and investing activities. (In UK terms this means 'corporation tax', not the 'income tax' paid on behalf of employees).

IAS 7 is silent on whether cash flows such as receipts from debtors and payments to suppliers should be shown inclusive or exclusive of VAT or other sales tax. If VAT is included then the net payment to or refund from the tax collecting authority would also need to be included.

The UK equivalent, FRS 1 says that although strictly speaking VAT represents a cash flow (the organization either pays over VAT or receives a refund at the end of a period) it is only a short-term timing difference and the inclusion of VAT could distort the figures. It therefore recommends that cash flows are shown net of sales taxes. If sales tax paid is irrecoverable, as it may be on certain assets, it should be included. (Likewise, of course, for all transactions if the business is not registered for VAT.) This is consistent with the treatment of VAT in other financial statements.

Investing activities

These cash flows represent expenditure on resources intended to generate future income and cash flows. Examples include acquiring or disposing of property and plant and equipment, and buying or selling shares in other companies, for example buying or disposing of a subsidiary company; shares that are just bought for dealing or trading purposes are regarded as similar to inventory bought for resale, so they are classified under operating activities.

Possibly included under investing activities are various financial instruments such as futures, options and swaps, although not if held for trading or dealing purposes (operating activities) or if they are classified as financing activities. In other words they may be classified under any of the headings, depending on circumstances: we shall be explaining these sorts of transactions in much more detail in a later chapter.

Exercise 3.2

SOPHIA LTD

Sophia Ltd sold a machine during the year ended 31 July 20X1; no purchases of fixed assets were made. Below are shown extracts from the financial statements of Sophia Ltd for the year ended 31 July 20X1.

PROFIT AND LOSS ACCOUNT

	20X1 £
Depreciation	(10,000)
Profit on sale of machine	1,000

BALANCE SHEET

	20X1 £	20X0 £
Fixed assets at net book value (NBV)	80,000	100,000

Required

What amount should be disclosed in the cash flow statement under investing activities?

Solution

We can work out the cash inflow for the machine by using the following information:

	£
Fixed assets (NBV) 31.07.X0	100,000
Less depreciation	(10,000)
	90,000
Fixed assets (NBV) 31.07.X1	80,000

We can see that if no assets had been sold, the balance at 31.07.X1 would have been £90,000, but it is actually £80,000 so a machine with a net book value (NBV) of £10,000 must have been sold.

The profit and loss account tells us that a £1,000 profit was made on the sale, therefore the machine must have been sold for £11,000, which is the cash flow that will be reported.

	£
Profit on sale	1,000
NBV at sale	10,000
Sale proceeds (cash inflow)	11,000

If you are using the indirect method the profit on sale will be one of the items adjusted for in the reconciliation of profit to operating cash flow.

Financing activities

These cash flows give an indication of future claims on the company's future cash flows by the providers of capital. Examples include:

(a)   cash receipts from issuing shares and cash payments to redeem shares;

(b)   cash receipts from issuing debentures, bonds and so on, and cash repayments of amounts borrowed;

(c)   cash payments relating to finance leases.

Interest and dividends

Cash flows from interest and dividends paid and received must be disclosed separately, but the heading used depends on circumstances.

(a)   Dividends paid may be classified as a financing cash flow. This is logical, on the grounds that they are a cost of obtaining equity finance. IAS 7 also permits dividends paid to be shown as an operating cash flow, to help users to assess the company's ability to pay dividends out of operating cash flows.

(b)   For a financial institution (such as a bank) interest paid and interest and dividends received are usually classified as operating activities.

(c)   For other entities interest paid and interest and dividends received may be treated as operating activities on the grounds that they are a component of profit or loss, or alternatively interest paid may be treated as a financing cash flow and interest and dividends received as an investing cash flow.

In an exam question, unless you are specifically instructed otherwise, we recommend the following approach, which is the most intuitively obvious one.

Item	Most entities	Financial institutions
Interest paid	Operating	Operating
Interest received	Investing	Operating
Dividends received	Investing	Operating
Dividends paid	Financing	Financing

Exercise 3.3

The following extracts are taken from the financial statements of Maria Ltd for the year ended 30 June 20X1.

MARIA LTD

PROFIT AND LOSS ACCOUNT (EXTRACT)

	£
Interim preference dividend	50,000
Final preference dividend	100,000

BALANCE SHEET (EXTRACT)

	20X1	20X0
	£	£
Dividends payable	100,000	80,000

Required

What amount should be shown in the cash flow statement for dividends paid?

Solution

The amount of dividend paid in cash during the year ended 30 June 20X1 can be calculated as a balancing figure, as follows.

	£
Outstanding at year end 30.06.X0	80,000
Plus amount proposed during the year ended 30.06.X1	150,000
Total outstanding during the period	230,000
Amount outstanding at 30.06.X1	(100,000)
Therefore amount paid	130,000

The same procedure can be used to work out how much interest has been paid.

Taxes on the organization's income

Cash flows arising from taxation such as corporation tax must be separately disclosed and are normally classified under operating activities. (There are circumstances in which certain tax cash flows may be classified as investing or financing activities but these are beyond the scope of the syllabus.)

Subsidiaries

There are detailed disclosure requirements relating to the acquisition or disposal of subsidiary companies; we shall return to these when we are dealing with group accounts in a later chapter.

Non-cash transactions

As you might expect, non-cash transactions should be excluded from cash flow statements. Examples include the acquisition of a subsidiary company by issuing shares or by assuming its liabilities.

Components of cash and cash equivalents

The components of cash and cash equivalents must be disclosed separately. If necessary there should be a reconciliation of the amounts in the cash flow statement with the equivalent amounts in the balance sheet.

Here is an example, adapted from the one given in IAS 7.

CASH AND CASH EQUIVALENTS

Cash and cash equivalents consist of cash on hand and balances with banks, and investments in money-market instruments. Cash and cash equivalents included in the cash flow statement comprise the following balance sheet amounts:

	20X6 $000	20X5 $000
Cash on hand and balances with banks	40	25
Short-term investments	190	135
Cash and cash equivalents as previously reported	230	160
Effect of exchange rate changes	–	(40)
Cash and cash equivalents as restated	230	120

The final figure ($230,000) is the one shown at the foot of the cash flow statement that we showed you at the beginning of this chapter, and it is also the figure shown for cash in the balance sheet.

This note may well be given as part of the balance sheet disclosures, in which case the cash flow statement could simply direct users to the relevant balance sheet note so long as it was clear how the amounts reconciled.

Exercise 3.4

Jasmine Ltd has a year-end of 30 June. Shown below is the profit and loss account for the year ended 30 June 20X1, together with the balance sheets as at 30 June 20X0 and 20X1.

JASMINE LTD
PROFIT AND LOSS ACCOUNT FOR THE YEAR ENDED 30 JUNE 20X1

	£000
Turnover	1,200
Cost of sales	(800)
Gross profit	400
Distribution costs	(50)
Administration costs	(110)
Operating profit	240
Interest received	80
Interest paid	(50)
Profit before tax	270
Taxation	(30)
Profit for the financial year	240
Equity dividends	(40)
Retained profit for year	200

JASMINE LTD
BALANCE SHEET

	30 June 20X1 £000	30 June 20X0 £000
Fixed assets	480	230
Current assets		
Inventories	110	100
Debtors	320	300
Cash	145	120
	575	520
Current liabilities		
Creditors	(230)	(200)
Taxation	(30)	(25)
Dividend	(40)	(30)
	(300)	(255)
Net current assets	275	265
Total assets less current liabilities	755	495
Financed by:		
Share capital	450	400
Profit and loss	305	95
	755	495

The depreciation charge for the year was £40,000 and no fixed assets were sold during the year.

Required

Prepare a cash flow statement for the year ended 30 June 20X1 using the indirect method. Show all workings.

Solution

JASMINE LTD
CASH FLOW STATEMENT FOR THE YEAR ENDED 30 JUNE 20X1

	£000	£000
Cash flows from operating activities		
Profit before taxation	270	
Adjustments for:		
Depreciation	40	
Investment income	(80)	
Interest expense	50	
	280	
Increase in trade and other receivables	(20)	
Increase in inventories	(10)	
Increase in trade payables	30	
Cash generated from operations	280	
Interest paid (W1)	(50)	
Taxation (W2)	(25)	
Net cash from operating activities		205
Cash flows from investing activities		
Purchase of property, plant and equipment (W3)	(280)	
Interest received (W1)	80	
Net cash used in investing activities		(200)
Cash flows from financing activities		
Proceeds from issue of share capital	50	
Dividends paid (W4)	(30)	
Net cash used in financing activities		20
Net increase in cash and cash equivalents		25
Cash and cash equivalents at beginning of period		120
Cash and cash equivalents at end of period (Note 1)		145

NOTES TO THE ACCOUNTS

1   Cash and cash equivalents

Cash and cash equivalents included in the cash flow statement comprise the following balance sheet amounts:

	20X1 £000	20X0 £000
Cash on hand and balances with banks	145	120

Workings

I   In the absence of other information it is assumed that interest paid and received in the year is the same as the amount shown in the profit and loss account.

2   **Taxation**

	£000
Brought forward	25
Charge to P & L	30
Carried forward	(30)
Paid in the year	25

3   **Fixed assets**

	£000
Opening balance of fixed assets (NBV)	230
Less depreciation	(30)
Balance if there were no additions	200
Actual closing balance	480
Therefore purchases must equal	280

4   **Dividends paid**

	£000
Brought forward	30
Charge to P & L	40
Carried forward	(40)
Paid in the year	30

Summary

Now that you have completed this chapter you should be able to:

♦ **explain the purpose and structure of the cash flow statement, using either the direct or the indirect approach; and**

♦ **demonstrate knowledge and understanding of the following accounting standards:**
   IAS 1 *Presentation of Financial Statements*
   IAS 7 *Cash Flow Statements.*

Four

Additional disclosures

Syllabus

This chapter is the third of three relating to syllabus Section 2: The Primary Financial Statements. Particular attention is paid to the various components of these statements and to the interrelationships between them.

Objectives

After studying this chapter you should be able to:

♦ explain various additional components of financial statements; and

♦ demonstrate knowledge and understanding of the following accounting standards:

IAS 1 *Presentation of Financial Statements*

IAS 8 *Accounting Policies, Changes in Accounting Estimates and Errors*

IAS 14 *Segment Reporting.*

4.1 Statement of Changes in Equity

IAS 1 includes a fourth financial statement – the Statement of Changes in Equity – that should be regarded as part of a complete set of financial statements. This is not mentioned specifically in your syllabus so we will not go into great depth here. In any case, some of the items included such as 'cash flow hedges' are not intuitive things that you are likely to know about already. They are covered in later chapters.

The Statement of Changes in Equity is designed to show the profit for the period together with other gains and losses attributable to shareholders. There are two possible methods of presentation. Shown below is an adaptation of the first example given in IAS 1.

Statement of Changes in Equity

	Share capital	Other reserves	Translation reserve	Retained earnings	Total
Balance at 31 December 20X5 brought forward	X	X	(X)	X	X
Changes in accounting policy				(X)	(X)
Restated balance	X	X	(X)	X	X
Changes in equity for 20X6					
Loss on property revaluation		(X)			(X)
Available-for-sale investments:					
Valuation gains/(losses) taken to equity		(X)			(X)
Transferred to profit or loss on sale		X			X
Cash flow hedges:					
Gains/(losses) taken to equity		X			X
Transferred to profit or loss for the period		(X)			(X)
Transferred to initial carrying amount of hedged items		(X)			(X)
Exchange differences on translating foreign operations			(X)		(X)
Tax on items taken directly to or transferred from equity		X	X	X	X
Net income recognized directly in equity		(X)	(X)		(X)
Profit for the period				X	X
Total recognized income and expense for the period		(X)	(X)	X	X
Dividends				(X)	(X)
Issue of share capital	X				X
Equity share options issued		X			X
Balance at 31 December 20X6	X	X	(X)	X	X

'Equity' means the owners' interest in the company's assets after liabilities have been deducted, but as the columns above suggest, it can be divided into different categories. At the very least equity consists of shareholders' capital (the amount they paid for their shares) and the accumulated retained earnings of the company.

In addition this part of the balance sheet often also includes other 'reserves' that are created for various reasons – often because accounting standards require them. For example if an asset such as a building is restated at its current market value the double entry to reflect this in the financial statements under IAS 16 is:

DEBIT   Asset

CREDIT   Revaluation Reserve

A reserve might be 'recognized' in this way in the financial statements, but it will not be 'realized' until it is turned into cash (for example if the building is sold).

Alternative presentation

The alternative presentation is as shown below. This was formerly called a 'Statement of Recognized Gains and Losses' (and still is, in the equivalent UK standard, FRS 3). If this method is used, a reconciliation of opening and closing balances of share capital, reserves and accumulated profit must still be provided in the notes

Statement of Recognized Income and Expense

	20X6	20X5
Gain/(loss) on revaluation of properties	(X)	X
Available-for-sale investments:		
Valuation gains/(losses) taken to equity	(X)	(X)
Transferred to profit or loss on sale	X	(X)
Cash flow hedges:		
Gains/(losses) taken to equity	X	X
Transferred to profit or loss for the period	(X)	X
Transferred to the initial carrying amount of hedged items	(X)	(X)
Exchange differences on translation of foreign operations	(X)	(X)
Tax on items taken directly to or transferred from equity	X	(X)
Net income recognized directly in equity	(X)	X
Profit for the period	X	X
Total recognized income and expense for the period	X	X
Attributable to equity holders:	X	X
Effect of changes in accounting policy:	(X)	—

If you compare this with the previous example you will see that effectively the choice is between showing all the information in a single statement with lots of columns or in an easier to read primary statement and a series of underlying notes.

Relationship with other statements

The Statement of Changes in Equity is supposedly on a par with the balance sheet, cash flow statement and the income statement. The standard-setting bodies promote the Statement as a key indicator used in assessing a company's financial performance.

In practice, in published accounts, the Statement of Changes in Equity is often relegated to a misunderstood and largely ignored section or note to the accounts. The reason why it is not felt to be overly useful is because of the questionable additivity of the Statement. We are adding a profit earned over the current financial year to property revaluations which may have been earned over 40 years but recognized only in the current year. We then add to that an adjustment for exchange gains/losses, usually relating to external exchange-rate factors unrelated to the trading performance of the business. It is arguable that the overall total is of little use.

4.2   Additional disclosures

As well as the primary financial statements – the income statement, the balance sheet, the cash flow statement and the statement of changes in equity – standards require a seemingly ever-increasing number of additional notes and disclosures to help the user of accounts.

As we saw in Chapter 2 many of the notes to the accounts simply expand on the summarized figures that appear in the primary statements. Many others give new information and may not have any bearing on the double entry.

In the remainder of this chapter we will look at certain key disclosures to see what they can add to our understanding of the business. As we do so we will introduce a number of ideas that are crucial to your understanding of what follows.

Later chapters contain details of information that must be disclosed in a wide variety of specific circumstances.

4.3 IAS 8 Accounting Policies

Typically the very first note in a set of financial statements is a lengthy narrative one that explains the accounting policies that the organization has used.

> An accounting policy is a specific principle, base, convention, rule or practice that is applied when preparing and presenting financial statements.

The policy for different items will often be dictated by specific accounting standards, but there is also a general standard on the subject: IAS 8 *Accounting Policies, Changes in Accounting Estimates and Errors*.

Selecting accounting policies

IAS 8 makes the priorities clear:

♦ if there is a Standard on a particular type of transaction then the organization should apply it;

♦ if there is no standard that deals with a particular type of transaction the organization should use its 'judgement' to develop and apply an accounting policy that results in information that is relevant to the needs of users and is reliable – in other words gives a faithful representation of the economic substance of the transaction and is neutral (unbiased), prudent and complete;

♦ in making this judgement:

    – the organization should consider how other standards deal with similar issues or, if there are none, the general guidance in the IASB Framework; and

    – consideration may also be given to the most recent pronouncements of other standard-setting bodies, if any; to other accounting literature (eg the work of academics); or to usual industry practices, so long as none of these conflicts with international standards.

Changes in policies

Once an accounting policy has been adopted it should normally be applied consistently from year to year but change may be necessary if a new standard requires an existing type of transaction to be dealt with differently. A change may also be allowed if it would result in more reliable and relevant information for users (for example if the circumstances of the organization change).

If a change is necessitated by a new standard, the standard will often explain how the change should be accounted for.

If not, or if the change is voluntary, it should be applied retrospectively. This means that any opening balances affected by the change should be adjusted and comparative amounts for the previous years should also be adjusted as if the revised accounting policy had always applied, so far as this is practicable.

Besides providing a statement of the new policy the organization must also disclose certain additional matters, most notably the nature of the change and the reasons for it, and the amount of the adjustment for the current period and for each prior period presented in the accounts. If this is not practicable that fact must be disclosed.

Changes in accounting estimates

IAS 8 also explains what to do in the event that estimates that were made in preparing the accounts are changed. This may often be necessary because certain items in the accounts require the organization to make assumptions about uncertain future events. For example a debt recognized at the end of a period may turn out not to be recoverable in the next, or stock may become obsolete because of events beyond the organization's control.

The effect of any change in estimate should be included in profit or loss in the period of the change and future periods if they are affected, but the prior year figures do not have to be adjusted. Small changes will be made silently, but if a change in estimate has a material effect the nature and amount should be disclosed.

Errors

Obviously errors should not normally occur, but if they do they should be corrected as soon as they are discovered. This should be done retrospectively by restating the comparative amounts and adjusting the opening balance of retained earnings.

4.4   Events after the balance sheet date

Occasionally an incident may occur between the company's year-end and the publication of the company's accounts. IAS 10 *Events after the Balance Sheet Date* indicates that the financial statements need to take account of circumstances arising after the reporting year-end. (IAS 10 is not in your syllabus but we mention it to ensure that you do not confuse such incidents with changes in estimates or errors.)

IAS 10 identifies two types of event:

- ◆ adjusting events; and
- ◆ non-adjusting events.

The distinction between the two is that adjusting events provide additional evidence about conditions existing at the balance sheet date and therefore will lead to the figures being amended.

Examples of adjusting events:

- ◆ debtor insolvency;
- ◆ evidence concerning the net realizable value of stock;
- ◆ evidence concerning the profitability of a long-term contract; and
- ◆ a change in the valuation of property.

Non-adjusting events are those that have occurred since the year-end but which do not relate to a condition existing at the year-end. Here are some examples:

- ◆ disasters such as fire or flood;
- ◆ shares or loan stock issues;
- ◆ takeovers/mergers;
- ◆ major purchases or disposals of fixed assets;
- ◆ closure or opening of areas of operation.

Accounting treatment

Adjusting events

IAS 10 requires that adjusting events be adjusted in the financial statements for the year.

For example suppose that Doublespeak Ltd's year-end is 31 December 20X0. At the year-end debtors stood at £1,400,000, including £300,000 owed by Truth Limited. On 1 March 20X1, Doublespeak discovers that Truth has gone into administrative receivership and that creditors are likely to get only 10p in the £. At 31 December 20X0, Truth owed Doublespeak £360,000, none of which had been received by 1 March 20X1.

In the year-end accounts Doublespeak should write off 90% of the year-end debts owed by Truth, ie £300,000 x 90% = £270,000. The £270,000 should be charged to Doublespeak's income statement.

Non-adjusting events

Non-adjusting events should not be incorporated in the year end accounts. If the event is material, however, the entity should disclose the nature of the event and give an estimate of its financial effect, so that readers can get a fuller picture of the company's activities.

Going concern

Finally, a non-adjusting event could effectively turn into an adjusting event. This would be under the unusual circumstances where the non-adjusting event was so serious that it called into question the going concern concept.

For example suppose that Julia Ltd's year-end is 31 December 20X0. On 13 February 20X1 a catastrophic fire destroyed the company's main centre of operations. The company was insured only for the physical damage and not the resulting loss of turnover and profits.

Normally such a post year-end fire would be a non-adjusting event, disclosed in the accounts if the estimated was material, but because of the catastrophic nature of the fire, the appropriateness of the going concern concept has been called into question: the accounts would have to be redrafted on the basis that the going concern basis was no longer appropriate. The company would have to account for the effects of the fire, any penalty clauses arising from cancelled contracts, revaluing the assets to realizable values, provisions for redundancy, insolvency costs, etc.

Window dressing

This term is used to describe alterations to the balance sheet, made just before the year-end and reversed just after, which have the effect of making the balance sheet look healthier. A fairly innocuous example would be issuing cheques to creditors before the year-end thereby reducing year-end creditors, but not actually sending out the cheques. After the year-end the cheques would be either sent out or cancelled.

Other, more sophisticated, schemes might involve the sale of an asset, at a large profit, prior to the year-end, with a repurchase shortly after the year-end. We will consider such issues in more detail in Chapter 8 in the context of substance over form.

4.5 IAS 14 *Segment Reporting*

Most large organizations derive their income from a number of different activities, and often from many different countries. This means that a figure in the financial statements for, say, revenue, may actually represent revenue earned from significantly different types of business activity in widely different trading conditions.

IAS 14 *Segment Reporting* therefore requires that specified elements of reported accounts information be analysed into segments. The segments required are classes of business and geographical areas of operation. The information to be segmented is Revenue, Profit before taxation and Net Assets. Thus, key ratios of Turnover/Assets, Profit/Assets and Profit/Sales can be calculated for each segment of the business.

Transactions between segments of the business should also be shown (intersegment sales).

Segments

A class of business is a distinguishable part of a business that provides a separate service/product or group of services/products.

A geographical segment is a geographical area comprising a country or group of countries in which the business operates.

The overall purpose of the standard is to assist in the provision of useful information to accounts users to assess the performance of the business. As can be seen by the information required, the user will be able to compare the performance of the various segments of the business and to ascertain their relative performance in profit and profit/asset terms.

The segments are chosen by the directors by considering the organization's internal organization structure and management reporting system. Therefore, it is likely that every company will segment its business in different ways. One of the problems that can appear in attempting to use this information is that the segments chosen can be too wide to be of any great use.

Here is a simple example (adapted from IAS 14) of a segment report.

Classes of business

	Total	Paper products	Office products	Pub-lishing
Turnover				
Total sales	X	X	X	X
Inter-segment sales	(X)	(X)	(X)	(X)
Sales to third parties	X	X	X	X
Profit before taxation				
Segment profit/(loss)	X	X	X	X
Common costs	(X)			
Operating profit	X			
Net interest	(X)			
Profit before tax	X			
Net assets				
Segment net assets	X	X	X	X
Unallocated assets	X			
Unallocated non-current liabilities	(X)			
Total net assets	X			

Geographical segments

	Total	Europe	North America	Middle East
Sales to third parties	X	X	X	X

4.6   Historical summaries

One of the uses to which reported accounts information is put is the identification and analysis of medium- to long-term trends. The Companies Act requires companies to present accounts showing the current year's figures and the previous year's comparative figures. This is often insufficient to identify a trend because either of the two years visible may be unusual. Therefore, large companies will present a five-year summary of results in an appendix to the main accounts. This is required by the Stock Exchange listing rules.

Preparing a five-year summary may not be as simple as it first appears. For example, at some stage there may have been a change in accounting policy, and as we know this should be dealt with by means of a prior year adjustment. To retain comparability, all of the years in the summary should be adjusted to show the change. It is usually possible to identify if the appropriate changes have been made because the figures will generally be marked as adjusted if they have been.

Assuming the figures are found to be reliable, they can be extremely useful because:

♦ the turnover figures will give a good overview of the amount of growth in the period;

♦ profit can be assessed to see if it has stayed in line; and

♦ ratios calculated over the period available will give a good impression of overall trend and should avoid distraction from an abnormal result.

Care should be exercised when using these figures however:

♦ turnover and profit declining may be the result of demerging or disposing of non-core businesses rather than poor performance;

♦ it is not always possible to distinguish between organic growth and growth through acquisition; and

♦ if the company has changed the nature of its business the ratios may be misleading. Typical gross margins are industry specific, a company reporting an increased margin may simply have switched from manufacturing to retailing, for example.

4.7   Related parties

Fair value and arm's length transactions

In many of the following chapters you will find that transactions are often required to be reported at 'fair value', which is defined as the amount for which an asset could be exchanged between knowledgeable, willing parties in an arm's length transaction. To put it simply, if you buy a car, say, from a car dealer, this would normally be an arm's length transaction. If you buy your brother's car, and furthermore you do so because your brother is in financial difficulties, this is not an 'arm's length' transaction and quite possibly neither you nor your brother would have willingly entered into it in normal circumstances.

Given the importance of this idea it will be helpful to look in a little more detail at what is – or rather what is not – an arm's length transaction. Fortunately there is a standard to help us out: IAS 24 *Related Party Disclosures*.

This standard was introduced in a climate of various corporate governance scandals. It was felt that some companies were not as independent as their incorporated status would suggest. Parties are considered to be related if one party has the ability to control the other party or to exercise significant influence or joint control over the other party in making financial and operating decisions. For the protection of creditors and to help users of accounts to understand more fully the circumstances of the company, IAS 24 requires various details of related parties to be disclosed

From a banker's perspective this information is very useful. It might well indicate relationships of which the bank was unaware and which may have a bearing on the bank's dealings with the company.

Related parties

Transactions between companies that form a group of companies (see Chapter 9) are usually considered to be related-party transactions.

Other related parties include:

♦ members of the key management personnel of the entity or its parent; and
♦ close members of family.

Some parties are specifically deemed *not* to be related, including:

♦ providers of finance, trade unions, public utilities, government departments and agencies in the course of their normal dealings with an enterprise; and
♦ a single customer, supplier, franchiser, distributor, or general agent with whom an enterprise transacts a significant volume of business merely by virtue of the resulting economic dependence.

The above exemption means that a bank does not become a related party simply by lending the company money, even though it may exercise some influence over the company as a consequence of the lending.

Disclosure

If there have been transactions between related parties, the entity should disclose the nature of the related-party relationship as well as information about the transactions and outstanding balances necessary for an understanding of the potential effect of the relationship on the financial statements. This information would include:

♦ the amount of the transactions;
♦ the amount of outstanding balances, including terms and conditions and guarantees;
♦ provisions for doubtful debts related to the amount of outstanding balances; and
♦ expenses recognized during the period in respect of bad or doubtful debts due from related parties.

If related-party transactions were made on terms equivalent to those that prevail in arm's length transactions, a statement should be made to this effect, but only if it can be substantiated.

4.8 Reports to employees

One of the main user groups is the company's employees. The purpose of corporate reporting is to furnish useful information to assist decision-making.

It is arguable whether the company's full statutory financial statements are either relevant or understandable to the majority of the company's employees. Therefore some companies have produced additional employee-focused reports. The main features of these reports are usually:

♦ a summary of the full accounts;

♦ employee information, eg analyses of average numbers of employees, pay levels, total pay/pension data;

♦ a narrative description of the company's results, operations and prospects especially in relation to employment issues; and

♦ comparative pay information, information relative to any pay claims, health and safety, promotion/grading issues, etc.

4.9 Glossy brochures

Hopefully by now you have followed up our suggestion in Chapter 2 that you should obtain some published accounts via the *Financial Times* Annual Reports Service (http://ftcom.ar.wilink.com) or from WILink (http://www.wilink.com).

If so you will now have a collection of glossy brochures and, depending on which companies you chose, you may well be wondering what on earth these have to do with the various requirements that we have been describing!

Typically a company's annual report will include a fair bit of what might be called 'marketing puff' – photographs of smiling employees, articles by various people saying what a wonderful year the company has had, and so on.

Even a relatively conservative annual report will seem to contain a lot of information that we have not mentioned as belonging in the financial statements. For example, you will find overleaf the contents page of the most recent accounts of LloydsTSB:

2003 highlights	Five-year financial summary
Profit before tax by main businesses	The board
Presentation of information	Directors' report
Chairman's statement	Corporate governance
Group chief executive's review	Statement of directors' responsibilities
The community and our business	Directors' remuneration report
Description of business	Report of the independent auditors
Introduction and development	**Financial pages**
Strategy of Lloyds TSB Group	**Notes to the accounts**
Businesses and activities	Shareholder information
Management and resources	Taxation
Employees	Other information
Competitive environment	Glossary
Risk factors	Reference information for shareholders
Operating and financial review and prospects	

The financial statements proper are highlighted in bold, but as you can see these are dwarfed by all the other information, so what is it doing there?

- ♦ Some of the additional items are required by company law, for example the Director's Remuneration Report and, from 2005, the Operating and Financial Review, as mentioned in Chapter 2.
- ♦ Most of the others items are either required by the UK Listing Rules (notably the information on corporate governance) or recommended by the Listing Rules. As you might expect, therefore, these items provide a variety of information that is intended to be useful to shareholders.

The LloydsTSB example is fairly representative of the type of additional information you will find, but be aware that there is generally greater scope for different interpretation of the recommendations, so you may not find the same information in all annual reports.

We do not cover the Listing Rules in detail in this book because they are not mentioned in your syllabus, and in any case rules vary from country to country. This does not mean that in practice you should ignore the additional information provided – depending on what decision you are making it may well be useful.

Summary

Now that you have completed this chapter you should be able to:

♦ explain various additional components of financial statements; and

♦ demonstrate knowledge and understanding of the following accounting standards:

IAS 1   *Presentation of Financial Statements*

IAS 8   *Accounting Policies, Changes in Accounting Estimates and Errors*

IAS 14 *Segment Reporting.*

Five

Tangible assets

Syllabus

This chapter is the first of two relating to syllabus Section 3: Fixed Assets. Attention is paid to the economic nature of tangible fixed assets. The section then focuses on the principles of recognition, valuation (and re-valuation) and depreciation, recognizing that these are areas where different regulatory regimes can (and do) adopt (sometimes very) different accounting bases.

Objectives

After studying this chapter you should be able to:
- explain the factors that determine what items of expenditure should be capitalized as tangible assets;
- explain how tangible assets are valued, and revalued, and depreciated;
- explain alternative bases of depreciation; and
- demonstrate knowledge and understanding of the following accounting standards:
  - **IAS 16** *Property, Plant and Equipment*
  - **IAS 17** *Leases*
  - **IAS 36** *Impairment of Assets*
  - **IAS 40** *Investment Property*
  - **IFRS 5** *Non-current Assets Held for Sale and Discontinued Operations*
  - **(IAS 17 is dealt with in more detail in Chapter 8).**

5.1   Tangible assets

Assets

The IAS Framework defines an asset as follows:

> 'a resource controlled by the entity as a result of past events and from which future economic benefits are expected to flow to the entity'.

The key things to note about the definition are that it does not depend on ownership of the asset – assets held under finance leases, for example, meet the definition – and it does not require that cash must change hands.

Accounts users such as banks would look primarily at this aspect of the balance sheet before entering into secured lending, so clearly the basis of recognition and valuation of the company's assets is very important.

Tangible and intangible assets

It is usually easy to identify *tangible* assets because they have physical substance – you can touch them – and because you know that you intend to keep them and use them for several years. The desk you may be leaning on right now and the chair you are sitting on are tangible assets because otherwise you would fall on the floor, and because you very rarely get a new desk or chair (unless, perhaps, you are in the furniture business).

Intangible assets are assets that do not have physical substance. For example you may pay an author a sum of money to obtain the rights to make a film of one of his or her books. Although the agreement may be written on paper, the physical paper and ink are not the assets. It is the information conveyed by the writing – what various parties may and may not do – that is the asset.

Some assets are harder to pin down. For example a computer program is not something you can touch and computer software would therefore seem to be an intangible asset. But a computer (something tangible) will not function as a computer without boot-up and operating system software (both intangible), so you might argue that it is most reasonable to treat the BIOS and the operating system software as inseparable parts of the tangible asset.

You should appreciate that not every case is clear-cut, but we will not worry about these more questionable cases for the remainder of this chapter: we will save the debate for the next chapter which is devoted to intangible assets.

Fixed (non-current) and current assets

The Companies Act defines fixed assets as those intended to be held on a 'continuing basis'. International standards tend not to use the term 'fixed asset', preferring to distinguish between 'current' and 'non-current' assets.

IAS 1 explains as follows.

(a) A current asset:

    (i) is expected to be realized in, or is intended for sale or consumption in, the entity's normal operating cycle;

    (ii) is held primarily for the purpose of being traded;

    (iii) is expected to be realized within 12 months after the balance sheet date; or

    (iv) is cash or a cash equivalent.

(b) All other assets are non-current.

Property, plant and equipment

Most of a business's tangible non-current assets will fall into category of *property* (an office building and the land it stands on, say), plant (a car production line, say, or the office carpet), and *equipment* (for example desktop computers, power tools, and so on). The dividing line between 'plant' and 'equipment' is blurred, but this is not significant for financial accounting purposes.

IAS 16 *Property, Plant and Equipment* says that property, plant and equipment are tangible items that are held for use in the production or supply of goods, for rental to others, or for administrative purposes; and that are expected to be used during more than one period.

Therefore it is not the precise nature of the tangible asset that is important, but the intended use by the company. A company car, for example is usually accounted for as a fixed asset, because the business intends to keep and use it for some time. The same is true of the cars held by a car rental company: it may not use them itself, but it keeps them so as to make money by allowing customers to use them. For a car dealer, however, the cars they intend to sell will be current assets – inventory.

Investment property

Investment property is land or a building that is held so as to earn rental payments or because it is expected to appreciate in value, as opposed to being held to produce or supply goods or for administrative purposes and as opposed to being held with the intention of selling it.

Investment property is the subject of a separate standard – IAS 40 *Investment property* – because there are a certain additional matters to be considered that do not apply to property in general.

Non-current assets held for sale

If the intention is to sell a particular non-current asset (a building, or a subsidiary company, say, although these are not the only examples) it should not be grouped together in the financial statements with similar assets that are not to be sold. There are also various matters that need to be considered relating to how the asset is valued, and, given that a transaction such as this is likely to be very large in value, extra disclosure in the financial statements is desirable, so that users can assess its potential effects.

These matters are dealt with in IFRS 5 *Non-current Assets Held for Sale and Discontinued Operations.*

Leased assets

Businesses often enter into leasing agreements to obtain items for use in the business so that they do not have to pay the full purchase price up front. Instead they pay for the use of the item over time.

In this case the item is not 'controlled' by the business in the sense that it owns the legal title to it. The accounting treatment depends on the nature of the financial arrangement.

♦ If ownership of the item will eventually pass to the business, once all the payments have been made (a finance lease), it is treated in the same way as assets that the business owns.

♦ If not, the payments are simply treated as an expense (an operating lease): the asset itself is an investment property of the company that leases it, and it is dealt with as an asset in their accounts, not in the accounts of the company that currently happens to be paying an expense for the use of the asset.

This matter is dealt with in IAS 17 *Leases* and we will explain it in more detail in Chapter 8 on liabilities.

The capitalization decision

The term 'capitalization' – meaning to treat a cost as representing a fixed asset rather than writing it off as an expense of the period – is not actually used in international standards (which talk in terms of 'recognition'). It is, however, common to use the term in this sense and it occurs in your syllabus.

Let us take as an example an item such as a company car.

♦ The cost is, say, $20,000. The financial statements therefore recognize an asset of $20,000. In other words the $20,000 is 'capitalized'.

♦ It is expected to be used for three years before it needs to be replaced (so it is a non-current asset). At the end of three years it is expected to have a second-hand value of $5,000.

♦ The financial statements therefore also charge an expense of ($15,000/3) = $5,000 per year for each of the next three years, so that the asset is written down to its disposal value over its useful life. This charge is known as 'depreciation'.

This treatment follows the accruals principle: the income statement is not distorted by an extra large charge in the year the asset is acquired, so understating the profit for that year, and then by no charge at all, overstating the profit for subsequent years.

It also follows the going concern principle, because it values the car on the assumption that it will continue to be used for the next three years, not that it is likely to be sold off before that, for whatever its current second-hand value may be.

Complications arise when we start to consider the subsequent costs of owning the car:

♦ it will need to be serviced;

♦ it may need to be repaired if it breaks down or is involved in an accident;

♦ it may need to be altered in some way, for example so that it can use some new kind of ultra-clean fuel, or if safety enhancements are fitted;

♦ it may eventually be sold for far more or far less than was anticipated at the beginning of its life.

What is the accounting treatment in these cases? Which costs should be capitalized? How should depreciation be calculated? When should the value of the asset in the financial statements be amended, and when not?

As we will see in the remainder of this chapter, the various standards exist to provide answers to these questions for different types of assets.

5.2   IAS 16

As noted above, IAS 16 *Property, Plant and Equipment* says that property, plant and equipment are tangible items that are held for use in the production or supply of goods, for rental to others, or for administrative purposes; and that are expected to be used during more than one period.

Recognition

Items of property, plant, and equipment should be recognized as assets when it is probable that the future economic benefits associated with the asset will flow to the enterprise, and the cost of the asset can be measured reliably. The cost includes costs incurred initially to acquire or construct the item, and costs incurred subsequently to add to, replace part of, or (in some circumstances) to service it.

IAS 16 requires entities to account separately for components of assets that have a cost that is material in relation to the total. This might have an impact on the accounts in the case of, for example, an office building that is expected to have a useful life of 50 years. Within the cost of the building there are likely to be costs associated with, say, the air conditioning system. It is unlikely that the air conditioning will last 50 years and IAS 16 requires that, where the cost of such a component is material and the useful life is substantially different, the component should be separately identified and depreciated over its useful life.

Measurement at the time of recognition

Initial costs

The initial cost includes:

 ♦ the purchase price;
 ♦ any directly attributable costs necessary to bring the item into operation (such as site preparation costs, delivery, installation and testing, surveyors' fees); and
 ♦ if necessary, an estimate of the costs of dismantling the item and restoring the site.

The last item is most relevant in the case of, say, a mine and associated heavy mining equipment. You do not need to include the cost of dismantling most items since that task would not normally be your responsibility: effectively it is recognized in your estimate of the value of the asset at the end of its useful life.

Subsequent costs

As we have mentioned, it is often difficult to identify whether expenditure on fixed assets represents an enhancement of the asset or whether it is simply routine maintenance. In principle companies would tend to prefer to expense costs where tax relief is available and capitalize them if not, because capitalizing improves reported profit in the year the expenditure is incurred.

Under IAS 16 the cost of regular servicing is treated as an expense. This is simply expenditure necessary to ensure that the required standard of performance is maintained, and so it should be recognized in the income statement when incurred.

Under IAS 16 subsequent expenditure should be capitalized:

♦ if it results in an enhancement of economic benefits, beyond those previously recognized (for example if you add an extension to an existing building);
♦ where a component that is accounted for separately (as in the example of the air conditioning, above), is replaced or restored. The cost of the replaced item is written off in full if it has not been written off already.

Capitalization is also allowed where the subsequent expenditure relates to a 'major inspection'. This mainly applies in the case of assets such as aircraft, where such inspections are mandatory (to obtain a certificate of airworthiness so that the asset can continue to be operated), and it applies whether or not items are actually replaced. Any remaining capitalized costs of a previous inspection should, of course, be written off in full.

Interest costs

The Companies Act permits, but does not require, the capitalization of interest costs when calculating the production cost of fixed assets. The Act requires that any capitalized interest be disclosed. On this topic IAS 16 refers to IAS 23 *Borrowing Costs*, which covers (among other things) assets that take a substantial period of time to get ready for their intended use. It says that borrowing costs in relation to the acquisition, construction and production of such an asset may be treated as part of the cost of the asset.

The argument for capitalization is twofold: firstly, the cost of borrowing funds to construct a major fixed asset is an intrinsic part of the overall cost of that asset and should not be written off to the income statement, any more than the purchase price of a fixed asset should be; secondly, capitalization enhances comparability between companies constructing assets and companies purchasing assets. This is because the purchase price of an asset will indirectly include interest, because the seller will take into account all of the costs it incurred when pricing the asset.

Note that care is needed when analysing the accounts where interest has been capitalized. The effect of interest capitalization is to defer the charge in the profit and loss account for interest, to spread it over future periods, rather than charging it to the accounts when it is incurred. Thus in comparing a company that does capitalize interest with one that does not, the former will have higher profits initially, followed by lower profits later as the asset is depreciated. The depreciation charge will be higher than it would have been if interest had not been capitalized.

One other noticeable effect of a policy of capitalizing interest costs is that there will be a difference between interest costs appearing in the income statement and the figure for interest paid in the cash flow statement.

Measurement after recognition

IAS 16 permits two accounting models:

♦ under the *cost model* the asset is carried at cost less accumulated depreciation and impairment;
♦ under the *revaluation model* the asset is carried at a revalued amount, being its fair value at the date of revaluation less subsequent depreciation, provided that fair value can be measured reliably.

We will need to look at the concepts of depreciation and impairment before we can consider revaluation.

5.3 Depreciation

Depreciation is the method used to write off the cost of the asset over the time it will be used in the business – this is called its 'useful economic life' (UEL). (The term 'amortization' is used instead of 'depreciation' in the context of intangibles, as we will see in the next chapter.)

IAS 16 defines depreciation as 'the systematic allocation of the depreciable amount of an asset over its useful life.' Depreciable amount is 'the cost of an asset, or other amount substituted for cost, less its residual value'. The IAS requires that all items of property, plant and equipment except land should be depreciated and that the useful life and the residual value should be reviewed and revised if necessary at each period end.

Land is regarded as having an unlimited useful life, except for obvious exceptions such as quarries (which are eventually emptied) and landfill sites (which are eventually filled up).

It is critical to appreciate that depreciation is a measure of consumption or usage, not valuation. For example, it is often observed that a new car loses around 15% of its value immediately it is driven out of the showroom, but as it has not yet been used in the business, no depreciation would yet be charged. Depreciation is based on the matching concept: matching the asset's cost to the periods expected to benefit from the use of the asset.

If the resulting net book value is felt to overstate the value of the asset then that would be dealt with by IAS 36 *Impairment of Assets,* covered later in this chapter.

Depreciation methods

IAS 16 requires that depreciation be recognized in a way that reflects the way in which the asset is used up. Several methods have been developed, the two main ones being straight line and reducing balance.

Straight-line depreciation

Straight-line depreciation writes off the cost of the fixed asset in equal instalments over the UEL of the asset. Thus, for example, a five-year lease costing $200,000 would be written off at $40,000 ($200,000/5) per annum.

If the asset has an anticipated residual value, this is deducted from the cost of the asset to give the depreciable amount. For example, a piece of machinery costing $40,000 might have an estimated scrap value of $1,000. The depreciable amount is therefore $39,000 ($40,000 less $1,000).

The residual value and the useful life must be based on the user's intentions. For example, if a company kept its company cars for only three years the residual value would be relatively high, reducing the depreciable amount to only the part of cost that the company will use up.

Reducing-balance method

The reducing-balance method writes off a proportion of the net book value (NBV) of the asset each year, and gives a higher charge in the earlier years. It is typically used for assets that are felt to be most effective in the early years of their life and lose a lot of value early on. The NBV is the cost of the asset less accumulated depreciation to date. For example, a car costing $10,000 may be written off using a 20% reducing-balance rate. At the end of Year 1, the car will be depreciated down to $8,000 ($10,000 less 20% x $10,000). At the end of Year 2 its net book value will be $6,400 ($8,000 brought forward less 20% x $8,000). The percentage applied is selected to leave the appropriate residual value at the end of the asset's UEL.

Other methods

Other, less commonly used, often industry-specific, methods of calculating depreciation include the following.

◆ *Usage-based methods* for example, Galton Limited purchases a widget-making machine for $200,000 in 20X0. The capacity of the machine over its life is estimated at two million widgets. Using the usage-based method for depreciating the asset, the machine will be written off at the rate of 10 cents per widget produced ($200,000/2m widgets). Thus if in 20X0 Galton produces 300,000 widgets using the machine, depreciation of $30,000 (300,000 x 10 cents) will be charged.

◆ *Extractive-based methods* these are similar to usage-based methods but are commonly used for mines or quarries and compare the amount extracted in a year with the total expected capacity.

◆ *Sum of the digits method* this method is related to the reducing-balance method; it writes off the cost of the fixed asset in a way that gives a higher charge in the early years.

Exercise 5.1

Cuttings Limited purchased a digger on 1 January 20X1 for $15,400. The company intends to keep the digger for eight years, when it will have an estimated scrap value of $1,000. Calculate the depreciation charges over the asset's useful life, using the sum of the digits method.

Solution

The key to this method is to allocate a digit to each year in which the asset will be depreciated, in this case 8, with the first year being given the highest number.

Depreciable amount: $15,400 less $1,000 = $14,400.

Sum of the digits

8 + 7 + 6 + 5 + 4 + 3 + 2 + 1 = 36

There is a formula that can be used to calculate this easily:

n/2 x (n + 1) where n is the number of digits

In this case n = 8, therefore the calculation becomes (8/2) x (8 + 1) = 4 x 9 = 36. In the first year, we depreciate by 8/36ths; in the second year by 7/36ths, etc.

	20X1	20X2	20X3	20X4	20X5	20X6	20X7	20X8
Depreciation $14,000 x	8/36	7/36	6/36	5/36	4/36	3/36	2/36	1/36
	3,200	2,800	2,400	2,000	1,600	1,200	800	400
Year end Net Book Value	12,200	9,400	7,000	5,000	3,400	2,200	1,400	1,000

Analysis

Different depreciation methods give different depreciation charges in the accounts; over the life of the asset the total depreciation charged will be the same, the depreciable amount. A study of a company's depreciation methods is important in analysing their accounts because depreciation is often one of the biggest costs and different methods do have an impact on the pattern of profitability.

Compared to the straight-line method, the reducing-balance method gives a higher depreciation charge in the early years of an asset's life (hence lower profits) and lower charges (higher profits) in the later years. It is also worth comparing the useful lives that have been assumed: the longer the useful life, the lower the annual depreciation charge and the higher the profit.

Adjustments to depreciation

When a company purchases a fixed asset its useful life and any residual value are estimated, using information available at the time of purchase. All of these assumptions are to be reviewed regularly and adjusted when necessary. The adjustment is always done prospectively, ie the changed depreciation rate is applied from the date the decision is made, never as a prior-year adjustment.

This regular review should mean that companies do not end up with the problem of fully depreciated assets still in use.

5.4   Impairment

IAS 36 *Impairment of assets* introduced the concept of impairment. An impairment loss is defined as:

> 'the amount by which the carrying amount of an asset or a cash-generating unit exceeds its recoverable amount'.

IAS 36 applies to all assets (including intangible assets: see the next chapter) unless there is another standard dealing with similar issues, as there is, for example, for inventories, financial instruments, investment properties and non-current assets held for sale.

The general requirement is that companies should assess at each reporting date whether there are any indications that an asset may be impaired. These indications include evidence of obsolescence or physical damage to the asset, a significant decline in the market value of the asset during the period, or losses arising in a business division.

Where an indication of impairment is seen the company must then estimate the 'recoverable amount' of the asset and write off the amount of the impairment loss immediately in the income statement.

The impairment review

Impairment reviews should be conducted in relation to individual assets where possible. If it is not possible the review should be conducted at the level of cash-generating units. A cash-generating unit is the smallest part of the business that can be identified as giving independent cash inflows, for example, one shop out of a chain.

We saw that the definition of an impairment loss involves the comparison of the carrying amount (the amount at which it is recorded in the financial statements) and 'recoverable amount'.

Recoverable amount and discounted future cash flows

Recoverable amount is defined as the higher of the asset's:

♦ net selling price; and
♦ value in use.

Value in use is the discounted future cash flows, including ultimate sale proceeds, arising from the asset or cash-generating unit. Discounting converts future amounts into present values using the formula:

$$\text{Present value} = \frac{\text{Sum receivable in Year } n}{(1 + \text{Interest rate})^n}$$

So if an asset is expected to generate $1,000 receivable in two year's time and the interest rate is 5% the present value is $1,000/1.05² = $907.02. (The principle is that if you had $907.02 right now you could invest it at 5% and it would be worth $1,000 in two years time.)

Discounting and present values may be familiar from your earlier studies. If not, there is an appendix on the subject at the end of this book, because it is relevant in a variety of contexts.

Stages of an impairment review

The stages in conducting an impairment review of an asset are therefore as follows.

(a) Calculate net selling price, in other words the amount that would be received if it were sold today less any costs of selling it.

(b)   Calculate value in use.

(c)   Identify recoverable amount, ie the higher of (a) and (b). What we are checking is whether it is worth keeping the asset or not. If net selling price is the higher amount we should sell the asset now, to recover that amount. If value in use is higher, the asset is worth keeping because that will generate more money.

(d)   Compare recoverable amount to current carrying value.

   (i)   If carrying value is lower then we need do nothing.

   (ii) If recoverable amount is lower, then the asset has suffered an impairment loss and will need to be written down.

One of the benefits of this approach is that a fall in general property prices, as has been seen at various times in the past, will not automatically lead to the recognition of an impairment loss. If the asset is operating successfully within the business we would expect to find that value in use would be higher than NRV and value in use would therefore be used as recoverable amount.

Accounting for the impairment

The write down will be recognized within operating profit in the profit and loss account and shown as an exceptional item if material. The only exception to this is where the impaired asset has been revalued, in which case it is primarily recognized in the statement of total recognized gains and losses.

5.5   Revaluation of assets

As noted earlier, IAS 16 permits two accounting models for the valuation of property, plant and equipment: the cost model, discussed above, and the revaluation model. IAS 16 says that the revaluation model should be used only if the fair value of an item can be measured reliably.

Valuation bases

There are different bases of valuation and indeed different methods of valuation.

Companies Act 1985

The Companies Act 1985 Schedule 4 contains 'alternative accounting rules' which allow departures from the normal historical cost basis.

- 'Market value' is much the same as what IAS 16 calls 'fair value' and will be covered soon.
- The Companies Act also allows the directors to use their judgement and discretion in selecting an appropriate base to value the fixed asset. This is generally the least satisfactory basis for valuation, and it is questionable whether such a valuation could be regarded as 'reliable', in which case IAS 16 would require either a market value or the cost model to be used.
- 'Current cost' is also permitted under the Companies Act. This is not defined in the act but it can be explained by means of a diagram. To get the current cost, you should work from bottom to top.

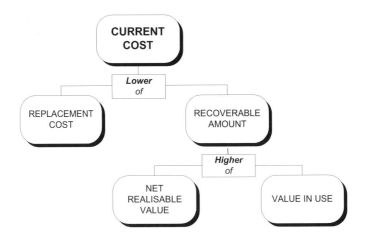

There may be problems in obtaining all the individual figures within this valuation base.

- The net realizable value is at best an estimate. There may be no ready market for the particular asset.
- The value in use involves estimating the future cash flows that the asset will generate – always likely to be at least in part subjective.
- Obtaining the current replacement cost may be difficult if the asset is specialized or if that particular asset is no longer made because of technological advances or consumer preference.

In effect, therefore, it is often likely to be questionable whether current cost is a 'reliable' measurement, and if not IAS 16 would require either market value or the use of the cost model instead.

IAS 16: Fair value and market value

Under IAS 16's revaluation model, so long as the measurement is reliable an asset may be carried at its 'fair value' at the date of the revaluation less any subsequent depreciation and impairment losses. Fair value is the amount for which an asset could be exchanged between knowledgeable, willing parties in an arm's length transaction. This is usually its market value.

If one item is revalued then the entire class of assets to which that item belongs should also be revalued. This means that the business cannot cherry-pick: it cannot just revalue assets whose value has increased and ignore a fall in value of similar assets.

Where it is difficult or impossible to obtain a market value for an asset (for instance if it is specialized or rarely traded) the depreciated replacement cost may be used. For example, for land and buildings this is based on the market value of the land (in its existing use) together with an estimated replacement cost of the building. This figure is then 'depreciated', taking into account the building's age, condition, and other factors affecting its useful economic life.

The frequency of valuations depends on the volatility of the fair value. Most assets will need a revaluation only every three to five years, but annual revaluation may be necessary for assets where the fair value changes frequently and significantly.

Valuers

Surprisingly it is not a requirement of the Companies Act that the valuers be professionally qualified. The Act states that the name or the qualification of the valuer should be disclosed in the financial statements. Also, if the valuer is an employee this should be noted.

IAS 16 says that the fair value of land and buildings should normally be appraised by professionally qualified valuers, while for items of plant and equipment the fair value is the market value (determined by the relevant 'market', of course). IAS 16 requires comprehensive disclosure if revalued amounts are used, including the date of the revaluation, whether an independent valuer was used, the methods used and any significant assumptions made.

Increase in value

Let us suppose that on 1 January 20X0 Hancock plc purchased freehold land and buildings for $700,000. The land element was valued at $100,000, the buildings at $600,000. At the time of purchase the estimated UEL of the buildings was 40 years.

At the end of 20X0 the net book value of the asset will be as follows.

	$
Cost	700,000
Depreciation ($700,000 – $100,000)/40)	15,000
Net book value ($700,000 – $15,000)	685,000

At the end of 20X1 Hancock decided to show the asset at its market value, which was $1,000,000 including $280,000 for the land. By the end of the year a further year's depreciation of $15,000 has been incurred so the net book value immediately before the revaluation was $670,000.

The asset must therefore be revalued by $330,000 ($1m less $670,000). The revaluation is effected by debiting the asset in the balance sheet and crediting a revaluation reserve also in the balance sheet. The revaluation should also be shown in the Statement of Changes in Equity (see Chapter 4).

Position immediately after revaluation

The normal practice is to write back any accumulated depreciation and to uplift the cost to the revalued amount:

	$
Valuation	
Cost at 1/1/X1	700,000
Revaluation	300,000
Adjusted at 31/12/X1	1,000,000
Accumulated depreciation	
At 1/1/X1	15,000
Charge for the year	15,000
Revaluation	(30,000)
Adjusted at 31/12/X1	0
Net book value	1,000,000

Thus a net $330,000 ($300,000 plus $30,000) is credited to revaluation reserve and will be reported in the Statement of Changes in Equity.

The revaluation reserve is unrealized: it represents a gain that has been recognized but not yet realized in cash terms. Thus it cannot be paid out as a dividend.

Position in subsequent years

In subsequent years depreciation must be charged on the revalued amount, not on the original cost. Consider the situation, one year later, at the end of 20X2. (Assume that the original UEL of 40 years still applies: this means that there will be 38 years remaining unless we reassess the useful life and find it should be different.)

The depreciation charge is ($1m − $280,000)/38 = $18,947.37 as opposed to $15,000. Under IAS 16 the difference is considered to represent the amount by which the revaluation surplus has been used up: it does not pass through the income statement. In 20X2 therefore, $15,000 depreciation will be charged to the income statement as usual and the remaining $3,947 will be transferred from the revaluation reserve to retained earnings.

If you are a bit confused about how this works look at the balance sheets for the three years. For simplicity we will assume that there are no other assets or liabilities and no other income or expenses.

	20X0	20X1	20X2
	$	$	$
Tangible Assets:			
Land	100,000	280,000	280,000
Buildings	600,000	720,000	720,000
Accumulated Depreciation	(15,000)	(0)	(15,000)
	685,000	1,000,000	985,000
Equity	700,000	700,000	700,000
Revaluation reserve:			
Land	0	180,000	180,000
Buildings	0	150,000	146,053
Retained earnings	(15,000)	(30,000)	(41,053)
	685,000	1,000,000	985,000

Over the next 37 years, 37 × $3,947.37 = $146,053 will be written off, the part of the revaluation reserve relating to the buildings. This, of course, is in the very unlikely event that there are no further revaluations.

Retained earnings are calculated as follows.

	20X0	20X1	20X2
	$	$	$
Retained earnings brought forward	0	(15,000)	(30,000)
Loss for the year	(15,000)	(15,000)	(15,000)
Transferred from revaluation reserve	0	0	3,947
Retained earnings carried forward	(15,000)	(15,000)	(41,053)

Decrease in value

A decrease in value is the same as an impairment loss and is dealt with in the same way unless the asset has previously been revalued upwards.

Suppose that on 1 January 20X0 James Co purchased freehold land and buildings for $500,000. The land element cost $75,000, the buildings $425,000. At the time of purchase the estimated UEL of the buildings was 50 years.

On 31 December 20X0 James Co decided to show the asset at its current market value of $450,000, including $70,000 for the land.

The effect of this decrease in value is that $50,000 is charged directly to the income statement.

Reversals

Suppose an asset that was revalued at a higher amount than its original cost a few years ago (an increase in value) is revalued again today and is now worth less than the previous revalued amount. Or vice versa: suppose an asset that was revalued at a lower amount than its original cost a few years ago (a decrease in value) is revalued again today and is now worth more than the previous revalued amount.

The balance sheet value of the asset should of course always reflect the latest valuation, but where do the changes go?

Common sense and accurate reporting to users always prevail.

	Increase followed by decrease	Decrease followed by increase
Year 1		
Asset NBV	$570,000	$500,000
Value on revaluation	$720,000	$450,000
Asset value	Debit $150,000	Credit $50,000
Revaluation reserve	Credit $150,000	No effect
Income statement	No effect	Debit $50,000
Year 2		
Asset NBV b/f	$720,000	$450,000
Value on revaluation	$520,000	$525,000
Asset value	Credit $200,000	Debit $75,000
Revaluation reserve	Debit $150,000	Credit $25,000
Income statement	Debit $50,000	Credit $50,000

5.6 Disclosure

The fixed assets notes in a set of financial statements will often be extensive, although this depends on the type of business.

For the figures, the layout below is typically used, with a total column and as many separate columns as necessary for different classes of non-current asset.

	Total	Land and buildings	Plant and equipment
	$	$	$
Cost or valuation			
At 1 January 20X5	130,000	104,000	26,000
Revaluation surplus	31,200	31,200	–
Additions in year	10,400	–	10,400
Disposals in year	(2,600)	–	(2,600)
At 31 December 20X5	169,000	135,200	33,800
Depreciation			
At 1 January 20X5	(41,600)	(26,000)	(15,600)
Charge for year	(10,400)	(2,600)	(7,800)
Eliminated on disposals	1,300	–	1,300
At 31 December 20X5	(50,700)	(28,600)	(22,100)
Net book value			
At 31 December 20X5	118,300	106,600	11,700
At 1 January 20X5	88,400	78,000	10,400

IAS 16

For each class of property, plant, and equipment, IAS 16 requires that the following information is disclosed:

♦ the basis for measuring the carrying amount;
♦ the depreciation method(s) used;
♦ useful lives or depreciation rates;
♦ gross carrying amount and accumulated depreciation and impairment losses;
♦ a reconciliation of the carrying amount at the beginning and the end of the period, showing:
  – additions;
  – disposals;
  – acquisitions through business combinations (covered in later chapters);

- revaluation increases;
- impairment losses and reversals of impairment losses;
- depreciation;
- net foreign exchange differences on translation; and
- other movements.

Where applicable the following information must also be disclosed:

♦ any restrictions on title to an asset;
♦ expenditures on the construction of property, plant, and equipment;
♦ any commitments to acquire property, plant, and equipment;
♦ any compensation receivable from third parties for items of property, plant, and equipment that were impaired, lost or given up that is included in profit or loss.

If property, plant, and equipment is stated at revalued amounts, further disclosures are required as follows:

♦ the effective date of the revaluation;
♦ whether an independent valuer was involved;
♦ the methods and significant assumptions used in estimating fair values;
♦ the extent to which fair values were determined directly by reference to observable prices in an active market or recent market transactions on arm's length terms or were estimated using other valuation techniques;
♦ the carrying amount that would have been recognized had the assets been carried under the cost model; and
♦ the revaluation surplus, including changes during the period and any restrictions on distribution.

IAS 36

IAS requires disclosure by class of assets of impairment losses recognized in the income statement and impairment losses reversed in the income statement.

If an individual impairment loss (reversal) is material the entity must disclose:

♦ the events and circumstances resulting in the impairment loss;
♦ the amount of the loss; and
♦ the nature of the asset and the business segment to which it relates.

If the recoverable amount is fair value less costs to sell, the entity should disclose the basis for determining fair value. If the recoverable amount is value in use, it should disclose the discount rate used.

5.7   Investment properties

Investment property is land or a building that is held so as to earn rental payments or because it is expected to appreciate in value, as opposed to being held to produce or supply goods or for administrative purposes and as opposed to being held with the intention of selling it. This includes property that is held under a finance lease (leased assets are covered later).

This type of asset is covered by IAS 40 *Investment Property*. Most of the issues have been covered already in this chapter, so the key points can be summarized very simply:

♦   initial recognition is as in IAS 16 (initial cost is used);
♦   subsequently the entity should account for the asset using either the fair-value model or the cost model:
   −   under the fair-value model the asset is measured at current market value and any changes from one period to the next are recognized in the income statement;
   −   under the cost model the asset is accounted for in accordance with IAS 16, except that additional disclosures are required, notably the fair value;
♦   whatever model is chosen must be applied to all investment properties.

Given that land and buildings generally increase in value it would be attractive for companies to classify all property as investment property and use the fair-value model. They could then not only avoid charging depreciation, but also recognize increases in value as income.

IAS 40 therefore makes it clear that certain specific items should not be treated as investment property, including the following:

♦   property held for sale in the ordinary course of business (dealt with by IAS 2 *Inventories*);
♦   property being constructed or developed on behalf of third parties (IAS 11 *Construction contracts*);
♦   owner-occupied property (IAS 16 *Property, Plant and Equipment*);
♦   property being constructed for future use as investment property (IAS 16 until complete, then IAS 40).

We will be looking at IAS 2 and IAS 11 in Chapter 7.

Change of use

An asset that is originally classified as an investment property may start to be used within the business. In this case IAS 40 is applied up until the date of the change and IAS 16 thereafter. The cost used should be the fair value at the date of the change.

Conversely, a building that was originally owner-occupied may cease to be used by the business for its own purposes, but be retained either to earn rentals or for capital appreciation. In this case IAS 40 will start to apply from the date of the change.

Note that any difference between carrying value and fair value at the date of a change from an owner-occupied to an investment property is treated as a revaluation under IAS 16, not as income or expense. The one exception is if the property has previously suffered an impairment loss. If that is the case the previous impairment loss is written back to profit and loss, and only the excess above that is credited to the revaluation reserve.

Leased property

There are certain provisions in IAS 40 about leased property. We will return to this topic when we deal with IAS 17 *Leases*, in Chapter 8.

Disclosure

IAS 40 requires the following information to be disclosed for investment properties:

- ♦ whether the fair-value model or the cost model is used;
- ♦ if classification is difficult, the criteria used to distinguish investment property from owner-occupied property and from property held for sale;
- ♦ the methods and significant assumptions applied in determining the fair value of investment property;
- ♦ the extent to which the fair value of investment property is based on a valuation by a qualified independent valuer. If there has been no such valuation, that fact must be disclosed;
- ♦ rental income from investment property and direct operating expenses (including repairs and maintenance) arising from the investment property;
- ♦ the amounts recognized in profit or loss for any restrictions on the realisability of investment property or the remittance of income and proceeds of disposal and any contractual obligations to purchase, construct, or develop investment property or for repairs, maintenance or enhancements.

The figures in the notes are likely to be shown in a similar way to those for property, plant and equipment.

- ♦ For the fair-value model IAS 40 requires a reconciliation between the carrying amounts of investment property at the beginning and end of the period, showing additions, disposals, fair-value adjustments, net foreign exchange differences, transfers to and from inventories and owner-occupied property, and other changes.

♦ For the cost model the entity must disclose depreciation methods, rates and amounts, impairment recognized or reversed, foreign exchange differences, transfers to and from inventories and owner-occupied property, and other changes.

Most notably, even if the cost model is used, the entity must disclose the fair value of investment property (or a range of likely estimates if the fair value of an item of investment property cannot be measured reliably). This last requirement means that an entity cannot avoid considering the fair-value issue and providing information, whichever method it adopts.

5.8   Non-current assets held for sale

Imagine a situation where a company moves its head office from one city to another. There could well be a point at which it still owns its old head office building but only because it has not yet sold it: the entity is not occupying the old building for its own purposes, nor intending to use it to generate rental income or to hold it for capital appreciation, and it is not in the business of dealing in property on a regular basis. It is just waiting for the often lengthy process of selling a property to be completed.

This type of asset falls into the category of non-current assets held for sale and these are dealt with in IFRS 5 *Non-current Assets Held for Sale and Discontinued Operations* (we will look at 'discontinued operations' in the context of group accounts later in this book).

IFRS 5 says that an asset should be classified as a non-current asset held for sale if its carrying amount will be recovered principally through a sale transaction rather than continuing use. The following factors indicate that this is so:

♦ management is committed to a plan to sell and the plan is unlikely to be changed or withdrawn;
♦ the asset is available for immediate sale;
♦ an active programme to locate a buyer has been initiated;
♦ the sale is highly probable within 12 months of classification in the accounts as 'held for sale';
♦ the asset is being actively marketed for sale at a price reasonable in relation to its fair value.

Accounting treatment and disclosure

Under IFRS 5 a non-current asset held for sale should be measured at the lower of its carrying amount and its fair value less costs to sell the asset. 'Fair value' is as previously defined in this chapter. Costs to sell means 'the incremental costs directly attributable to the disposal of an asset' excluding finance costs or tax expenses.

If the fair value is less than the carrying amount an impairment loss should be recognized in profit and loss. Note that this is different to the rules in IAS 36, where an impairment loss is recognized by reference to 'value in use' if that is higher than the net selling price.

The other key points in the accounting treatment are that:

♦ non-current assets held for sale should not be depreciated; and
♦ non-current assets held for sale should be shown separately from other assets on the face of the balance sheet, and the notes should include a description of the type of asset held for sale and the circumstances surrounding the sale.

Summary

Now that you have completed this chapter you should be able to:

♦ **explain the factors that influence when tangible assets are capitalized and how they are valued, and revalued, and depreciated;**
♦ **explain alternative bases of depreciation; and**
♦ **demonstrate knowledge and understanding of the following accounting standards:**
  IAS 16 *Property, Plant and Equipment*
  IAS 17 *Leases*
  IAS 36 *Impairment of Assets*
  IAS 40 *Investment Property*
  IFRS 5 *Non-current Assets Held for Sale and Discontinued Operations*
  (IAS 17 is dealt with in more detail in Chapter 8).

Six

Intangible assets

Syllabus

This chapter is the second of two relating to syllabus Section 3: Fixed Assets. Attention is paid to the economic nature of intangible fixed assets. The section then focuses on the principles of recognition, valuation (and re-valuation) and amortization, recognizing that these are areas where different regulatory regimes can (and do) adopt (sometimes very) different accounting bases.

Objectives

After studying this chapter you should be able to:
- ♦ explain issues surrounding the recognition and valuation of intangible assets and the **IASB** position on intangibles;
- ♦ explain how intangible assets are amortized; and
- ♦ demonstrate knowledge and understanding of the following accounting standards:
  IAS 38 *Intangible Assets*
  IFRS 3 *Business Combinations.*

6.1   Intangible assets

As we explained in the previous chapter, intangible assets are assets that do not have physical substance, for example a sum of money paid to an author to obtain the rights to make a film of one of his or her books. Although the agreement may be written on paper, the physical paper and ink are not the assets. It is the information conveyed by the writing – what various parties may and may not do – that is the asset.

As you will remember from Chapter 2, the Companies Act balance sheet format includes a section for intangible assets as follows.

1   Development costs.

2   Concessions, patents, licences, trade marks and similar rights and assets.

3   Goodwill.

4   Payments on account.

Because of their nature, intangible assets have historically been of less interest to accounts users such as bankers. Their perceived lack of marketability and difficulty in valuing them means that they are less suitable for use as loan collateral.

This does not mean, however, that such assets are insignificant. In some businesses, particularly those in service industries, the major assets may be intangible. Consider the most valuable assets of an advertising agency. They are likely to be its reputation, its creative staff and its client base. None of those assets is 'easy' to identify and value. None of those assets is likely to be recognized on the balance sheet, but they do contribute significantly to the success or otherwise of the business.

6.2   IAS 38 Intangible assets

Intangible assets are the subject of IAS 38 *Intangible assets*. This standard applies to all intangible assets other than financial assets, mineral rights and exploration and development costs for minerals, insurance contracts, intangible assets covered by another IAS (such as non-current assets held for sale), and goodwill.

Goodwill is covered by IFRS 3.

Examples of possible intangible assets include:

- ◆ patents;
- ◆ copyrights;
- ◆ computer software (if it is not an integral part of computerized equipment);
- ◆ films;
- ◆ customer lists;

- licenses;
- import quotas;
- franchises;
- customer and supplier relationships;
- marketing rights.

Identifiability, control and future economic benefits

If you consider the items in the previous list you will realize that some intangibles are much harder to value than others: a patent has a cost and could be sold, but a relationship with a customer is highly nebulous – it depends as much on the customer as it does on the entity that has the relationship.

For this reason IAS 38 specifies three critical attributes that an intangible asset must possess:

- identifiability;
- control;
- future economic benefits.

'Future economic benefits' means revenues from the sale of products or services as a result of using the asset or reduced future costs.

An intangible asset is *identifiable* in the following circumstances:

- if it is separable, in other words if it is capable of being sold, transferred, licensed, rented, or exchanged, either individually or as part of a package;
- if it arises from contractual or other legal rights, whether or not those rights are transferable or separable from the entity or from other rights and obligations.

The *control* criterion means that the entity must be able to enjoy future economic benefits from the use of the asset and prevent others from getting access to those benefits. IAS 38 gives some examples.

- The organization may have technical knowledge that is likely to give rise to future economic benefits but this can be recognized only as an intangible asset if it is protected by legal rights such as copyright.
- The skills of staff may have been developed in house through training and experience, and these may lead to future economic benefits but it is unlikely that the entity could control whether or not those staff are retained.
- As mentioned above, an organization may enjoy a certain market share and good relationships with customers, but it cannot control the actions of those customers: they may go out of business, or they may not remain loyal if a competitor enters the market.

Recognition and initial measurement

An asset that meets the criteria above may be recognized in the financial statements if both the following also apply:

 ♦ it is probable, on the basis of reasonable and supportable assumptions, that the future economic benefits will indeed flow to the organization; and
 ♦ if the cost of the asset can be measured reliably.

When it is first recognized an intangible asset should be measured at cost.

 ♦ If it is acquired separately this means its purchase price plus any acquisition costs such as legal fees or other costs incurred to bring it into use.
 ♦ If it is acquired as a result of a business combination (eg taking over another company) its cost is its fair value at the date of the acquisition. As you know from the previous chapter, fair value means the amount for which the asset could be exchanged in an arm's length transaction, usually the market price.

Research and development expenditure

Growing organizations are constantly spending money on dreaming up new products and new ideas for services and may wish to argue that such expenditure represents an internally generated intangible asset.

In this regard IAS 38 distinguishes between a research phase and a development phase.

 ♦ *Research* is original and planned investigation undertaken with the prospect of gaining new scientific or technical knowledge and understanding (eg market research).
 ♦ *Development* is the application of research findings or other knowledge to a plan or design for the production of new or substantially improved products or services.

Research expenditure may not lead to any new product or service and IAS 38 says that it should be written off as an expense when it is incurred.

Development expenditure, however, may sometimes be recognized as an intangible asset, but IAS 38 sets strict conditions.

 ♦ The organization must be able to demonstrate that the asset is technically and commercially feasible (ie that it can be created and there is a market for it).
 ♦ The organization must be able to show that it intends to complete the intangible asset and has the technical, financial and other resources to do so.
 ♦ It must be able to demonstrate how the asset will generate future economic benefits.
 ♦ It must be able to measure reliably the expenditure attributable to the asset during its development.

Internally-generated goodwill

A business is normally worth more than the sum of its net assets. The excess is known as goodwill and is created by such diverse factors as a good reputation, full order book, loyal/talented employees, successful management team, good location, profitable product lines, good quality intellectual property, etc.

Goodwill has a constantly fluctuating value. It can even have a negative value. In this case a company would be worth more when broken up into its constituent assets and liabilities than as a whole entity.

Because of the inherent uncertainties, internally-generated goodwill may not be recognized as an intangible asset under either the Companies Act 1985 or IAS 38.

(As we shall see later, however, when acquiring another business the price paid will often be more than value of the net assets acquired. The difference is known as purchased goodwill and is dealt with in IFRS 3.)

Brands and similar internally-generated assets

Brands have always represented one of the bigger areas of controversy in the debate over intangibles. In the late 1980s several companies included brands on their balance sheet. One of the most famous was Rank Hovis McDougall plc which revalued its brands every year and ended up with more than half of its net assets value in the form of brands.

No-one disputes that a successful brand is valuable. Businesses may be bought purely to acquire the brand name, and in this case the goodwill provisions of IFRS 3 will apply, as we shall see later.

The difficulty is identifying a reliable value for a self-generated brand: there is no general agreement on how or whether this should be done.

The position of the standards is clear, however. IAS 38 specifically forbids the recognition of internally-generated brands, mastheads, publishing titles, customer lists and similar items, on the grounds that expenditure on such things cannot be distinguished from the cost of developing the business as a whole, in other words it cannot be measured reliably.

Subsequent measurement

After they have been recognized organizations can choose to value intangible assets using either the cost model or the revaluation model, applying the chosen model to all assets in the same class. This is exactly the same treatment as is applied to tangible assets, so we need not repeat the details of these models: see the previous chapter.

But IAS 38 does insist that revaluations of intangible assets should be determined only by reference to an active market (not by consulting a professional valuer, for example) and it is rare for an active market to exist. Intangibles are typically unique, and transactions in intangibles are relatively infrequent, so evidence of one transaction is not good evidence for the value of another.

Effectively, therefore, the cost model will usually be used.

Useful life and amortization

The writing down of intangible assets over their useful lives is conventionally called amortization rather than depreciation, but the principles are the same.

Useful life

Some intangible assets may have an indefinite useful life if, based on an analysis of all relevant factors, there is no foreseeable limit to the period over which the asset is expected to generate net cash inflows. IAS 38 gives a number of examples, such as a trademark that is renewable every ten years at little cost.

Other intangibles may have a very clearly defined useful life, for example if they arise from a legal contract that specifies that the entity is to enjoy the benefits of the contract for a specific period and no longer. If a legal right lasts for, say, 50 years, but the only expects to derive benefits for only, say, 30 years, the asset should be amortised over the shorter period, 30 years.

For most intangibles a number of factors will need to be taken into account when determining the useful life. Among other things IAS 38 mentions: expected usage; product life cycles; technical, technological and commercial obsolescence; expected actions by competitors; and the level of maintenance expenditure required.

Amortization (and impairment)

An intangible asset with an indefinite useful life should not be amortized.

An intangible asset with a finite useful life should be amortized over its expected useful life using an appropriate method (the straight-line method, the reducing-balance method, the unit-of-production method and so on), based on the expected pattern of consumption of the expected future benefits.

The residual value of an intangible asset is normally assumed to be zero unless there is clear commitment by a third party to purchase the asset at the end of its useful life or an active market is expected to exist and it is possible to determine residual value by reference to that market.

Both the amortization period and the method used should be reviewed at each financial year end and changed if appropriate. This applies to assets with both finite and indefinite useful lives. If an asset that was previously considered to have an indefinite useful life is not considered to have a finite life, this is an indication of impairment, and IAS 36 should be applied. In other words the entity should compare the carrying amount with the recoverable amount and recognize an impairment loss if necessary.

Disclosure

The figures will be laid out in the notes in a similar way to tangible assets (see the previous chapter).

IAS 38 requires the following information to be disclosed for each class of intangible asset:

♦ the useful life or amortization rate and the amortization method;
♦ the gross carrying amount;
♦ accumulated amortization and impairment losses;
♦ a reconciliation of the carrying amount at the beginning and the end of the period showing additions, assets held for sale, disposals, revaluations, impairments, reversals of impairments, amortization charge, and foreign exchange differences;
♦ the basis for determining that an intangible has an indefinite life, if applicable
♦ a description and carrying amount of individually material intangible assets;
♦ information about intangible assets whose title is restricted; and
♦ commitments to acquire intangible assets in the future.

IAS 38 also requires disclosures about:

♦ intangible assets carried at revalued amounts (date of revaluation, methods used, carrying amount if the cost model were used instead, and amount of any revaluation surplus and movements in the year); and
♦ the amount of research and development expenditure recognized as an expense during the period.

6.3　Purchased goodwill

As we have seen goodwill is the concept that a business is normally worth more than the sum of its parts due to factors such as a good reputation, a full order book, talented employees, a good location, and so on.

Goodwill is not normally recognized in the financial statements, but when one business acquires another for a premium price this creates an amount of 'purchased goodwill' which can be reliably measured at a specific point in time.

For example, suppose that Williams Ltd purchased 100% of Cheam Ltd's share capital for £3,000,000.

At the time of purchase Cheam's balance sheet, stated at fair value, was as follows:

	£m
Fixed assets:	
Intangible	0.5
Tangible	1.6
	2.1
Net current assets	1.1
	3.2
Creditors: due after one year	(0.5)
	2.7
Financed by:	
Share capital	1.0
Reserves	1.7
	2.7

Williams has paid £3m for separable net assets valued at £2.7m. The difference of £0.3m represents the premium Williams has paid – this is purchased positive goodwill.

IFRS 3 Business Combinations

IFRS 3 *Business Combinations* defines goodwill as 'future economic benefits arising from assets that are not capable of being individually identified and separately recognized'.

Initial measurement

The cost of goodwill is recognized as an asset in the financial statements. The cost is the excess of:

- ♦ the cost of bringing together separate entities into one entity; over
- ♦ the acquirer's interest in the net fair value of the identifiable assets (including identifiable intangible assets), liabilities and contingent liabilities.

To put it more simply it is the acquisition costs minus the fair value of the net assets. As usual fair value is the amount of an arm's length transaction between willing parties – usually market price.

Subsequent measurement

Previous standards had required goodwill to be amortized, usually over a period of 20 years or less, and also subjected to impairment reviews if circumstances suggested that impairment might have occurred.

IFRS 3, issued in March 2004, has tightened up on this rather arbitrary treatment. Under IFRS 3 purchased goodwill is not amortized, but must be tested at least annually for impairment. Any impairment loss is written off immediately as an expense. (See the previous chapter for details of what is involved in an impairment review.)

FRS 10 requires that goodwill be amortized over its useful life unless it is felt that it does not have a finite useful life. The standard encourages companies to amortize goodwill over a maximum of 20 years. It does this indirectly because there is a requirement for an annual impairment review where a period of more than 20 years is selected or where the goodwill is not amortized because it is felt that the useful life is infinite. In any case a company making an acquisition must undertake a limited impairment review one year after the acquisition.

An impairment review is a formal review, set out in FRS 11, performed as necessary or as required by accounting standards, to ensure that an asset's carrying value has not fallen below its recoverable amount. It is dealt with in more detail later in this chapter.

Negative goodwill

Negative goodwill arises where the acquisition cost is less than the fair value of the net assets acquired. For example, if Williams had paid £2m for its interest in Cheam, there would be negative goodwill of £0.7m.

IFRS 3 requires that negative goodwill is recognized immediately in the income statement as a gain. Before concluding that negative goodwill has arisen, however, the standard requires that the acquirer reassess the identification and measurement of the fair value of identifiable assets, liabilities, and contingent liabilities acquired and the measurement of the cost of the business combination.

Disclosure

IFRS 3 requires a reconciliation of the carrying amount of goodwill at the beginning and end of the period, showing the gross amount and any impairment losses. In the period in which the combination occurs extensive disclosures are required, including the following:

♦ names and descriptions of the combining entities or businesses;
♦ acquisition date;

♦ cost of the combination (with separate disclosures where the business was acquired by issuing shares to the previous owners);

♦ amounts recognized at the acquisition date for each class of assets, liabilities, and contingent liabilities acquired, and, unless impracticable, the carrying amounts of each of those classes, determined in accordance with international standards immediately before the combination;

♦ amount of any negative goodwill recognized in profit or loss; and

♦ details about the factors that contributed to recognition of goodwill.

Summary

Now that you have completed this chapter you should be able to:

♦ **explain issues surrounding the recognition of intangible assets and the IASB position on intangibles;**

♦ **explain various bases of amortization of intangible assets; and**

♦ **demonstrate knowledge and understanding of the following accounting standards:**
IAS 38   *Intangible Assets*
IFRS 3   *Business Combinations.*

Seven

Current assets

Syllabus

This chapter covers syllabus Section 4: Current Assets. It looks at the nature of current assets and their incorporation in financial statements. The focus is principally on the valuation of inventories and receivables using the lower of cost and net realizable value principle. Attention is paid to differing approaches to the measurement of cost (of inventories) and how to deal with long-term contracts, leading on to a broader discussion of the principles of revenue recognition.

Objectives

After studying this chapter you should be able to:

♦ **explain the components of inventories and discuss how their cost is measured by reference to absorption costing, direct costing and cost flow assumptions;**
♦ **explain the lower of cost and net realizable value principle;**
♦ **explain how profit is recognized on long-term contracts;**
♦ **discuss revenue recognition principles and valuation of receivables; and**
♦ **demonstrate knowledge and understanding of the following accounting standards:**
  IAS 2 *Inventories*
  IAS 11 *Construction Contracts*
  IAS 18 *Revenue.*

7.1 Current assets

In essence a current asset is cash already, or it is something that you expect to turn into cash before the end of the current year. According to IAS 1 a current asset is an asset that has one or several of the following characteristics:

(a) it is expected to be realized in, or is intended for sale or consumption in, the entity's normal operating cycle;

(b) it is held primarily for the purpose of being traded;

(c) it is expected to be realized within 12 months after the balance sheet date;

(d) it is cash or a cash equivalent.

Components of current assets

Here is the Companies Act format for the current assets section of the balance sheet.

CURRENT ASSETS
I   Stocks
    1   Raw materials
    2   Work in progress
    3   Finished goods and goods for resale
    4   Payments on account

II   Debtors
    1   Trade debtors
    2   Amounts owed by group undertakings
    3   Amounts owed by undertakings in which the company has a participating interest
    4   Other debtors
    5   Called-up share capital not paid
    6   Prepayments and accrued income

III   Investments
    1   Shares in group undertakings
    2   Own shares
    3   Other investments

IV Cash at bank and in hand

We will leave the 'Investments' part for later chapters, and likewise the group-related amounts (II(2) and II(3)).

In normal circumstances 'Cash' is not controversial: it is the actual cash held by the entity right now, the bulk of which sits in its current account(s) at the bank. The financial statements are generally several days more up-to-date than its bank's records at any particular point in time because of clearing systems that do not take advantage of modern technology, particularly in the UK. You will probably remember doing bank reconciliations, taking account of uncleared cheques and deposits, in your earlier studies.

The accounting treatment of stocks (which we will call 'inventories' in keeping with international standards) raises a variety of issues regarding how items are valued and when they are recognized. Much of this chapter is devoted to these issues.

Debtors raise the issue of revenue recognition: when is the entity entitled to include income in its financial statements? Although this is normally straightforward there are some transactions where there may be some room for interpretation as to when and whether ownership has passed to a customer, and there may often be doubts over whether income is really collectable.

7.2   Inventories

Inventory, more often called 'stock' in the UK, simply means 'things that come in' to the business, like tins of baked beans to resell.

Modern methods of management aim to save costs by reducing the amount of goods held in stores and warehouses to a bare minimum, but in spite of this inventory is still a major asset in the balance sheet of many companies.

The nature of inventory will depend on the type of organization involved.

- ♦ A retailer is likely to buy and sell only items of inventory. He will have only one sort of inventory – finished goods.
- ♦ A manufacturer will purchase raw materials, work on them and convert them into finished goods. Inventory that is part way through conversion is referred to as work in progress.
- ♦ A service company does not sell physical items so it may have no inventory in a conventional sense. It may instead have a large amount of work that is part-completed and on which it has incurred substantial costs, such as staff salaries.

Valuation

The valuation of inventory is an important issue. It directly affects both the balance sheet and reported profits – different inventory valuations will give different profits and different net assets.

Here is a simple example that illustrates the impact of inventory on reported figures. In this case it shows that the lower the opening inventory value and the higher the closing inventory value the higher the profits will be.

	Company A		Company B	
	€	€	€	€
Revenue		10,000		10,000
Cost of sales				
Opening inventory	1,000		0	
Purchases	5,000		5,000	
Closing inventory	(0)		(1,000)	
		(6,000)		(4,000)
Gross profit		4,000		6,000

This year's closing inventory is next year's opening inventory, so Company B will need to value its closing inventory at an even higher amount next year if it wants users to believe that it has maintained an increase in profits.

In terms of the balance sheet, the higher the closing inventory value the larger the net assets. To the unwary user of the financial statements this may make the company look very healthy, but high levels of inventory may include many items that are unsaleable.

You can probably see the temptation for a company to 'massage' the figures so that they report the results it wants to show. As with many of the other assets we have already looked at, valuation of inventory is an area where judgement needs to be exercised and great care taken in interpreting the results. Accounting standards exist to prevent companies from manipulating the figures to suit themselves.

Measuring cost

Inventory items should normally be valued at their cost, but if they cannot be resold for that amount they should be valued at the amount they can be sold for.

Under IAS 2 *Inventories* 'cost' comprises the costs incurred in bringing the inventory to its present location and condition. This is quite consistent with the definition of 'cost' used for non-current assets.

Cost will include:

♦ purchase price;

♦ carriage inwards, import duties etc; and
♦ conversion costs, including fixed and variable manufacturing overheads.

To understand IAS 2 properly you need to be aware of the distinction that is made in accounting between direct costs and indirect costs (overheads).

Direct costs

A direct cost is a cost that can be traced in full to the item whose cost is being determined.

♦ *Direct material* is all the material that becomes part of the product – steel, plastic, nuts and bolts, electrical components etc, unless used in negligible amounts and/or having negligible cost (eg a few drops of oil).
♦ *Direct wages* are all wages paid for labour expended on the work of making the product or providing the service. This includes the wages and salaries of the people involved directly in the work, but excludes the costs of support staff.
♦ *Direct expenses* are any expenses that are incurred on a specific product, other than direct material cost and direct wages. Examples of direct expenses include the cost of special designs, drawings or layouts for a specific job; the hire of tools or equipment for a particular job; and maintenance costs of tools, machines and so on, incurred on a specific job.

Indirect costs

Indirect costs, more commonly known as overheads, are all the costs that are not direct costs.

♦ *Manufacturing (or production) overhead* includes all indirect material costs, indirect wages and indirect expenses incurred in the factory from receipt of the order until its completion. Indirect materials are items such as consumable stores like cleaning materials. Indirect wages means all wages not charged directly to a product, for example the wages or salaries of non-productive personnel in the production department, such as foremen and supervisors. Indirect expenses typically include rent, rates and factory insurance, and depreciation charges for plant and machinery.
♦ *Administration overhead* relates to the administration of an undertaking, for example the costs of the accounts department.
♦ *Selling overhead* relates to expenses incurred in promoting sales and retaining customers.
♦ *Distribution overhead* is the expenses incurred in making the packed product ready for despatch and delivering it to the customer.

In 'traditional' costing systems, therefore, the unit cost of production can be calculated as the sum of the following items.

	€	€
Direct materials	X	
Direct labour	X	
Direct expenses	<u>X</u>	
Direct cost		X
Manufacturing overhead		<u>X</u>
Full production cost		X
Administration overhead		X
Selling and distribution overhead		<u>X</u>
Full cost of sale		<u>X</u>

Absorption costing

An absorption costing system measures the cost of items as the sum of direct costs plus overheads. 'Absorption' of overheads means assigning an appropriate share of overhead costs to each item, that share being an amount that reflects the amount of indirect resources that go into producing the item.

In many absorption costing systems only manufacturing overheads are added to product costs. Administration overheads and sales and distribution overheads are treated as separate expenses in the income statement.

Suppose that a company makes and sells 250 units of a product each week. The direct cost per unit is €5 and the sales price per unit is €10. Manufacturing overhead is €500 per week and administration, selling and distribution overhead is €250 per week.

The weekly profit is as follows.

	€	€
Sales (250 units x €10)		2,500
Direct costs (250 x €5)	1,250	
Manufacturing overheads	500	
Administration, selling, distribution overheads	<u>250</u>	
		<u>(2,000)</u>
Profit		<u>500</u>

In absorption costing, manufacturing overheads will be added to each unit of product manufactured and sold.

	€ per unit
Direct cost per unit	5
Manufacturing overhead (€500 per week for 250 units)	2
	7

The weekly profit would be calculated as follows.

	€
Sales	2,500
Cost of sales (250 × €7)	(1,750)
Gross profit	750
Administration, selling, distribution costs	(250)
Net profit	500

If an organization produces a single standard product the overhead cost per unit can be calculated by dividing the total overhead costs among the total units produced, as in the example above. Most companies produce a variety of products, or single products in different sizes, and a fair method of sharing overhead costs between them needs to be established. A common way of doing this is on the basis of the amount of time it takes to produce different items.

For example if the company works a total of 50 labour hours per week and incurs €500 in manufacturing overheads per week then the absorption rate is (€500/50) = €10 per labour hour. Suppose it produces two products, Product A, each unit of which takes 0.28 labour hours to produce, and Product B, each unit of which takes 0.12 labour hours.

	Units produced	Hours per unit	Absorption rate	O'head cost per unit
Product A	125	0.28	€10	€2.80
Product B	125	0.12	€10	€1.20

The weekly profit is as before, but now we have a more detailed analysis.

	€	€
Sales of A (125 × 10)		1,250
Sales of B (125 × 10)		1,250
		2,500
Cost of sales: Product A (125 × €(5 + 2.80))	975	
Cost of sales: Product B (125 × €(5 + 1.20))	775	
		(1,750)
Gross profit		750

We can see the relevance of this in the context of inventory if we assume that not all of the items produced are sold. Let us say we produce as before but sell only 100 units of each product.

	€	€
Sales of A (100 × 10)		1,000
Sales of B (100 × 10)		1,000
		2,000
Opening stock (A and B)	0	
Cost of sales: Product A (125 × €(5 + 2.80))	975	
Cost of sales: Product B (125 × €(5 + 1.20))	775	
Closing stock of A (25 × €(5 + 2.80))	(195)	
Closing stock of B (25 × €(5 + 1.20))	(155)	
		(1,400)
Gross profit		600

This approach is totally consistent with the matching principle: the overhead relating to the unsold items is carried forward to be matched against income in the next period. If stock were valued at direct cost only and all production overheads were written off in full as incurred this would understate profits.

	€	€
Sales of A (100 × 10)		1,000
Sales of B (100 × 10)		1,000
		2,000
Cost of sales: Product A (10 × €5)	625	
Cost of sales: Product B (125 × €5)	625	
Closing stock of A (25 × €5)	(125)	
Closing stock of A (25 × €5)	(125)	
		(1,000)
Production overhead		(500)
Gross profit		500

IAS 2 and conversion cost

Although IAS 2 does not actually use the term 'absorption costing', this is the approach it requires in valuing inventory. It says that cost should include 'conversion costs' and these in turn include fixed and variable manufacturing overheads.

Cost flow assumptions: FIFO and other methods

Defining cost can be problematic where the purchase price of inventory bought is fluctuating. Consider the following example.

During the week Kerr Ltd purchased the following identical inventory items.

		€ per kg	Total
Monday am	4 kg	2.00	8.00
Tuesday am	8 kg	2.10	16.80
Wednesday am	3 kg	2.15	6.45
Thursday am	10 kg	2.16	21.60
Friday am	6 kg	2.20	13.20
TOTAL			66.05

On Wednesday afternoon Kerr sold 6 kg and on Thursday afternoon 12 kg. Calculate Kerr's cost of sales.

Three methods of valuing inventory are commonly identified, FIFO, LIFO and weighted average cost.

FIFO

The most obvious method to use is first-in, first-out (FIFO), which assumes that the oldest inventory is sold first and we are left with the newest inventory. This is what would happen in practice in most cases.

			€/kg	Cost of sales (€)
Monday am	Purchase	4 kg	2.00	
Tuesday am	Purchase	8 kg	2.10	
Wednesday am	Purchase	3 kg	2.15	
Wednesday pm	Sale (6 kg)	(4 kg)	2.00	8.00
		(2 kg)	2.10	4.20
Remaining		6 kg	2.10	
		3 kg	2.15	
Thursday am	Purchase	10 kg	2.16	
Thursday pm	Sale (12 kg)	(6 kg)	2.10	12.60
		(3 kg)	2.15	6.45
		(3 kg)	2.16	6.48
Remaining		7 kg	2.16	
Friday am	Purchase	6 kg	2.20	
TOTAL				37.73

Thus we will be left with:

kg	€/kg	€
7	2.16	15.12
6	2.20	13.20
13	TOTAL	28.32

LIFO

Now consider the position using last-in, first-out (LIFO). This method assumes that we sell the newest inventory and keep the oldest.

			€/kg	Cost of sales (€)
Monday am	Purchase	4 kg	2.00	
Tuesday am	Purchase	8 kg	2.10	
Wednesday am	Purchase	3 kg	2.15	
Wednesday pm	Sale (6 kg)	(3 kg)	2.15	6.45
		(3 kg)	2.10	6.30
Left remaining		4 kg	2.00	
		5 kg	2.10	
Thursday am	Purchase	10 kg	2.16	
Thursday pm	Sale (12 kg)	(10 kg)	2.16	21.60
		(2 kg)	2.10	4.20
Left remaining		4 kg	2.00	
		3 kg	2.10	
Friday am	Purchase	6 kg	2.20	
TOTAL				38.55

Thus we will be left with:

kg	€/kg	€
6	2.20	13.20
3	2.10	6.30
4	2.00	8.00
13	TOTAL	27.50

Weighted average cost

Finally consider using weighted average cost, sometimes called AVCO. With this method we re-calculate the average cost of inventory at every purchase or sale. For example, as at the end of Tuesday we have 12 kg and this cost €24.80 so the weighted average cost is (€24.80/12) = €2.067.

			€/kg	Total	Cost of sales (€)
Monday am	Purchase	4 kg	2.00	8.00	
Tuesday am	Purchase	8 kg	2.10	16.80	
Inventory at AVCO		*12 kg*	*2.067*	*24.80*	
Wednesday am	Purchase	3 kg	2.15	6.45	
Inventory at AVCO		*15 kg*	*2.083*	*31.25*	
Wednesday pm	Sale	(6 kg)	2.083	(12.50)	12.50
Thursday am	Purchase	10 kg	2.16	21.60	
Inventory at AVCO		*19 kg*	*2.124*	*40.35*	
Thursday pm	Sale	(12 kg)	2.124	(25.48)	25.48
Friday am	Purchase	6 kg	2.20	13.20	
Inventory at AVCO		*13 kg*	*2.159*	*28.07*	
TOTAL					37.98

Thus we will be left with:

kg	€/kg	€
13	2.159	28.07

To compare the effect of the three methods, assume that all inventory was sold for €3.00 per kg.

	FIFO €	LIFO €	AVCO €
Sales (18 kg @ €3.00)	54.00	54.00	54.00
Cost of sales			
Opening inventory	0	0	0
Purchases	66.05	66.05	66.05
Closing inventory	(28.32)	(27.50)	(28.07)
Cost of sales	37.73	38.55	37.98
Gross Profit	16.27	15.45	16.02

In summary, in times of rising prices, FIFO will give the highest inventory values and consequently the highest profit, AVOC will give a lower value and a lower profit and LIFO will give the lowest inventory value and the lowest profit.

IAS 2 *does not allow the use of LIFO,* because of its inherent understatement of inventory values and the fact that it does not follow what happens in practice in terms of inventory rotation. In addition the Inland Revenue will not accept LIFO as a method of inventory valuation for use in inventory valuation, mainly because it understates inventory values and consequently taxable profits.

Cost and net realizable value (NRV)

IAS 2 states that inventory should be valued at the lower of cost, as calculated on the principles explained above, and net realizable value (NRV). NRV is the estimated selling price of the inventory less estimated future costs of completion, if any, and estimated costs to enable the inventory to be sold. For example if it is old stock it may have to be adapted in some way to conform to the latest product standards.

The comparison between cost and NRV is made on the grounds of prudence and in the interests of users: it would be imprudent and misleading to show a value for inventory that was greater than the amount it could really be sold for.

The comparison should be made for each item of inventory – not globally. Consider the following example.

James Limited holds three types of inventory; their cost and NRVs are as follows:

Inventory	Cost (€)	NRV (€)
A	2,000	2,900
B	1,400	1,200
C	3,800	5,000
Total	7,200	9,100

In total the estimated sale proceeds are more than the cost. Examining each inventory line individually, we should value the inventory as follows:

Inventory	€	
A	2,000	(Cost)
B	1,200	(NRV)
C	3,800	(Cost)
Total	7,000	

Why might NRV be less than cost – surely we are in business to make a profit?

Some of the reasons might be:

 ♦ loss leaders, eg tins of baked beans sold for 20 cents to attract custom into the shop;

♦ old/obsolete/damaged inventory;
♦ collapse in the market – this might apply to high fashion goods where the market is volatile and fluctuating.

Disclosure

IAS 2 requires disclosure of the following in the financial statements:

♦ the accounting policy for inventories;
♦ the carrying amount of inventory. IAS 2 says that this will typically be classified as merchandise, supplies, materials, work in progress, and finished goods, but the classifications depend on what is appropriate for the enterprise;
♦ the carrying amount of any inventories carried at NRV;
♦ the amount of any write-down of inventories recognized as an expense in the period;
♦ the amount of any reversal of a write-down to NRV and the circumstances that led to this reversal;
♦ the carrying amount of inventories pledged as security for liabilities.

The financial statements must also disclose one or other of the following, whichever is felt to be more appropriate to the business:

♦ the cost of inventories recognized as expense (in other words cost of goods sold);
♦ the operating costs recognized during the period by nature of the cost (raw materials and consumables, labour costs, other operating costs and the amount of the net change in inventories for the period).

There is a choice because IAS 1 *Presentation of Financial Statements* permits different ways of presenting the income statement.

7.3   IAS 11 *Construction Contracts*

Certain companies are engaged in long-term contracts that straddle more than one accounting period. For example, a construction company may build a power station that takes three years to complete. Under the realization principle, we cannot recognize the profit on the project until it is complete (ie it turns from work in progress to finished goods). This can lead to a distortion of the company's results. Consider the following example.

Suppose that Jacques plc is a construction company building a dam. It is the only project the company is currently engaged in. Apart from the project, the company incurs general overheads and interest of €0.5m per year. The contract price is €10m. Total costs of the project are €8m, spread €4m in Year 1, €3m in Year 2 and €1m in Year 3. The contract specifies that the client will pay Jacques half of the contract price at the end of Year 2, with the remainder upon satisfactory completion of the project.

If we account for this project in the normal way the results will be as follows:

Income statement

	Year I €m	Year 2 €m	Year 3 €m
Sales	–	–	10
Cost of sales	–	–	(8)
Gross Profit	–	–	2
Overheads	(0.5)	(0.5)	(0.5)
Net profit/(loss)	(0.5)	(0.5)	1.5

Balance sheet

	Year I €m	Year 2 €m	Year 3 €m
Inventory	4	7	0
Creditors – payments in advance	0	5	0

Without knowing the story behind this company we might have difficulty in interpreting its performance. A loss for two years is converted into a profit in Year 3. One might get the impression its performance is improving from a poor start. In reality the company has performed similarly for all three years. The above treatment conflicts with the accruals concept.

The provisions of IAS 11 *Construction Contracts* cater for this. They allow the company to recognize part of the contract revenue before it has been realized (ie before the end of the contract). Thus the revenue is spread over the three years, not all taken in Year 3. Concurrently, the contract costs are also spread over the three years – and taken to the income statement – using the same method used to allocate the contract revenue.

This is commonly called the percentage of completion method.

How to determine the stage of completion

This can be done in several ways.

The cost basis

The stage of completion is determined with reference to the proportion of costs incurred to date compared with estimated total contract costs. In the case above, at the end of Years 1, 2 and 3 we will have incurred respectively 4/8ths, 7/8ths and

8/8ths of the total costs. Thus we will take those proportions of sales, cost of sales and consequently gross profit to the income statements for the three years.

Income statement

		Year 1 €m		Year 2 €m		Year 3 €m
Sales	4/8ths x €10m)	5.00	(7/8ths x €10m = €8.75m less €5m already taken)	3.75	(8/8ths x €10m less €8.75m already taken)	1.25
Cost of sales	(4/8ths x €8m)	4.00	(7/8ths x €8m = €7m less €4m already taken)	3.00	(8/8ths x €8m less €7m already taken)	1.00
Gross profit		1.00		0.75		0.25
Overheads		(0.50)		(0.50)		(0.50)
Net profit/(loss)		0.50		0.25		(0.25)

These results may reflect more accurately the company's results – declining profitability over the three years as the project activity decreases.

Balance sheet extract

	Year 1 €m	Year 2 €m	Year 3 €m
Inventory			
Costs incurred	4.00	7.00	8.00
Taken to P/L a/c	(4.00)	(7.00)	(8.00)
WIP	0.00	0.00	0.00
Debtors			
Sales	5.00	8.75	10.00
Progress payments received	(0.00)	(5.00)	(10.00)
Debtors	5.00	3.75	0.00

The survey basis

An architect/quantity surveyor's opinion may be used to ascertain the current value of the contract in selling terms. For example, in this case an architect may value the contract at €2m, €7m and €10m for Years 1, 2, and 3, respectively.

Income statement

		Year 1 €m		Year 2 €m		Year 3 €m
Sales		2.0	*(€7m less €2m already taken)*	6.0	*(€10m less €7m already taken)*	3.0
Cost of sales	*(4/8ths x €8m)*	(1.6)	*(7/10ths x €8m = less €1.6m taken in Year 1)*	(4.0)	*(10/10ths x €8m less €5.6m already taken)*	(2.4)
Gross profit		0.4		1.0		0.6
Overheads		(0.5)		(0.5)		(0.5)
Net profit/(loss)		(0.1)		0.5		0.1

These results may reflect more accurately the nature of the company's activity – reflecting the increased value of the project in sales terms in Year 2.

Balance sheet extract

	Year 1 €m	Year 2 €m	Year 3 €m
Inventory			
Costs incurred	4.0	7.0	8.0
Taken to P/L a/c	(1.6)	(5.6)	(8.0)
WIP	2.4	1.4	0.0
Debtors			
Sales	2.0	7.0	10.0
Progress payments received	(0.0)	(5.0)	(10.0)
Debtors	2.0	2.0	0.0

Physical proportion completed

The physical proportion of work done may be measurable, eg 15%, 65%, 100%.

You would then take 15% of the contract price as sales in Year 1, 50% (65% less the 15% taken in Year 1) in Year 2, and 35% (100% less 65% taken in Years 1 and 2) in Year 3. Similarly, you would take 15% of total contract costs in Year 1, 50% in Year 2 and 35% in Year 3.

Note, however, that under all methods, even the original method of not taking attributable profit, the total contract profit over the three years will be the same. The difference in the methods is in the allocation of that profit to the various accounting periods. Once again different methods of allocation will lead to different asset valuations and different profits.

What constitutes a long-term contract?

IAS 11 defines a construction contract as a contract specifically negotiated for the construction of an asset or a group of interrelated assets. This may include a contract for providing services directly related to the construction, such as an architect's services.

A construction contract need not exceed one year, but it must straddle at least one year-end, otherwise the accounting problem does not arise.

It is also an overriding requirement that if we are accounting for a contract under IAS 11 it must be possible to estimate the outcome of the project reliably. This will be so if the following conditions are satisfied:

♦ total contract costs can be measured reliably;
♦ it is probably that the economic benefits will flow to the entity;
♦ both the remaining costs to completion and the stage of completion can be measured reliably; and
♦ costs incurred so far that are attributable to the contract can be identified clearly and reliably measured, so that actual costs can be compared with previous estimates.

If the outcome cannot be measured reliably IAS 11 says that the following treatment should be adopted:

♦ contract costs should be recognized as an expense as they are incurred; and
♦ contract revenue should only be recognized to the extent of contract costs incurred that are expected to be recoverable.

The net effect would normally be nil, assuming that the entity will not be foolish enough to incur further costs unless it expects to recover them.

Losses on construction contracts

Another application of the prudence concept occurs if the project is estimated to show a loss. Any loss should be recognized as an expense as soon as it is foreseen. The amount of the loss will be the difference between the total contract costs and the total contract revenues.

Using our example above, and assuming we have used the survey basis, consider the situation at the end of Year 2 if the cost profile were as follows:

	Year 1 €m	Year 2 €m	Year 3 €m
Costs	4 (actual)	3 (actual)	4 (estimated)

At the end of Year 2, Year 3 costs are now estimated at €4m instead of the original estimate of €1m. We would have accounted to date as follows:

Income statement (original)

	Year 1 €m	Year 2 €m
Sales	2.0	5.0
Cost of sales	1.6	4.0
Gross profit	0.4	1.0
Overheads	(0.5)	(0.5)
Net (loss)/profit	(0.1)	0.5

We will now need to rework Year 2's figures in line with the new estimate.

Income statement (revised)

	Year 1 €m	
Sales	5.0	(as before)
Cost of sales (W2)	(6.4)	
Gross loss (W1)	(1.4)	
Overheads	(0.5)	
Net loss	(1.9)	

Workings

1   We account for the whole of the anticipated loss immediately as well as writing back any profit we have recognized in earlier periods. Thus:

	€m
Total contract revenue	10.0
Costs to date	(7.0)
Costs to complete	(4.0)
Anticipated total project loss	(1.0)
Write off of gross profit taken in Year 1	(0.4)
Gross loss for Year 2	(1.4)

2   Cost of sales is a balancing figure, following on from the calculation in Working 1.

Balance sheet

As always the balance sheet entries follow on from the income statement calculations.

	Year 2 €m
Inventory	
Costs incurred	7
Taken to P/L a/c	(8)
WIP/(Provisions for losses on construction contracts)	(1)
Debtors	
Sales	7
Progress payments received	(5)
	2

In Year 3, in case you are wondering, sales will be €3m, as previously determined, and cost of sales will be €11m less the €8m costs recognized to date which is also €3m, so the overall effect in Year 3 is nil.

Disclosure

IAS 11 requires the following matters to be disclosed:
- ♦ the amount of contract revenue recognized in the period;
- ♦ the method used to determine contract revenue; and
- ♦ the method used to determine the stage of completion of the contract.

For contracts in progress at the balance sheet date the entity should disclose the aggregate costs incurred and recognized profits less recognized losses to date; the amount of advances received; and the amount of 'retentions', which are progress billings that are not paid until certain conditions are satisfied, such as the rectification of defects.

If costs incurred plus recognized profits and losses is greater than progress billings the entity should show the gross amount due from customers as an asset.

If progress billings exceed costs incurred plus recognized profits and losses the entity should show the amount due to the customer as a liability.

7.4   Receivables

The recognition of revenue is usually straightforward in principle: the organization makes a sale and expects to be paid under normal business terms, so revenue is recognized at the point of sale.

It is not that uncommon, however, for a sale to be agreed but the items not delivered until some time afterwards. Construction contracts are an extreme example of this, but there are many others.

IAS 18 *Revenue* lays down the procedures to follow when recognizing and measuring the revenue that the entity can show as received or receivable in its accounts. It applies to common transactions that are not dealt with in other standards:

♦ sale of goods;
♦ rendering of services;
♦ interest, royalties and dividends receivable.

(Although the standards appear to come at the issue from an income statement point of view, we are still talking about current assets because revenue that is receivable will be recognized amongst debtors until it is actually received, and when it is received it will form part of cash.)

Revenue recognition principles

IAS 18 defines revenue as the gross inflow of economic benefits arising from the ordinary operating activities of an enterprise. It excludes amounts collected on behalf of third parties, most notably VAT.

Sale of goods

In the case of sale of goods revenue should be recognized when all of the following conditions have been satisfied:

♦ the significant risks and rewards of ownership of the goods have been transferred to the buyer;
♦ the entity does not have any managerial involvement or control over the goods of the kind normally associated with ownership;
♦ the amount of revenue can be measured reliably;
♦ it is probable that the economic benefits will flow to the entity; and
♦ the costs incurred in respect of the transaction can be measured reliably (revenue and expenses relating to the same transaction should be recognized simultaneously under the matching principle).

Risks and rewards normally pass to the buyer when the item is in its possession and the buyer has legal title to it: this is what happens when you buy something in a shop. An example of a situation where the entity may retain the significant risks and rewards of ownership is a sale or return arrangement: the entity should not recognize the revenue until the buyer sells the goods and consideration has been received.

Bad debts and refunds

Sometimes the entity retains what is considered an 'insignificant' risk, if for example it retains legal title until the goods are paid for, or if one aspect of the transaction is that the customer can take the goods back and get a refund if not satisfied. In such cases revenue can be recognized at the point of sale provided that a liability is recognized to cover the risk based on previous experience and any other factors that might help to determine the amount of the potential liability.

For example, as well as writing off known bad debts immediately – amounts owed by specific customers that are definitely not collectable, typically because that customer has gone out of business – organizations also usually need to make a general provision for bad debts. This would be calculated as a percentage (say 2%) of total trade debts, based on previous experience of non-payment.

Services

Revenue from rendering services is recognized on a similar basis to that from construction contracts. Revenue is recognized when it can be estimated reliably and this will be when all of the following conditions are satisfied:
- the amount of revenue can be measured reliably;
- it is probable that the economic benefits will flow to the entity;
- the stage of completion can be measured reliably; and
- the costs incurred in respect of the transaction to date and the costs to completion can be measured reliably.

In practice for many services revenue and expenses can usually be recognized as received (or receivable) and as incurred. As with construction contracts, however, in some cases it may be more appropriate to measure the stage of completion on a proportion of cost incurred basis, via a survey, or on a percentage basis.

Again, as with construction contracts, if the outcome cannot be measured reliably revenue should be recognized only to the extent of costs incurred that are recoverable.

Interest, royalties and dividends

These items are included in IAS 18 because the revenue arises from the use by others of assets (including cash) belonging to the entity. As usual revenue is recognized when it can be measured reliably and it is probable that economic benefits will flow to the entity.

- ◆ Dividends are recognized when the shareholder's right to receive payment is established.
- ◆ Royalties are recognized on the basis that they accrue under the relevant agreement. There are usually agreed methods for industries where this applies, for example for actors and musicians.
- ◆ As for interest, the situation can be highly complex in the world of high finance, and therefore IAS 18 refers to IAS 39 which deals with financial instruments in great depth. We will look at this standard in a later chapter. In normal circumstances, in practice, interest such as bank interest can be recognized on the normal accruals basis.

Valuing receivables

As noted above, revenue excludes amounts collected on behalf of third parties, most notably VAT.

IAS 18 says that revenue should be measured at the fair value of the consideration received or receivable, taking into account discounts if any. Fair value is defined as usual as the amount for which an asset could be exchanged between knowledgeable, willing parties in an arm's length transaction.

- ◆ An exchange for goods or services of a similar nature and value is not regarded as a transaction that generates revenue. (This provision is included mainly to cater for practices in commodities-based businesses.)
- ◆ In certain circumstances, for instance if the seller is providing interest-free credit to the buyer, the fair value of the consideration receivable is less than the nominal amount of cash and cash equivalents to be received, and discounting is appropriate.

Disclosure

IAS 18 requires disclosure of the following items:

- ◆ the accounting policy for recognizing revenue, including methods used to determine the stage of completion of transactions where applicable;
- ◆ the amount of revenue recognized in respect of sale of goods, rendering of services, interest, royalties and dividends; and
- ◆ within each of the above categories, the amount of revenue arising from exchanges of goods or services, if any.

Summary

Now that you have completed this chapter you should be able to:

♦ explain the components of inventories and discuss how their cost is measured by reference to absorption costing, direct costing and cost flow assumptions;

♦ explain the lower of cost and net realizable value principle;

♦ explain how profit is recognized on long-term contracts;

♦ discuss revenue recognition principles and valuation of receivables; and

♦ demonstrate knowledge and understanding of the following accounting standards:

IAS 2   *Inventories*

IAS 11   *Construction Contracts*

IAS 18   *Revenue.*

Eight

Liabilities

Syllabus

This chapter focuses on syllabus Section 5: Liabilities. It covers accounting for liabilities, both short- and long-term. It raises issues relating to the nature of liabilities and when they should be recognized in financial statements. In this regard, attention is paid to the 'substance versus form' debate.

Objectives

After studying this chapter you should be able to:

- explain when certain liabilities should be recognized;
- explain the meaning and nature of contingent liabilities;
- explain the meaning and nature of provisions;
- outline the substance over form debate and the nature of off-balance sheet finance;
- explain how different types of leases should be accounted for; and
- demonstrate knowledge and understanding of the following accounting standards:
  IAS 17   *Leases*
  IAS 37   *Provisions, Contingent Liabilities and Contingent Assets.*

8.1   Liabilities

Liabilities are amounts owed, or potentially owed, to those who provide the resources to enable a business to do its work: typically trade suppliers, employees, providers of finance other than equity finance, and the authorities under whose regime the business operates, such as the Inland Revenue.

As we saw in Chapter 1 the IASB *Framework* tells us that a liability is a present obligation of the enterprise arising from past events, the settlement of which is expected to result in an outflow from the enterprise of resources embodying economic benefits.

Components of liabilities

Here is the Companies Act format for the current assets section of the balance sheet.

The Companies Act format has the same headings under both creditors falling due within one year and after more than one year.

H   CREDITORS
  1   Debenture loans
  2   Bank loans and overdrafts
  3   Payments received on account
  4   Trade creditors
  5   Bills of exchange payable
  6   Amounts owed to group undertakings
  7   Amounts owed to undertakings in which the company has a participating interest
  8   Other creditors including taxation and social security
  9   Accruals and deferred income *(may be shown as item E(9) or J)*

I   PROVISIONS FOR LIABILITIES AND CHARGES
  1   Pensions and similar obligations
  2   Taxation, including deferred taxation
  3   Other provisions

J   ACCRUALS AND DEFERRED INCOME *(may be shown as item E(9) or H(9))*

Debenture loans come into the category of 'financial instruments': these are dealt with in the next chapter.

There are standards dealing with taxation (IAS 12) and employee benefits such as pensions (IAS 19) but these topics and standards are not within your syllabus.

The group-related amounts will be covered in later chapters.

Recognition

The principles of dealing with amounts paid or payable to trade creditors are normally the same as those for dealing with revenue received or receivable from debtors, as explained in the previous chapter. In essence a liability is recognized (and simultaneously an expense) when it is probable that an outflow of resources embodying economic benefits will occur and the amount can be measured reliably.

8.2   Contingent liabilities

Contingencies

Contingent means 'depending on an uncertain event'.

IAS 37 *Provisions, Contingent Liabilities and Contingent Assets* defines a contingent liability as:

(a)   a possible obligation that arises from past events and whose existence will be confirmed only by the occurrence or non-occurrence of one or more uncertain future events not wholly within the control of the entity; or

(b)   a present obligation that arises from past events but is not recognized, either because it is not probable that an outflow of resources embodying economic benefits will be required to settle the obligation; or because the amount of the obligation cannot be measured with sufficient reliability.

To put it more simply, in the first case the obligation is only possible; in the second it is actual but there is a reason for not recognizing it in the accounts. Part (b) of the definition is relevant to deciding whether an item is a 'contingency' or a 'provision', as we shall see later.

An entity may also have a contingent asset. This is defined in the same way as (a) above, as 'a possible asset …' and so on. Part (b) of the definition does not apply to assets: it would be highly imprudent to include any information in the accounts about improbable assets that cannot be measured!

The most common examples of contingencies are court cases – when the entity is being sued or is suing someone else, and damages may be awarded.

Recognition and disclosure

Under IAS 37 the entity should *not recognize* either a contingent liability or a contingent asset in the financial statements. Contingent assets should not even be disclosed in the notes, unless an inflow of economic benefits is 'probable', in which case the nature of the asset and its estimated financial effect should be shown.

Contingent liabilities, however, *should* be disclosed in the notes. The entity should explain the nature of the item and if possible give an estimate of its financial effect. The entity should also explain what the uncertainties are about the amount or timing of any possible outflows and say if there is the possibility of any reimbursement.

There is an exception to these disclosure rules if disclosure might prejudice the interests of the entity (as perhaps in a court case). IAS 37 says that this would be 'extremely rare', and in any case the entity should still disclose the general nature of the contingency and say why all the required information has not been disclosed.

Fortunately the standard gives an example of this seemingly rather ungenerous exception.

> 'Litigation is in process against the company relating to a dispute with a competitor who alleges that the company has infringed patents and is seeking damages of £100 million. The information usually required by IAS 37 Provisions, Contingent Liabilities and Contingent Assets, is not disclosed on the grounds that it can be expected to prejudice seriously the outcome of the litigation. The directors are of the opinion that the claim can be successfully resisted by the company.'

Measurement

The financial effect of a contingency should be measured in accordance with the rules for provisions (see below).

8.3   Provisions

The word provision is used in two very different contexts. One use of the word implies the reduction in carrying value of an asset, as in doubtful debt or depreciation provisions.

These provisions are not covered by IAS 37. The other use of provision is the target of IAS 37. This kind of provision is defined as:

> 'a liability of uncertain timing or amount'.

Take care here: it may sound as if a provision is the same thing as a contingent liability (except with a more succinct definition) but the difference is that an item is recognized as a provision if it is *probable* that an outflow of resources embodying economic benefits will be required to settle the obligation and the amount of the obligation can be measured with sufficient reliability. So, an obligation that was once a contingent liability and therefore not recognized in the accounts may, as a result of events, later become a provision, and at that point it should be recognized.

IAS 37 was introduced in part as a response to the misuse of provisions that had become fairly widespread. The creation of provisions was often driven by the fact that tax relief was available, or the desire to smooth profits, rather than by any accounting theory.

To this end IAS 37 gives very clear criteria for when a provision needs to be created. If the criteria are met a provision must be created.

Recognition

The most important point is that a provision is being defined as a form of liability. Stemming from this, the criteria, which have all to be met before an entity is permitted to create a provision, are as follows:

- ♦ there is a present obligation as a result of a past event;
- ♦ it is probable that an outflow of resources will be required to settle the obligation; and
- ♦ a reliable estimate can be made of the amount of the obligation.

The first point was very controversial when introduced. The significance of the phrase 'present obligation' is that the obligation has to exist now rather than being expected in the future.

As an example, prior to IAS 37, it was fairly common for companies to provide for a major overhaul of an asset that they intended to undertake in, say, five years' time. Under IAS 37 this would not be permitted because there is no obligation to undertake the overhaul – a mere intention is not enough.

The rationale is that the company could avoid the need for the overhaul by its own actions, presumably selling the asset. Although this may not seem particularly realistic, remember that this standard was in part trying to stop the worst excesses of creativity associated with provisions where, in a year of (too) high profit, some companies would create provisions on the most tenuous bases. IAS 37 also interacts with IAS 16 on property plant and equipment on this point because IAS 16 requires that the costs of the overhaul suggested above be recognized as part of the asset and then depreciated over the period until the next overhaul.

An example of circumstances that would require a provision would be where a property lease gave a company an obligation at the end of the lease to remove the partitioning they had put up when they moved in. Here we have a present obligation, it is a requirement of the lease. In this case the company would provide for their best estimate of what it would cost to undertake the remedial work.

Not all present obligations will give rise to provisions, however, because the other two criteria also have to be met. Take the example of the guarantee given for another company's borrowings, as is typically seen in a group situation. In this case we do have a present obligation but we would need to provide only if there was the likelihood of an outflow of resources. In the case of a guarantee this would require an assessment of how likely it was that the other company would default on the loan, and if the other company is under the control of the first this likelihood can be readily assessed. If default is unlikely, no provision will be necessary.

The third criterion, relating to the 'reliable estimate' looks as if it might give a useful escape route from the requirement of the standard, however, the standard itself makes very clear that this can be used to escape the obligation to create a provision only in extremely rare circumstances.

Accounting and measurement

The double entry for a provision is to DEBIT the appropriate expense heading in the profit and loss account and CREDIT provisions for liabilities and charges in the balance sheet.

The amount recognized should be the entity's best estimate of the expenditure required, taking into account the risks and uncertainties. In making the estimate management should consider similar transactions, and perhaps independent expert advice.

Expected values

If the provision is related to a number of items the amount may need to be measured using expected values. For example, suppose a company offers a warranty on its products but experience shows that only a certain proportion of those sold develop faults.

Extent of defects	Proportion of products sold %	Cost of rectifying €000		Expected value €000
None	80	0	80% × 0 =	0.0
Minor	15	30	15% × 30 =	4.5
Major	5	169	5% × 169 =	8.5
				13.0

Present values

If the effect of time on the amount to be paid is material, the amount should be discounted to its present value (see Appendix 1 if you do not know what discounting is and what 'present value' means).

For example, let us say the company mentioned above with the property lease obligation expects the cost of the remedial work to be €20,000 but the lease does not end for another five years. The company's cost of capital is 10%. The amount payable in present value terms would be €20,000/1.105 = €12,418. If the difference (nearly €7,600) is material for the company it should make provision for the present value amount, not for €20,000.

Future events

The passage of time may also be relevant in the sense that future events such as a government's planned new legislation may affect an obligation. If it is sufficiently certain that the future events will occur and if the effect can be measured reliably the amount of the provision should be adjusted accordingly. An example might be legislative proposals regarding company pension schemes.

Onerous contracts

This term refers to a situation where a company has entered into a contract which it now appears will definitely generate a loss. It would not apply where, for example, the company buys a shipment of oil and the world oil price then falls, because it is felt that is a normal commercial risk.

The most common example by far of an onerous contract has been the case where a company has leased a property that it then wants to leave to move to another, it does so but cannot find a sub-tenant, or cannot find a sub-tenant prepared to pay the full rent. The commitment to carry on paying the rent to the lessor creates an onerous contract and IAS 37 requires that provision be made for the best estimate of the amount the company will have to pay.

8.3   Substance over form

The concept of substance over form is the idea that a transaction should be treated in the accounts in accordance with its underlying commercial substance, rather than its technical legal form.

In most transactions, the economic substance and the legal form are the same, but the IASB *Framework* requires that where the two differ the economic substance should govern the accounting rather than the legal form.

Various standards cater for situations where matters could otherwise be arranged to artificially affect the presentation of items in the financial statements, usually with the aim of understating liabilities.

Off-balance sheet financing

Such situations are sometimes referred to as 'off-balance sheet' financing. The following is a simple example.

Richardson plc wishes to purchase a new fixed asset for $10m. The company does not have any spare funds and has to borrow the money. Richardson currently has a level of gearing (the relationship between debt and equity, see Chapter 12) which it considers high enough. In fact, Richardson's bankers are already concerned at the level of borrowing. A further increase in borrowing would not be tolerated.

Richardson's balance sheet is as follows:

	$m
Fixed assets	13
Net current assets	2
Long-term loans	(5)
	10
Capital and reserves	10

Currently, using the ratio long-term loans/capital and reserves, gearing is 50% ($5m/$10m). Assuming that Richardson borrows $10m long term and buys the fixed asset, its balance sheet will be:

	$m
Fixed assets ($13m + $10m)	23
Net current assets	2
Long-term loans ($5m + $10m)	(15)
	10
Capital and reserves	10

Gearing is now 150% ($15m/$10m x 100). This would probably be unacceptable to the company and the bank and indeed might also be unacceptable to the company's investors. High gearing is perceived as being risky and the company's share price could fall as a result.

As a way around this dilemma, the company could set up an enterprise to lend the money and buy the asset on its behalf. Assume that Mortimer Enterprises is set up to do this. Richardson would control Mortimer, but because it is a separate legal entity Mortimer would prepare its own accounts. The accounts of the two enterprises would be as follows.

	Richardson	**Mortimer**
	$m	**$m**
Fixed assets	13	10
Net current assets	2	0
Long-term loans	(5)	(10)
	10	0
Capital and reserves	10	0

In effect Richardson's gearing and balance sheet would be unaffected by the acquisition of the asset. Richardson, through its control of Mortimer, would benefit from the use of the asset.

Can you see where the application of the doctrine of substance over form would affect this situation? In substance Richardson controls Mortimer (and its only asset). Legally Mortimer owns the asset not Richardson. Applying the doctrine of substance over form, Richardson would have to bring the asset and the loan back on the balance sheet; and would end up with a balance sheet showing gearing at 150%.

The standard-setting bodies have long been involved in trying to eliminate such perceived abuses, examples of misleading creative accounting. One of the first actions was to compel companies to incorporate controlled enterprises, such as Mortimer above, into the accounts of Richardson.

This topic is dealt with in IAS 27 *Consolidated and Separate Financial Statements* under which controlled enterprises, such as Mortimer above, would have to be consolidated with the accounts of Richardson.

At one time it seemed that as quickly as the standard-setting bodies introduced standards so some accounts' preparers and their advisers devised new ways of circumventing them, in order to mask the true situation. Usually the aim was to present an overly favourable impression of the balance sheet – chiefly to reduce gearing. To reiterate, high gearing implies high risk which in turn can lead to a number of unwelcome consequences for the company: higher borrowing costs, pressure on loan covenants, investor reluctance, depressed share price, etc.

To deal with this situation standard-setters now draft standards in such a way that there is no question that accounts should report the economic substance rather than the strict legal form. In particular the IASB Framework definitions of assets and liabilities must be employed to determine whether a transaction has resulted in the creation of an asset or liability.

As a reminder, an asset is a resource controlled by the enterprise as a result of past events and from which future economic benefits are expected to flow to the enterprise. Legal title is not even mentioned: economic rights and control over those rights are the important criteria.

We will look at a few more examples of off-balance sheet financing before concluding this section, and there are other examples in subsequent chapters.

Sale and repurchase

A key determinant of the true nature of a transaction is to ascertain where the risks and rewards lie. Consider this example.

The McFee Distillery Limited sells its inventory consisting of $20m worth of whisky to a finance house. The agreement specifies that the distillery can repurchase the inventory in three years for $22m.

The strict legal interpretation is that there has been a sale of inventory with a receipt of cash. Depending on the terms of the agreement, the substance of the transaction may well be that McFee has entered into a three-year secured loan, with $2m ($22m − $20m) of interest paid.

The terms of the agreement would have to be considered. For example, how likely is it that the Finance House will exercise its option to sell the inventory back to the distillery? Is it an option or is it compelled to re-sell the inventory?

If in our judgement the whisky is going to be sold back to the distillery, it does look more like a financing arrangement and McFee would have to bring the whisky back on the balance sheet. Thus McFee would continue to recognize the whisky as stock of $20m, and the $20m cash received would be recorded (Dr Cash) along with a three-year secured loan of $20m (Cr Creditors falling due after more than one year). Over the three years the $2m of interest payable would be charged to the profit and loss account, and added to the carrying value of the loan in McFee's accounts. No sale would be recorded.

Legally there has been a sale and the finance house owns the stock. In substance, McFee has borrowed $20m over three years, using the whisky as security.

To make a judgement we need to ascertain where the risks and rewards lie. This is a good indicator of what the economic substance of the transaction is. For instance, in the above example if the market value of whisky doubles in the three-year period, who would reap the benefits? McFee or the Finance House? Who is responsible for insuring the whisky?

Options

The terms of any agreement need to be carefully examined. Consider for instance another sale and repurchase situation, organized differently this time. First you will need to understand the following terms:

♦ a *put* option is a contract to sell a specified amount of a commodity at an agreed price and time at any time until the expiration of the option;

♦ a *call* option is a contract that entitles the buyer to buy a fixed quantity of commodity at a stipulated basis or striking price at any time up to the expiration of the option.

Suppose Hawkins sells Asset X to Booth for $20m. Both Hawkins and Booth have a put and call option at the same price, say $23m, exercisable between 12 and 36 months.

Hawkins has the right, at any time between 12 and 36 months, to exercise its call option and repurchase Asset X. If, say, the market value of X rises to $30m, Hawkins will exercise its option and repurchase.

Booth also has the right to exercise its put option between 12 and 36 months and sell the asset to Hawkins. So if, for example, the market price falls to $15m, then Booth will exercise its option at the price of $23m.

It is, therefore, certain that Asset X will return to Hawkins and there has been no genuine sale. The sale should not be recognized and Asset X should remain on Hawkins' balance sheet.

Consignments

'Consignments' occur frequently in the motor industry where a dealer is consigned items of stock (inventory) by the manufacturer on a sale or return basis. The inventory is held on the dealers' premises, where they can later:

♦ adopt it, eg by using the car as a demonstration model;
♦ transfer it to another dealer;
♦ sell it to a customer; or
♦ return it to the manufacturer.

As usual, the terms of the agreement would need to be examined to ascertain if, in substance, the inventory is an asset of the dealer or the manufacturer, for example, judging which party bears the risk of obsolescence. Can the dealer return the item to the manufacturer at the original value if, say, a new model is brought out and the value of the old model falls? Is a finance charge payable by the dealer contingent upon the length of time the inventory is held?

One of the critical features is the ability to return cars to the manufacturer. Where a dealer can do that, then avoid the biggest risk, that of being left with cars it cannot sell. This would suggest that the inventory should be in the books of the manufacturer rather than the dealer.

As you may remember from the previous chapter, under IAS 2 when an entity retains the significant risks and rewards of ownership of inventory it should not recognize the revenue (and therefore expense the consignment stock) until the buyer sells the goods and consideration has been received.

8.4   Leasing

IAS 17 *Leases* is intended to ensure that certain leased assets (and of course the associated liability) are shown meaningfully on the balance sheet. The motive for companies attempting to exclude leased assets from the balance sheet was to improve its appearance, and in particular the gearing ratio – the extent to which it appeared to be in debt.

Leased assets are legally owned by the lessor – the person leasing it out – and, therefore, applying the strict legal form, they should not appear on balance sheet of the lessee – the person that has the use of the asset. But in certain circumstances leased assets are, in substance, assets of the lessee; the risks and rewards of holding the asset fall on the lessee not the lessor.

IAS 17 outlines the principles on which a situation should be judged. The criterion is to examine whether the significant risks and rewards of holding the asset have been transferred from the lessor (legal owner) to the lessee (the user).

Contrast, for example, the difference between leasing a car for five years from a manufacturer, with renting a car for the weekend:

♦ in the former case, the user of the car is likely to be responsible for the insurance and maintenance of the car. He is likely to be able to benefit from any gain in value or suffer if the value falls; he is likely to be able (legally) to buy the car at the end of the five years;

♦ conversely, the car rental company rather than the user is likely to be responsible for the maintenance of the rented car. The user is unlikely to have any exposure to the risks in renting that car over the weekend. The user would certainly not be responsible for any fall in the market value of that model over the weekend, nor benefit from any rise.

Finance leases

Under IAS 17 if a lease transfers 'substantially all the risks and rewards of ownership' to the lessee it should be classified as a 'finance lease'.

The implication of the name is that the lease arrangement is a means of financing something that should be regarded as the lessee's asset. If it is held under a finance lease the asset should be recognized on the balance sheet of the lessee and the obligation (to pay amounts to the lessor) should be likewise recorded as a liability. Any interest element of the amounts paid is treated as an expense and is written off over the period of the lease (explained in more detail below).

'Risks' of ownership would include the responsibility for insuring the asset and keeping it in good working order. 'Rewards' would include any gains from the profitable operation of the asset and from any rise in its value.

IAS 17 goes into the question of how to spot a finance lease at some length. There may be many variations, but typical characteristics of a finance lease include the following:

♦ it transfers legal ownership of the asset to the lessee at the end of the lease, or gives the lessee an option to purchase the asset at an advantageously low price after, say, three years;

♦ the lease term is for the major part of the economic life of the asset; and

♦ the lease term has a primary period, during which the amounts paid are sufficient to reimburse the lessor for the cost of the asset plus interest, and a secondary period during which only nominal amounts are paid and if the asset is sold the sales proceeds go to the lessee.

Operating leases

A lease that does not meet the criteria of a finance lease is called an 'operating lease'.

If a lease is an operating lease no asset or liability is shown in the balance sheet and all amounts paid are written off immediately to the income statement as an expense.

Accounting for finance leases by lessees

Having seen how to identify finance leases, let us look at an example showing how we account for such transactions. First we will look at the lease from the lessee's point of view.

Suppose that Downend Limited leases a machine, on a finance lease, on 1 January 20X0. The terms are for eight payments of $1,000, half-yearly, in advance. The fair value of the machine is $5,868. The useful economic life of the machine is five years. The interest rate implicit in the lease is 10% per half year.

Asset

Initially the machine should be capitalized in the balance sheet at its fair value, with a corresponding amount recorded in creditors, as a lease liability:

Fixed assets

	$
Cost	
At 1 January 20X0	–
Addition	5,868
At 31 December 20X0	5,868

Accumulated depreciation

At 1 January 20X0	–
Charge ($5,868/4 years *)	1,467
At 31 December 20X0	1,467

Net book value

At 31 December 20X0	4,401

*Note the leased asset is written off over the shorter of the estimated useful life and the lease period.

Liability

The lease liability can be calculated by setting up a lease schedule as shown below. In this case we have used the interest rate implicit in the lease (10% per half year), because this is actually given in the question.

If you did not happen to have this information an acceptable alternative would be to use the sum of the digit method, as explained in the chapter on non-current assets in the context of depreciation.

Lease schedule

Payment	Opening balance	Cash flow	Sub-total	Interest @ 10%	Closing balance
	$	$	$	$	$
20X0 – Jan	5,868	(1,000)	4,868	487	5,355
20X0 – July	5,355	(1,000)	4,355	435	4,790
20X1 – Jan	4,790	(1,000)	3,790	379	4,169
20X1 – July	4,169	(1,000)	3,169	317	3,486
20X2 – Jan	3,486	(1,000)	2,486	249	2,735
20X2 – July	2,735	(1,000)	1,735	174	1,909
20X3 – Jan	1,909	(1,000)	909	91	1,000
20X3 – July	1,000	(1,000)	0		

In the balance sheet, at the end of 20X0, under Creditors, 'Obligations under finance leases' will be the year-end balance – $4,790 – split between Creditors: due within one year and Creditors: due after more than one year.

		$
Initial liability		5,868
Capital element of January payment ($1,000 – $487)	513	
Capital element of July payment ($1,000 – $435)	565	
		(1,078)
Liability carried forward		4,790

Income statement

In 20X0, there will be a profit and loss account charge of $922 ($487 plus $435) representing the interest element of the lease payments. In addition, depreciation on the leased asset of $1,467 will be charged.

As can been seen the finance charge falls over the term of the lease, reflecting the decreasing lease liability.

Disclosure by lessees

The disclosure requirements under IAS 17 are quite elaborate. Look at the notes in the published accounts of real companies if you can: this will give you more of a feel for the requirements.

Finance leases

For finance leases the entity must provide information including the following:

♦ the carrying amount of the asset;
♦ a reconciliation between the total minimum lease payments and their present value (see Appendix 1 if you do not know what present values are);
♦ the amounts of minimum lease payments at balance sheet date for:
  – the next year
  – years 2 to 5 combined
  – beyond five years
  the present values of these amounts must also be given; and
♦ a general description of significant leasing arrangements.

Note the stress on 'minimum lease payments'. A lease may allow early termination but there will usually be some kind of financial penalty, to protect the lessor's leasing income, and this should be recognized.

Operating leases

For operating leases the entity must provide the following information:

♦ as for finance leases, the amounts of minimum lease payments at the balance sheet date under non-cancellable operating leases. again this must be split between amounts for the next year, for years 2 to 5 combined, and beyond five years; and

♦ a general description of significant leasing arrangements.

Accounting for leases by lessors

You might expect the lessor's financial statements to be a mirror image of those of the lessee, and this is broadly true, although the detailed requirements of IAS 17 are more complex than this. The following is just an outline.

Finance leases

At the start of the lease term, the lessor should record a finance lease in the balance sheet as a receivable (debtor), at an amount equal to the 'net investment in the lease'. Typically this is the same as the cost of the leased item but might include the costs attributable to negotiating and arranging the lease.

The amounts received from the lessee should be applied both to reduce the debtor and to recognize finance income. Formally, finance income should be recognized based on a pattern giving a 'constant periodic rate of return' on the lessor's net investment. In practice, again, this is likely to be similar to the pattern by which the lessee recognizes interest expense.

Operating leases

Assets held for operating leases should be presented in the balance sheet of the lessor as non-current assets according to the nature of the asset: in effect this means that the normal IAS 16 rules apply.

Operating lease income should be recognized over the lease term on a straight-line basis, unless another basis is more representative. In other words income is recognized as it is received or becomes receivable.

Disclosure by lessors

Again the disclosure requirements under IAS 17 are elaborate and if you can get hold of the published accounts of a real company that leases assets you should have a good look at the relevant notes.

Here are some of the key items.

Finance leases

◆ A reconciliation between the gross investment in the lease and the present value of minimum lease payments.

◆ The gross investment and present value of minimum lease payments receivable for the next year, years 2 to 5 combined and beyond five years.

◆ Unearned finance income.

◆ A general description of significant leasing arrangements.

Operating leases

◆ Amounts of minimum lease payments at the balance sheet date under non-cancellable operating leases in aggregate and for the next year, years 2 to 5 and beyond five years.

◆ A general description of significant leasing arrangements.

Summary

Now that you have completed this chapter you should be able to:

◆ **explain when certain liabilities should be recognized;**

◆ **explain the meaning and nature of contingent liabilities;**

◆ **explain the meaning and nature of provisions;**

◆ **outline the substance over form debate and the nature of off-balance sheet finance;**

◆ **explain how different types of leases should be accounted for; and**

◆ **demonstrate knowledge and understanding of the following accounting standards:**

IAS 17   *Leases*

IAS 37   *Provisions, Contingent Liabilities and Contingent Assets*.

Nine

Financial instruments

Syllabus

This chapter spans the part of syllabus Section 5: Liabilities that refers to long-term debt and the parts of syllabus Section 6: Investments that deals with debt securities and derivatives and hedging.

Objectives

After studying this chapter you should be able to:

- ◆ explain the treatment of long-term debt and debt securities in financial statements;
- ◆ understand why entities use derivatives and the impact of hedge accounting; and
- ◆ demonstrate knowledge and understanding of the following accounting standards:
  IAS 32 *Financial Instruments: Disclosure and Presentation*
  IAS 39 *Financial Instruments: Recognition and Measurement.*

9.1 Financial instruments

The topic of financial instruments is both complex and controversial. Before the issue of IAS 32 and IAS 39, many of the more esoteric financial instruments were not recognized or disclosed in the financial statements at all.

Debt or equity?

One of the reasons for the issue of these standards was to control creative accounting. Certain companies were raising finance by means of 'instruments' that were enough like shares to have to be classified in accordance with Companies Act rules relating to shares, but which had more characteristics in common with debt. This kind of arrangement is effectively a form of off-balance sheet finance, not because it is actually off-balance sheet, but because it has the effect of making the debt invisible and hence disguising the gearing position of the firm.

For example, in the late 1980s there was a vogue for issuing so-called 'convertible capital bonds', which are a kind of debt eventually convertible into shares. More than one company issuing these included a note in their accounts which said that the company were confident that the debt would be converted (rather than being redeemed) and therefore they included the issue within the capital and reserves section of the balance sheet rather than within liabilities. It would be very easy, in analysing these accounts, to put this issue on the wrong side of the gearing ratio and understate the company's exposure to debt.

Convertible debt

In essence, therefore, the standards lay down a framework for distinguishing between debt and shares. Some instruments have features of both debt and equity. Consider again convertible debt, ie debt that at some point in the future may be converted into shares. Applying the principle of substance over form this can be likened to normal debt with a warrant attached enabling shares to be acquired in the future. The accounting should follow this and as long as the debt characteristic exists it should be classified as debt, albeit separately disclosed within the liabilities section.

Redeemable preference shares

The Companies Act requires that all shares be accounted for within shareholders funds. Some share issues have characteristics of debt, which can be described as carrying a service cost and an obligation to repay the principle. Redeemable cumulative preference shares, for example, have very little to distinguish them in terms of their commercial effect from loan stock; they carry a regular service cost and will have to be repaid.

Financial markets

The situation is made more complex by the continual inventiveness of financial institutions. The growth of new and different kinds of financial instruments over recent years – options, swaps, swaptions, and so on – outstrips the development of guidance on how to account for them.

Standards

The IASC has issued two standards to deal with the issues:

♦ IAS 32 *Financial Instruments: Disclosure and Presentation,* which deals with the classification of financial instruments between liabilities and equity, the presentation of certain 'compound instruments', and the disclosure of information about financial instruments;

♦ IAS 39 *Financial Instruments: Recognition and Measurement*, which deals with recognition, measurement and what is known as 'hedge accounting'.

9.2   Definitions

The definitions given in IAS 32 and IAS 39 are extremely difficult to understand, partly because they are written in very broad terms to cover all likely situations, and partly because each definition uses one or more of the other definitions to explain itself!

Before you start ...

Before you read on we suggest that you take as long as you need to learn the following examples. This will give you a much better chance of understanding what follows without having to re-read everything several times.

	Simple examples	**Complex examples**
Equity instrument	Shares in the entity itself	–
Financial asset	Cash Trade debtors A portfolio of shares such as an individual might hold	A loan made to another company
Financial liability	Trade creditors	Corporate bonds Preference shares
Derivative	–	Options, futures, interest rate swaps etc

It may also help if you think of one of the parties to the transactions described as being a financial institution such as a merchant bank.

Note that everyday items such as cash and ordinary trade debtors are examples of financial assets, and trade creditors are examples of financial liabilities, but in ordinary circumstances accounting for these is straightforward. It is better for the purposes of this chapter if you are thinking in terms of high finance.

Now here come the formal definitions.

Financial instrument

Any contract that gives rise to both a financial asset of one entity and a financial liability or equity instrument of another entity.

Equity instrument

Any contract that evidences a residual interest in the assets of an entity after deducting all of its liabilities.

Financial asset

Any asset that is:

(a) cash;

(b) an equity instrument of another entity;

(c) a contractual right to receive cash or another financial asset from another entity; or to exchange financial instruments with another entity under conditions that are potentially favourable to the entity; or

(d) a contract that will or may be settled in the entity's own equity instruments and is:

    (i) a non-derivative for which the entity is or may be obliged to receive a variable number of the entity's own equity instruments; or

    (ii) a derivative that will or may be settled other than by the exchange of a fixed amount of cash or another financial asset for a fixed number of the entity's own equity instruments.

Financial liability

Any liability that is:

(a) a contractual obligation to deliver cash or another financial asset to another enterprise, or to exchange financial instruments with another enterprise under conditions that are potentially unfavourable; or

(b) a contract that will or may be settled in the entity's own equity instruments and is:

    (i) a non-derivative for which the entity is or may be obliged to deliver a variable number of the entity's own equity instruments; or

    (ii) a derivative that will or may be settled other than by the exchange of a fixed amount of cash or another financial asset or a fixed number of the entity's equity instruments.

Derivative

A financial instrument or other contract with all three of the following characteristics:

(a) its value changes in response to the change in a specified interest rate, financial instrument price, commodity price, foreign exchange rate, index of prices or rates, credit rating or credit index, or other variable …;

(b) it requires no initial net investment or an initial net investment that is smaller than would be required for other types of contracts that would be expected to have a similar response to changes in market factors; and

(c) it is settled at a future date.

Exceptions

IAS 32 makes it clear that the following items are *not* financial instruments:

- physical assets such as inventory, property, plant and equipment, leased assets and intangible assets (patents, trademarks etc);
- prepaid expenses, deferred revenue and most warranty obligations;
- liabilities or assets that are not contractual in nature; and
- contractual rights/obligations that do not involve transfer of a financial asset, such as operating leases.

IAS 32 does not apply to interests in subsidiaries, associates, and joint ventures. Other standards apply in these cases: see the chapters that follow this one.

9.3   Presentation and disclosure

IAS 32 should be applied in the presentation and disclosure of all types of financial instruments, whether recognized or unrecognized.

Liabilities and equity

IAS 32 makes it clear that financial instruments should be presented according to their substance, not merely their legal form. In particular, entities that issue financial instruments should classify them (or their component parts) as either financial liabilities, or equity.

♦ The critical feature of a liability, as you know from the IAS *Framework* definition, is an obligation to transfer economic benefit. A financial instrument is therefore a financial liability if there is a contractual obligation on the issuer either to deliver cash or another financial asset to the holder or to exchange another financial instrument with the holder under potentially unfavourable conditions to the issuer.

♦ If this critical condition is not met the financial instrument is an equity instrument.

The classification of the financial instrument is made when it is first recognized and this classification will continue until the financial instrument is removed from the entity's balance sheet.

Contingent settlement provisions

An entity may issue a financial instrument where the way in which it is settled depends on:

♦ the occurrence or non-occurrence of uncertain future events; or
♦ the outcome of uncertain circumstances.

Uncertainties are generally beyond the control of both the holder and the issuer of the instrument. For example, an entity might be in such a position in the future that it has to deliver cash instead of issuing equity shares, or *vice versa*. In this situation it is not immediately clear whether the entity has an equity instrument or a financial liability.

IAS 32 says that such financial instruments should be classified as financial liabilities unless the possibility of settlement is remote.

Settlement options

When a derivative financial instrument gives one party a choice over how it is settled (eg in cash or by issuing shares) the instrument is a financial asset or a financial liability unless all the alternative choices would result in it being an equity instrument.

Compound financial instruments

As mentioned, some financial instruments contain both a liability and an equity element. One of the most common types of compound instrument is convertible debt. In such cases, IAS 32 requires the component parts of the instrument to be classified separately, according to the substance of the contractual arrangement and the definitions of a financial liability and an equity instrument.

This is done as follows:

♦ calculate the value for the liability component;
♦ deduct this from the instrument as a whole to leave a residual value for the equity component.

The reasoning behind this follows the definitions given earlier: an entity's equity is its residual interest in its assets amount after deducting all its liabilities.

The split between the liability and equity components remains the same throughout the term of the instrument, even if there are changes in the likelihood of the option being exercised. This is because it is not always possible to predict how a holder will behave. The issuer continues to have an obligation to make future payments until conversion, maturity of the instrument or some other relevant transaction takes place.

Treasury shares

If an entity reacquires its own equity instruments (ie buys back its own shares), those instruments (treasury shares.) should be deducted from equity.

No gain or loss should be recognized in profit or loss on the purchase, sale, issue or cancellation of an entity's own equity instruments.

Consideration paid or received shall be recognized directly in equity.

Interest, dividends, losses and gains

IAS 32 also considers how financial instruments affect the income statement. The treatment depends on whether interest, dividends, losses or gains relate to a financial liability or an equity instrument.

♦ Interest, dividends, losses and gains relating to a financial liability should be recognized as income or expense in profit or loss.

♦ Distributions to holders of equity instruments should be debited directly to equity by the issuer.
♦ Transaction costs of an equity transaction shall be accounted for as a deduction from equity (unless they are directly attributable to the acquisition of a business, in which case they are accounted for under IAS 22).

9.4 Disclosure

The disclosure requirements of IAS 32 are very extensive. They include specific monetary disclosures, fair value information, and narrative commentary. The intention is to help users to understand management's attitude to financial risk and the extent to which the entity is exposed to various types of risk relating to both recognized and unrecognized financial instruments.

We will not go into the disclosure requirements in detail, but it is worth dwelling on the different types of risk identified in IAS 32, because this will help you to understand the underlying concerns of the standard – in other words what might go wrong!

♦ **Market risk**: there are three types of market risk: currency risk, interest-rate risk and price risk:
  – *currency risk* is the risk that the value of a financial instrument will fluctuate due to changes in foreign exchange rates;
  – *interest rate risk* is the risk that the value of a financial instrument will fluctuate due to changes in market interest rates;
  – *price risk* is the risk that the value of a financial instrument will fluctuate as a result of changes in market prices whether those changes are caused by factors specific to the individual instrument or its issuer or factors affecting all securities traded in the market.
  The term 'market risk' embodies not only the potential for loss but also the potential for gain.
♦ **Credit risk**: the risk that one party to a financial instrument will fail to discharge an obligation and cause the other party to incur a financial loss.
♦ **Liquidity risk** (or **funding risk**): the risk that an entity will encounter difficulty in raising funds to meet commitments associated with financial instruments. Liquidity risk may result from an inability to sell a financial asset quickly at close to its fair value.
♦ **Cash flow interest-rate risk**: the risk that future cash flows of a financial instrument will fluctuate because of changes in market interest rates. In the case of a floating-rate debt instrument, for example, such fluctuations result in a change in the effective interest rate of the financial instrument. usually without a corresponding change in its fair value.

9.5 Recognition of financial instruments

IAS 39 *Financial instruments: Recognition and Measurement* establishes principles for recognizing and measuring financial assets and financial liabilities.

Initial recognition

Financial instruments should be recognized in the balance sheet when the entity becomes a party to the contractual provisions of the instrument. This means that all derivatives should be on the balance sheet.

This is strikingly different from the recognition criteria in most standards, where items are normally recognized when there is a probable inflow or outflow of resources and the item has a cost or value that can be measured reliably.

Derecognition

Derecognition means removing a previously recognized financial instrument from an entity's balance sheet.

An entity should derecognize a financial asset when:

♦ the contractual rights to the cash flows from the financial asset expire; or
♦ it transfers substantially all the risks and rewards of ownership of the financial asset to another party.

Financial liabilities should be derecognized when they are 'extinguished', in other words when the obligation specified in the contract is discharged or cancelled or expires.

There could be occasions when only part of a financial asset or liability should be derecognized. A corporate bond, for example, gives the right to two separate sets of cash inflows, relating to the principal on the one hand and the interest on the other. The entity could sell one set of rights to someone else while retaining the other set.

On derecognition the amount to be included in profit or loss for the period is calculated as:

	$	$
Carrying amount of asset/liability (or the portion of asset/liability) transferred		X
Less: Proceeds received/paid	X	
Any cumulative gain or loss reported in equity	X	
		(X)
Difference to net profit or loss		X

9.6   Measurement

Again we are only scratching the surface of some very complex requirements here.

Initially, financial instruments are measured at fair value (usually cost) plus any transaction costs that are directly attributable to the acquisition or issue of the financial instrument.

Subsequently, financial assets and liabilities (including derivatives) should normally be measured at fair value, but there are a number of exceptions including the following:

♦ loans and receivables, held-to-maturity investments, and non-derivative financial liabilities should be measured at amortized cost using the effective interest method. The effective interest rate is the rate that exactly discounts estimated future cash payments or receipts through the expected life of the financial instrument to the net carrying amount of the financial asset or liability (see Appendix 1 if you do not understand what discounting and present values are);

♦ investments in equity instruments with no reliable fair value measurement (and derivatives that derive from such equity instruments) should be measured at cost.

Impairment

As with other assets an entity is required to assess at each balance sheet date whether there is any objective evidence of impairment. If any such evidence exists, the entity is required to do a detailed impairment calculation to determine whether an impairment loss should be recognized.

The amount of the loss is measured as the difference between the asset's carrying amount and the present value of estimated cash flows.

If, in a subsequent period, the amount of the impairment loss decreases due to an event occurring after the impairment was originally recognized, the previously recognized impairment loss is reversed through profit and loss.

9.7 Practical examples

This has been a highly abstract chapter so far, so you would probably appreciate seeing some numbers.

Bonds

On 1 January 20X0 Winston Smith Ltd raised £100m (net of issue expenses) by issuing a five-year bond, carrying interest at 5% payable annually in arrears. The bond is redeemable at £130.50 per £100 at the end of five years. (The rate of interest inherent in the bond is 10% per annum.)

The loan schedule would be as follows.

Year ending 31 December	Opening balance £m	Finance charge (10%) £m	Cash flow £m	Closing balance £m
20X0	100.0	10.0	(5) interest	105.0
20X1	105.0	10.5	(5) interest	110.5
20X2	110.5	11.0	(5) interest	116.5
20X3	116.5	11.7	(5) interest	123.2
20X4	123.2	12.3	(5) interest	
			(130.5) redemption	0

As can be seen from the loan schedule, we have applied the principle of substance over form. The interest on the bond is recorded at the effective rate of 10%, not the coupon rate of 5%. Using 10% gives a constant rate on the carrying amount of the loan. Using the effective rate recognizes that the premium on redemption is part of the total finance cost and should be added to the coupon interest of 5%.

In the accounts, the finance charge would be debited to the income statement and credited to the balance sheet account for the bond. The closing balance will be shown within creditors in the balance sheet, split between creditors: amounts falling due within one year and amounts falling due after more than one year. In the example above, all of the balance is due after more than one year.

Zero-coupon bonds

This is a modification of the example above, where in fact the capital instrument carries no annual interest.

On 1 January 20X0 Bernard Marx plc issues a zero-coupon bond for consideration of £100m. The bond is redeemable at £161 per £100 in five years' time. (The rate of interest inherent in the bond is 10% per annum.)

The loan schedule would be as follows.

Year ending 31 December	Opening balance £m	Finance charge (10%) £m	Cash flow £m	Closing balance £m
20X0	100.0	10.0		110.0
20X1	110.0	11.0		121.0
20X2	121.0	12.1		133.1
20X3	133.1	13.3		146.4
20X4	146.4	14.6	(161) redemption	0

Although technically no interest is payable on the loan, the accounts should recognize that the premium on redemption is part of the finance cost and therefore should be allocated to accounting periods over the term of the loan.

Convertible debt with varying interest

Savage plc issues convertible debt on 1 January 20X0 for £100m. The debt carries a coupon rate of 5.9% for the first five years and a coupon rate of 14.1% for the next ten years, after which it is redeemable at par. (The rate of interest inherent in the debt is 10% per annum.)

The loan schedule would be as follows:

Year ending 31 December	Opening balance £m	Finance charge (10%) £m	Cash flow £m	Closing balance £m
20X0	100	10	(5.9)	104.1
20X1	104.1	10.4	(5.9)	108.6
20X2	108.6	10.9	(5.9)	113.6
20X3	113.6	11.4	(5.9)	119.1
20X4	119.1	11.9	(5.9)	125.1
20X5	125.1	12.5	(14.1)	123.5
20X6	123.5	12.4	(14.1)	121.8
20X7	121.8	12.2	(14.1)	119.9
20X8	119.9	12	(14.1)	117.8
20X9	117.8	11.8	(14.1)	115.5
20Y0	115.5	11.6	(14.1)	113
20Y1	113	11.3	(14.1)	110.2
20Y2	110.2	11	(14.1)	107.1
20Y3	107.1	10.7	(14.1)	103.7
20Y4	103.7	10.4	(14.1)interest (100)redemption	0

As can be seen, although the debt carries variable interest, the income statement should reflect a constant rate on the carrying value of the loan, in this case 10% per annum.

Deep-discounted bonds

These are a variation on the zero-coupon bonds above. The bonds (usually) carry no interest, rather they are issued at a substantial discount and redeemed at par.

On 1 January 20X0 Eurasia plc issues a £100m bond at a discount of 37.91%. The bond carries no interest and is redeemable at par in five years. (The rate of interest inherent in the bond is 10% per annum.)

The loan schedule would be as follows.

Year ending 31 December	Opening balance £m	Finance charge (10%) £m	Cash flow £m	Closing balance £m
20X0	(£100m less discount of 37.91%)			
	62.1	6.2		68.3
20X1	68.3	6.8		75.1
20X2	75.1	7.5		82.6
20X3	82.6	8.3		90.9
20X4	90.9	9.1	(100) redemption	0

Once again, although the debt carries no interest, the profit and loss account reflects the fact that the deep discount on issue is part of the finance cost of the loan. The loan is initially recorded at its fair value of £62.1m.

Debt issued with warrants

This is an example of the hybrid type of capital instrument mentioned earlier. The instrument has characteristics of both a liability and shareholders' funds.

On 1 January 20X0 Ingsoc plc issues debt and warrants together for a total consideration of £125m. The debt is redeemable at £125m in five years and carries interest of 4.7% per annum (£5.9 million on £125m).

The initial question is how to divide the proceeds between the debt (liability) and warrant (shareholders' funds) elements. Considering the market values of the debt and the warrants after the issue shows that the fair value of the debt and warrants is, say, £100m and £25m, respectively. (The rate of interest inherent in the debt/warrant issue is 10% per annum.)

Initially the debt should be recognized in the books at its fair value of £100m and the warrants in shareholders' funds at £25m.

1 January 20X0

Dr. Cash £125m

Cr. Liabilities – Creditors £100m

Cr. Shareholders' funds – Warrants £25m

The loan schedule will be as follows.

Year ending 31 December	Opening balance £m	Finance charge (10%) £m	Cash flow £m	Closing balance £m
20X0	100.0	10.0	(5.9)	104.1
20X1	104.1	10.4	(5.9)	108.6
20X2	108.6	10.9	(5.9)	113.6
20X3	113.6	11.3	(5.9)	119.0
20X4	119.0	11.9	(5.9) interest (125) redemption	

The profit and loss account should reflect the finance cost of the loan. That is, recognizing in effect that £100m was borrowed for five years with a premium on redemption of £25m together with annual interest of £5.9m.

Depending on their terms, the warrants may be exercised at any time during the currency of the debt or after. Assume, for example, that all the warrant-holders exercise their right to subscribe, for say 30m £1 ordinary shares in Ingsoc on consideration of one warrant and £1.50 per share.

Accounting treatment

Dr. Cash (30m x £1.50) £45m

Dr. Shareholders funds – Warrants £25m

Cr. Share capital £30m

Cr. Share premium account £40m

* Share issue @ £1.50 plus one warrant per share *

The premium on the share issue can be proved as follows:

	£m
Proceeds from original debt/warrant issue	125
Less debt element	(100)
Net proceeds from warrant issue	25
Warrant exercise proceeds	45
Total proceeds	70
Less nominal value of shares issued	(30)
Premium	40

Repackaged perpetual debt

Occasionally debt is issued carrying a relatively high interest rate for a period, followed by a period of nominal/zero interest. The debt may be irredeemable.

The high-interest early period is usually referred to as the primary period and the later period the secondary period.

On 1 January 20X0 Soma plc issued an irredeemable bond for proceeds of £125m. The bond carries interest of 16.275% per annum (£20.3m) for a primary period of ten years, with no further interest payments after that. (The rate of interest inherent in the bond is 10% per annum.)

In substance, we can see that Soma is borrowing £125m over a ten-year period – not indefinitely. The value of the bond at the end of the primary period will be zero because henceforth it will carry no interest. Therefore, to Soma, the finance cost of the bond incorporates the high interest payments in the primary period, mitigated by the fact that the principal of £125m never needs to be repaid. (The rate of interest inherent in the bond is 10%.)

The loan schedule would be as follows:

Year ending 31 December	Opening balance	Finance charge (10%)	Cash flow	Closing balance
	£m	£m	£m	£m
20X0	125.0	12.5	(20.3)	117.2
20X1	117.2	11.7	(20.3)	108.6
20X2	108.6	10.8	(20.3)	99.1
20X3	99.1	9.9	(20.3)	88.7
20X4	88.7	8.8	(20.3)	77.2
20X5	77.2	7.7	(20.3)	64.6
20X6	64.6	6.4	(20.3)	50.7
20X7	50.7	5.0	(20.3)	35.4
20X8	35.4	3.5	(20.3)	18.6
20X9	18.6	1.7 *	(20.3)	0

* rounding

Note that at the end of ten years the bond has been written down to zero, even though it is technically irredeemable. Note also, that although the bond carries a high coupon rate of 16.275%, the effect of the non-redemption brings the effective rate down to 10% per annum.

Variable rate/index-linked loans

Variable rates

Sometimes debt is issued that does not carry a specific interest/repayment rate. Instead the terms of the debt include a formula to base future repayments and interest. A simple example is a floating-rate loan at, say, 4% over base rate. To calculate the rate to be used in the financial statements, we would have to use the variable rate currently in force as well as adjusting for any premium on redemption or non-redemption variation seen above.

Index-linked loans

This type of loan has the feature that the repayable value of the loan is increased at each year-end with reference to an index – for example the Retail Price Index. The loan will usually also carry a nominal rate of interest as well.

On 1 January 20X0 Proles plc issues a loan for £125m, carrying 6% (£7.5m) interest. The loan is uprated at the end of every year with reference to an index. The loan is redeemable in five years' time.

Year	Index at end of year
20X0	100
20X1	106
20X2	108
20X3	116
20X4	122
20X5	132

The loan schedule would be as follows.

Year ending 31 December	Opening balance £m	Finance charge (balancing figure) £m	Cash flow £m	Closing balance £m	
20X0	125.0	15.0	(7.5)	132.5	125 x 106/100
20X1	132.5	10.0	(7.5)	135	132.5 x 108/106
20X2	135.0	17.5	(7.5)	145	135 x 116/108
20X3	145.0	15.0	(7.5)	152.5	145 x 122/116
20X4	152.5	20.0	(165) redemption		152.5 x 132/122
			(7.5) interest	0	

The financing charge comprises two elements (i) the uplift in relation to the index and (ii) the 6% nominal interest rate. Thus, for example, in 20X1 the index rises from 106 to 108. Therefore the index element finance charge is (108 – 106)/106 x carrying value £132.5m = £2.5m. Added to the 6% nominal interest of £7.5m (6% x £125m) this gives the total finance charge of £10m.

9.8   Derivatives

A 'derivative' is a financial instrument that 'derives' its value from the price or rate of an underlying item. Here are some examples:

♦ *options* are rights (but not obligations) that the option holder can exercise to do something at a predetermined price; the option writer loses out if the option is exercised;

♦ *forward contracts* are agreements to buy or sell an asset at a fixed price on a specific future date;

♦ *futures contracts* are similar to forward contracts except that contracts are standardized and traded on an exchange;

♦ *swaps* are agreements to swap one set of cash flows for another. The commonest examples are interest rate swaps and currency swaps.

We will see why you might want to do some of these things in the next section: basically derivatives can help to protect again the risk of changes in prices in the future.

The value of a derivative depends on movements in an underlying item that the entity cannot control, such as an exchange rate. This means that settlement of a derivative can lead to a very different result from the one originally envisaged and the impact on the financial statements could be very significant.

Because a derivative contract normally has little or no initial cost, under traditional accounting it may not be recognized in the financial statements at all, or it may be recognized at an amount that bears no relation to its current value. This can be highly misleading: users of the financial statements would be quite unaware of the level of risk that the company really faces.

IASs 32 and 39 were developed in order to correct this situation.

9.9   Hedging

Hedging means any technique designed to reduce or eliminate financial risk, such as, taking two positions that will offset each other if prices change.

For example, an Italian company might commission a large piece of machinery from a foreign manufacturer, priced at one million US dollars. If the exchange rate rises while it is waiting for the machinery to be built it will incur significant extra costs. It might therefore enter into an agreement now that would give it the option of purchasing the required amount of currency at a known exchange rate in the future. There would be a premium for doing this, but it would be nowhere near the amount of the potential loss. If the exchange rate changed in their favour they would not exercise the option.

Hedge accounting

Hedge accounting is best explained by way of an example. Suppose a company owns 500 tonnes of a commodity (oil, coffee, steel, etc) which cost $200,000 on 1 March 20X5.

In order to hedge the fluctuation in the market value of the commodity the company signs a futures contract to deliver 500 tonnes of steel on 30 June 20X5 at the futures price of $440 per tonne.

The market price of the commodity on 31 March 20X5 is $450 per tonne and the futures price for delivery on 30 June 20X5 is $460 per tonne.

The futures contract was intended to protect the company from a fall in the commodity prices, but prices have actually risen, so that the company has made a loss on the contract.

- ♦ Ordinarily the futures contract is a derivative and therefore must be re-measured to fair value under IAS 39. The loss on the futures contract is recognized in the income statement:
  DEBIT Income statement (500 € (460 – 440)) $10,000
  CREDIT Financial liability $10,000
- ♦ With hedge accounting, however, the loss on the futures contract is recognized in the income statement as before, but the inventories can be revalued to fair value:

	$
Fair value at 31 March 20X5 (500 x 450)	225,000
Cost	(200,000)
Gain	25,000

The gain is also recognized in the income statement:
DEBIT Inventory $25,000
CREDIT Income statement $25,000

The net effect on the income statement is a gain of $15,000 compared with a loss of $10,000 without hedging.

Types of hedge

In the numerical example we gave an example of a 'fair value hedge'. Other types are cash flow hedges and hedges of a net investment in a foreign operation, but the example given should be sufficient for you to understand the concept.

Conditions for hedge accounting

Under IAS 39, before a hedging relationship qualifies for hedge accounting, all of the following conditions must be met.

(a) The hedging relationship must be designated at its inception as a hedge based on the entity's risk management objective and strategy. There must be formal documentation (including identification of the hedged item, the hedging instrument, the nature of the risk that is to be hedged and how the entity will assess the hedging instrument's effectiveness in offsetting the exposure to changes in the hedged item's fair value or cash flows attributable to the hedged risk).

(b) The hedge is expected to be highly effective in achieving offsetting changes in fair value or cash flows attributable to the hedged risk. (Notice that the hedge need not necessarily be totally effective.)

(c) For cash flow hedges, a forecast transaction that is the subject of the hedge must be highly probable and must present an exposure to variations in cash flows that could ultimately affect profit or loss.

(d) The effectiveness of the hedge can be measured reliably.

(e) The hedge is assessed on an ongoing basis (annually) and has been effective during the reporting period.

Summary

Now that you have completed this chapter you should be able to:

♦ explain the treatment of long-term debt and debt securities in the financial statements;

♦ understand why entities use derivatives and the impact of hedge accounting; and

♦ demonstrate knowledge and understanding of the following accounting standards:

IAS 32 *Financial Instruments: Disclosure and Presentation*

IAS 39 *Financial Instruments: Recognition and Measurement.*

Ten

Investments: group accounts 1

Syllabus

This chapter is the first of two covering syllabus Section 6: Investments. This section of the syllabus looks at the types of investment undertaken by (typically) business enterprises and the accounting treatment of such investments. Particular attention is to investment in other business enterprises and how the financial performance and position of 'groups' of enterprises should be reported.

Objectives

After studying this chapter you should be able to:

♦ explain how companies should account for associated companies;
♦ outline the accounting implications of taking part in a joint venture;
♦ explain how companies should account for subsidiary companies;
♦ explain the issues surrounding fair value accounting in the case of a business combination; and
♦ demonstrate knowledge and understanding of the following accounting standards:
  IFRS 3   *Business Combinations*
  IAS 27   *Consolidated and Separate Financial Statements*
  IAS 28   *Investments in Associates.*

10.1 Investments

If a company wishes to expand its operations, it can do so by acquiring additional assets and liabilities, for example by buying new equipment or by buying the net assets of another business. This is often referred to as organic growth. The new assets acquired are incorporated in the company's balance sheet and should help to generate future profit.

An alternative policy is to take a shareholding in another company, and through that company expand its operations or receive investment income or, in many cases, both.

The way investments are accounted for depends on the level of involvement the shareholding entitles the investor to and the intentions of the investor. If a company acquires shares in another solely with the intention of selling them again in the near future and not exercising any control or influence in the meantime, the investment would be treated as a current asset irrespective of the level of investment. Where the investment is going to be held on an ongoing basis, ie as a non-current (fixed) asset, there are basically four ways of describing the holding. These are based on the level of involvement enjoyed by the investor. They are:

♦ trade investment;
♦ associate;
♦ joint venture;
♦ subsidiary.

10.2 Trade investment

This term is applied to holdings, generally less than 20% of the voting shares, which means that the investing company has no influence or control over any of the decision making in the company. Generally a company will hold such an investment for its growth potential and dividend income.

Accounting treatment

Treat the investment as a fixed asset. The usual rules for recognizing assets apply: initially it must be recognized at cost but it may subsequently be revalued to current value. If there is an impairment, the fixed asset should be correspondingly written down.

Income from such investments, principally dividends, should be recorded in the income statement as 'Income from fixed asset investments'.

10.3   Associated companies

An associated company is one where the investor actively exercises significant influence but not control and is dealt with by IAS 28 *Investments in Associates*. The Companies Act 1985 refers to such companies as related companies. As a rule of thumb a holding of between 20% and 50% of voting rights would result in an associated company but it is more important to determine whether significant influence arises and is exercised. For example, if the investing company held 15% of the shares but no other party held more than 5% it is possible that it would have significant influence; alternatively, a holding of 30% would allow no influence if all of the other 70% of shareholders always acted together.

Accounting treatment

The equity method of accounting should be used. This method requires the holding company to value the investment on an equity basis, ie reflecting the investing company's share of the associate's net assets and profit.

This is because the influence the investor is exercising means that recording simply the cost of the investment and the dividends paid would not reflect the degree of involvement of the company.

As an extreme example, the company in which the investment is made may decide, with the agreement of the investing company, that although it is successful it will not pay any dividends in order to retain cash for future expansion. This would mean that no income would be reflected in the income statement of the investing company, suggesting (wrongly) that the investment was performing badly.

It is felt that, once an investor is in a position to exercise influence, it more accurately reflects the performance of the investment if recognition is based on the investor's share of net assets and profit.

As you will see, the equity method is a modified and summarized form of acquisition accounting as applied to subsidiaries.

Equity accounting

Suppose, for example, that on 31 December 20X0 Henry Limited purchased 25% of the share capital of Katherine Limited for £10m. Katherine Ltd's balance sheet at that date shows:

	£m
Fixed assets – tangible	30
Net current assets	8
	38
Creditors due > one year	(6)
	32
Financed by:	
Share capital (£1 shares)	10
Reserves	22
	32

Thus Henry has spent £10m securing influence over Katherine's net assets of £32m. Although the exact level of the influence exercised by Henry may be more or less than 25% depending on the levels of other shareholdings, for the purposes of accounting, 25% is used.

Look at the following calculation:

		£m
Consideration paid		10
Katherine's assets	£32m	
x Henry's shareholding	x 25%	
		(8)
		2

Henry has paid £2m over the fair value of Katherine's net assets for goodwill.

Henry's balance sheet at 31 December 20X0 is as follows.

	£m
Fixed assets – tangible	50
Investment in Katherine	10
Net current assets	16
	76
Creditors due > one year	(12)
	64
Financed by:	
Share capital (£1 shares)	20
Reserves	44
	64

As can be seen, the investment in Katherine is shown (i) as a fixed asset and (ii) at cost. The former implies that Henry intends to keep the shares in Katherine for the foreseeable future. We can now see that showing the investment at cost does not accurately reflect the current value of the investment. We are going to show the investment using the equity method of accounting, ie reflecting Henry's share of the net assets of Katherine.

Balance sheet

Katherine should be valued using the following formula:

Investing company's share	x	Net assets of associated company at balance sheet date		
25%	x	£32m	=	£8m
Plus unamortized goodwill				£2m
				£10m

Another way of calculating this figure is to use the formula:

Cost	X
Less goodwill amortized	(X)
Plus investing company's share x increase in net assets of associate from date of purchase to balance sheet date	X

In our example:

		£m
Cost		10
Less goodwill amortized		(0)
Plus		10
Investing company's share x	25%	
Increase in net assets of Associate from date of purchase to balance sheet date	zero	0
Carrying value of associate		10

Look at the situation in one year's time; at the end of 20X1 Katherine's balance sheet is as follows:

	20X1	20X0
	£m	£m
Fixed assets – tangible	36	30
Net current assets	12	8
	48	38
Creditors due > one year	(4)	(6)
	44	32
Financed by:		
Share capital (£1 shares)	10	10
Reserves	34	22
	44	32

As can be seen, the balance sheet total of Katherine has risen by £12m. We would expect Henry's share in that increase to be £3m (25% x £12m).

For simplicity we will assume goodwill has not been amortized.

Valuation of Katherine

Using the formula:

Investing company's share	x	Net assets of associated company at balance sheet date		
25%	x	£44m	=	£11m
Plus unamortized goodwill				£2m
				£13m

Or using the alternative formula:

			£m
Cost			10
Less goodwill amortized			(0)
Plus			10
Investing company's share _		25% x	
Increase in net assets of Associate from date of purchase to balance sheet date	£44m – £32m		3
value of associate			13

As you can see, the equity method of accounting allows us to show Henry's interest in the overall position of Katherine. The increase/decrease in the carrying value of the investment is in direct relation to the carrying value of the associate's balance sheet.

Income statement

In a similar way the investing company (Henry) should account for its share of the Associate's (Katherine's) profits by using the following formula.

Include:

Investing company's share	x	Associate's operating profit
	x	Associate's interest charge
	x	Associate's tax charge

In 20X0, Henry did not purchase its investment in Katherine until the year-end, therefore Henry should not record any share of Katherine's profit or tax for that year.

In 20X1 Katherine's income statement (extract) was as follows.

	£m
Profit before tax/operating profit	32
Tax	(12)
Profit after tax	20
Dividends	(8)
Retained profit for financial year	12
Profit and loss reserve brought forward	22
Profit and loss reserve carried forward	34

Include the following in Henry's income statement:

Investing company's share	x	Associate's operating profit	
25%	x	£32m =	£8m

And

Investing company's share	x	Associate's tax charge	
25%	x	£12m =	£3m

Henry, of course, would have been a recipient of 25% of Katherine's dividends. When using the equity method of accounting, Henry should not show this dividend income in the income statement because to do so would mean counting the dividend twice, once as a part of the overall profit and then again when it was paid as dividend. It will appear in the cash flow statement.

Overall effect

	£m
Investing company's share of associate's operating profit	8
Less	
Investing company's share of associate's tax charge	(3)
Less	
Dividends received but not shown in P & L account (25% x £8m)	(2)
Increase in balance sheet valuation of Associate	3

Where there has been an impairment in any goodwill attributable to an associate or joint venture, the goodwill should be written down. The amount written off in the accounting period should be separately disclosed.

In the consolidated statement of changes in equity the investor's share of the recognized income and expenses of its associates should be included, shown separately under each heading where material.

10.4 Joint ventures

The difference between a joint venture and an associate is that in a joint venture the companies involved share control rather than having influence. Joint ventures are often of limited duration and activity. An example might be some commercial activity connected with the Athens Olympics.

Joint ventures are covered by IAS 31 *Interests in Joint Ventures* but this is not in your syllabus so we will not go into great detail.

For accounting purposes IAS 31 allows the equity method described above to be used although it prefers a method known as 'proportionate consolidation'. This is like normal consolidation, as used for subsidiaries (see below), except that only the relevant share of assets, liabilities, income and expenses are included – there is no minority interest.

10.5   Subsidiary

Definition

The implication when a company has a subsidiary is that it has control over that company. Thus it can control the other company's operations and consequently its net assets and profits.

Over the years the precise definition of what constitutes a subsidiary has been refined. Usually, owning 51% of the shares will give the investor control but this would not be the case if, for example, an investing company owned 51% of the non-voting 'A' shares, but did not own any of the voting 'B' shares.

It is also important to appreciate that, for a company that wishes to manipulate its published results, there are advantages to being able to avoid defining an investment as a subsidiary relationship. Where a subsidiary exists, group accounts must be prepared and being able to omit a loss-making subsidiary or one with high borrowings could be beneficial. For this reason the definition appears very long and complicated; however, it needs to be comprehensive to avoid what became known as 'controlled non-subsidiaries'.

The Companies Act defines a subsidiary undertaking as one in which the parent:

(a)   has a majority of the voting rights; or

(b)   is a member and can appoint or remove a majority of the board; or

(c)   is a member and controls alone a majority of the voting rights by agreement with other members; or

(d)   has the right to exercise a dominant influence through the memorandum and articles or a control contract; or

(e)   has a participating interest and either

    (i)   actually exercises a dominant influence over it, or

    (ii)   manages both on a unified basis.

You may have noticed that the phrase 'subsidiary undertaking' was used above. The Companies Act 1989 introduced this term, using the word 'undertaking' rather than 'company' to ensure that entities that were unincorporated could not escape the definition.

The definition of a subsidiary will also apply to companies in which subsidiaries have invested: sub-subsidiaries. Any subsidiary of a subsidiary is deemed to be a subsidiary of the ultimate parent for the purposes of the definition.

In an exam question, unless you are given further information to allow you to assess the degree of control or influence it is safe to assume that a holding of more than 20% will give an associate and more than 50%, a subsidiary.

One final point, if an investor owns, say, 60% of the shares of a company, what degree of control does the investor have? Not 60%. In fact the investor has total control of the company, he can outvote any other shareholders, and as long as he does not infringe their limited statutory rights as a minority, the investor can exercise that control unreservedly.

Consolidated accounts

The relevant international standard is IAS 27 *Consolidated and Separate Financial Statements.*

Where there is a subsidiary, consolidated accounts are required. These aggregate the individual assets and liabilities of the subsidiary with the individual assets and liabilities of the investing company, the parent or holding company. Instead of brief, essentially one-line, entries that we have with associated companies, we add in the subsidiary's fixed assets, current assets, current liabilities, etc.

If the parent company does not own 100% of the subsidiary, the accounts should also reflect that another party – called the 'minority' or 'minority interest' – has an ownership interest in the net assets of the subsidiary.

For example, suppose that on 31 December 20X0, Pistol plc purchased 80% of the share capital of Rifle Limited for consideration of £80m. At the time of purchase Rifle's accounts were as follows:

	£m
Fixed assets – tangible	40
Net current assets	20
	60
Creditors due >1 year	(10)
	50
Financed by:	
Share capital (£1 shares)	30
Reserves	20
	50

We can see that the investing company (Pistol) has paid a premium to invest in Rifle. Pistol has paid £80m for an 80% share in Rifle's assets of £50m. Thus a premium (called goodwill on acquisition) of £40m has arisen (£80m − [80% _ £50m]). We will deal with the accounting treatment of the goodwill later, but first let us consider how to incorporate the assets and liabilities of Rifle in Pistol's accounts.

Pistol's balance sheet at 31 December 20X0 is as follows:

	£m
Fixed assets – tangible	100
Investment in Rifle Limited	80
	180
Net current assets	40
	220
Creditors due > one year	(30)
	190
Financed by:	
Share capital (£1 shares)	100
Reserves	90
	190

We need to aggregate the assets and liabilities of Pistol and Rifle. Pistol owns 80% of the equity of Rifle; however it has control over all the assets and liabilities, not just 80% of them. Therefore we need to combine all of the assets and liabilities of both companies.

Simply adding together the accounts of Pistol and Rifle we get the following:

	Pistol	**Rifle**	**Group**
	£m	**£m**	**£m**
Fixed assets – tangible	100	40	140
Investment in Rifle Ltd.	80	–	80
	180	40	220
Net current assets	40	20	60
	220	60	280
Creditors due > one year	(30)	(10)	(40)
	190	50	240
Financed by:			
Share capital (£1 shares)	100	30	130
Reserves	90	20	110
	190	50	240

There are a few problems with the above approach.

(a) To include the cost of the investment in Rifle as well as all of its net assets is effectively double counting. We should eliminate the 'investment in Rifle' in the consolidated accounts. Pistol's investment represents two elements: (i) Pistol's share of Rifle's net assets and (ii) goodwill on acquisition. Thus it is illogical to include the investment as well. We have already calculated the amount of goodwill arising, above, but in terms of a formula the following is the simplest way of calculating goodwill:

Goodwill

	£m	£m
Cost of investment		80
Less: group share of		
Share capital (80% x £30m)	24	
Reserves (80% x £20m)	16	
at the date of acquisition		40
Positive goodwill		40

The amount of goodwill is fixed at the moment of acquisition, and therefore there is no need to recalculate it in later years. Positive goodwill must be accounted for as an intangible fixed asset. The accounting for goodwill is covered more fully below.

◆ We have failed to recognize that although Pistol has control of Rifle, it does not own all of it. There is a minority interest in Rifle's net assets at the balance sheet date and we need to acknowledge that; if the company were wound up at that time, the minority would be entitled to a certain amount. The calculation can be done simply as follows:

Minority interest (MI) = MI% x net assets of subsidiary at the balance sheet date,

in this case 20% x 50 = 10.

Unlike goodwill, this figure will change at each balance sheet date to reflect the proportion of the subsidiary's net assets owned by the minority at that point. The formula is always the same but the net assets of the subsidiary will have changed.

◆ Finally we need to look at the capital and reserves of the consolidated entity. In our simple attempt above we are showing share capital of £130m. No company we are dealing with has that amount of share capital so it cannot be correct. Pistol controls its own assets and the assets of Rifle and the group accounts are prepared from Pistol's perspective, therefore it is Pistol's share capital which is shown together with the reserves which Pistol owns and, in the case of Rifle's reserves, the reserves which have arisen under Pistol's control. Consolidated or group reserves are calculated as follows:

Group reserves

	£m		£m
Holding company	90		
Group share of post acquisition reserves of subsidiary			
Reserves now	20		
Reserves at acquisition	(20)		
	0	x 80%	0
			90

The above result makes sense because, at the moment of acquisition, there are no post-acquisition reserves in the subsidiary therefore the group reserves figure will include only the reserves of the holding company.

Incorporating all these adjustments the group balance sheet looks as follows:

	Group £m
Intangible assets – positive goodwill	40
Fixed assets – tangible (100 + 40)	140
Investment in Rifle Ltd.(80 x 80)	–
	180
Net current assets (40 + 20)	60
	240
Creditors due > one year (30 + 10)	(40)
	200
Finance by:	
Share capital (£1 shares) (Pistol only)	100
Reserves see working above	90
Minority interest (20% x 50)	10
	200

One year later

Consider the situation in one year's time. Let us look at our two balance sheets then.

Balance sheets as at 31 December 20X1

	Pistol £m	Rifle £m
Fixed assets – tangible	120	50
Investment in Rifle Ltd.	80	–
	200	50
Net current assets	50	30
	250	80
Creditors due > one year	(40)	(20)
	210	60
Financed by:		
Share capital (£1 shares)	100	30
Reserves	110	30
	210	60

If we want to prepare consolidated accounts for the Pistol Group as at 31 December 20X1, we have to consider minority interest, goodwill and group reserves as we saw above as well as simply combining the assets and liabilities of the two companies.

Minority interest

Using the formula, MI% x net assets of subsidiary, we get:

20% x £60m = £12m

Goodwill

As mentioned above goodwill is calculated at the date of acquisition and does not change thereafter. The goodwill figure is therefore £40m and, for simplicity, we will not amortize the balance in this example.

Group reserves

Using the formula:

	£m
Holding company reserves	X
Plus: group share of post-acquisition Revenue reserves of the subsidiary	X
Group reserves	X

We will get:

	£m	£m
Pistol reserves		110
Rifle – reserves now	30	
– reserves at acquisition	20	
Post-acquisition reserves	10	
Group share	80%	8
Group reserves		118

Incorporating these pieces of information and amalgamating the other figures as we did before, we end up with a group balance sheet as follows:

	Group £m
Fixed assets – Intangible – goodwill	40
Fixed assets – tangible (120+50)	170
	210
Net current assets (50+30)	80
	290
Creditors due > one year (40+20)	(60)
	230
Finance by:	
Share capital (£1 shares) (Pistol only)	100
Reserves per working above	118
	218
Minority interest per working above	12
	230

10.6   Fair value accounting

IFRS 3 *Business Combinations* requires that the assets of the acquired company be revalued to fair value prior to being consolidated and for the purpose of calculating goodwill.

In most acquisitions a large number of adjustments will probably have to be made to the subsidiary's balance sheet. For example, land and buildings will probably need to be revalued upwards, while inventory or debtors may need to be revalued downwards.

Procedure

The accounting for the revaluation adjustments is as normal. Revaluations of fixed assets would be shown in a revaluation reserve; other changes in valuations of current assets would be charged to or credited to the income statement.

For example suppose that on 31 December 20X0 Talbot plc purchased 90% of the share capital in Gloucester Limited for consideration of £100m. The two companies' balance sheets at that date were as follows.

	Talbot	Gloucester
	£m	£m
Fixed assets – tangible	400	20
Investment in Gloucester Ltd.	100	
	500	20
Current assets	210	30
Current liabilities	(120)	(10)
	590	40
Creditors due > one year	(100)	(10)
	490	30
Financed by:		
Share capital (£1 shares)	400	10
Revenue reserves	70	20
Revaluation reserve	20	
	490	30

At first glance Talbot has paid £100m for £27m (90% x £30m) of assets, generating positive goodwill of £73m. However, in agreeing the deal fair values of the various assets would have been considered rather than book values and we need to reflect those fair values in the balance sheet of the subsidiary. Let us say, for example, that the fair value of the fixed assets should be £50m; that inventory has been overvalued by £5m and that there should be additional provisions of £2m. Incorporating this into Gloucester's balance sheet we get:

	Before	Adjustments	After
	£m	£m	£m
Fixed assets – tangible	20	30 (W1)	50
Current assets	30	(5) (W2)	25
Current liabilities	(10)	(2) (W2)	(12)
	40		63
Creditors due > one year	(10)		(10)
	30		53
Financed by:			
Share capital (£1 shares)	10		10
Revenue reserves	20	(5) (W2)	13
		(2) (W2)	
Revaluation reserve		30 (W1)	30
	30		53

Workings

1   The uplift in the fixed asset valuation (Dr fixed asset) has been credited to a revaluation reserve.

2   The inventory write-down (Cr inventory) and the new provision (Cr Provision) have been charged (Dr) to the income statement.

Having made the fair value adjustments we can now prepare the consolidated balance sheet.

Goodwill

We will now use the formula in its full form:

fair value of the consideration given – fair value of the net assets acquired

which becomes:

£100m – (90% x £53m) = £52.3m

Note: the £53m was taken from the revised balance sheet total but can be reconciled to the original balance sheet by taking the original balance sheet total of £30m and adjusting for the fair value adjustments. We get £30m + £30m (revaluation of TFA) – £5m (inventory write-down) – £2m (new provision) = £53m.

Minority interest

The formula remains the same as before:

MI% x net assets of subsidiary at balance sheet date

but remember that at the date of acquisition the calculation would be done after the fair value adjustments had been incorporated.

In our example,

10% x £53m = £5.3m

Although we have created a new reserve because we revalued the tangible fixed asset upwards the minority are still entitled to 10% of its balance so there is no need to separate it out in the calculation. The only time the calculation becomes more complex is where there are different classes of shares in issue with different rights on a winding up. Where this is the case a separate calculation would need to be done for each category of minority rights.

Group reserves

The previous formula – holding company reserves plus the group share of the post-acquisition reserves of the subsidiary – still applies but we do one calculation for each reserve.

In our example:

Income statement	£	£
Talbot		70
Gloucester – reserve now	13	
– reserve at acq'n	13	
Post-acquisition reserves	0	
Group share 10%		0
Consolidated profit and loss reserve		70

Revaluation reserve	£	£
Talbot		20
Gloucester – reserve now	30	
– reserve at acq'n	30	
Post-acquisition reserves	0	
Group share 10%		0
Consolidated revaluation reserve		20

When we bring all of the above together, the consolidated balance sheet looks as follows. The workings show the fair value adjustments.

Consolidated balance sheet as at 31 December 20X0

	Group £m
Fixed assets – intangible – goodwill	52.3
Fixed assets – tangible (400+20+30)	450.0
	502.3
Current assets (210+30-5)	235.0
Current liabilities (120+10)	(130.0)
	607.3
Creditors due > one year(100+10)	(110.0)
Provision (2)	(2.0)
	495.3
Financed by:	
Share capital (£1 shares) (Talbot only)	400.0
Revenue reserves (see working above)	70.0
Revaluation reserve (see working above)	20.0
	490.0
Minority interest (see working above)	5.3
	495.3

Provisions and write-downs

One of the concerns of IFRS 3 is to prevent companies from using creative accounting either to manipulate the amount of goodwill that arises or to affect the post-acquisition balance sheet.

Consider the example above. Gloucester wrote £5m off inventories and made a provision of £2m. The obvious effect of these adjustments is to alter the look of the balance sheet at the date of acquisition. There is also an effect on post-acquisition profits: the write down of inventory will mean that when the goods are sold the profit on sale will be higher than if the original book value had been retained.

As regards the provision, when the relevant expenditure is incurred it will be set against the provision rather than being charged against the income statement, again increasing profit compared to what it would have been without the adjustment.

The particular benefit that occurs in this context arises because they are fair value adjustments. The increase in profit is reflected in the group income statement while the write down and creation of the provision were recognized in the individual accounts of the subsidiary in the period immediately before the acquisition took place, and not in the group accounts. Put another way, the expense was in the pre-acquisition accounts of the subsidiary, but the benefit or income is in the post-acquisition group accounts.

This phenomenon became the basis for some of the worst excesses of creative accounting: many companies used acquisitions to record as many provisions, for reorganization, integration etc, as they could, so that they could then use the provisions to boost post-acquisition profits over the next few years.

This has the effect of distorting the profit trends and giving a false impression of the performance of the combined entity post-acquisition. Consider the effect on the return on capital employed ratio. Simply put the ratio can be expressed as:

$$\frac{\text{Profits}}{\text{Net assets}}$$

The effect of either write-downs or provisions on acquisition is to boost post-acquisition profits (see above) and to depress asset values on acquisition. The effect is to unfairly increase the return on capital employed post-acquisition.

In the interest of fairness, it should be pointed out that revaluing assets upwards has the opposite effect as asset values rise and profits fall due to the larger depreciation charges that result.

IFRS 3 includes strict criteria regarding the type of provisions, in particular, that can be made on acquisition and also detailed guidance on the valuation of assets and liabilities. We will deal with provisions first.

The basic principle is that provisions cannot be made to reflect the 'restructuring' intentions of the acquiring company. In general, fair values have to be determined from the acquired company's perspective. This means that when looking at the balance sheet of the subsidiary, the assets and liabilities should be valued from that company's point of view – taking the hypothetical position that the take-over had not taken, nor was ever going to take place.

This is very much an attitude of mind and can be difficult to conceptualize. For example, the acquirer may be intending to merge product lines and to streamline the company's range of products. The effect of this policy could well be to depress the net realizable values of such inventory. Under IFRS 3 we have to adopt the acquired company's perspective – thus the plans of the acquirer are irrelevant. We must value the inventory on the basis that the take-over is not going to take place.

Similarly, even though the acquiring company may intend to close some of the acquired company's factories or offices, provision for this may not be made as a fair value adjustment. It can be recognized only in the post-acquisition period because this means that both the debit and the credit will appear in the group accounts.

Guidelines on fair values

IFRS 3 gives guidance on the valuation of various assets and liabilities, including the following.

Plant and equipment

The fair value of a tangible fixed asset should be based on the following:

♦ market value, if assets similar in type and condition are bought and sold on an open market; or
♦ depreciated replacement cost, reflecting the acquired business's normal buying process and the sources of supply, and prices available to it. The fair value should not exceed the recoverable amount of the asset.

Intangible assets

Where an intangible asset is recognized, its fair value should be based on its replacement cost, which is normally its estimated market value.

Inventories and work in progress

Value at the lower of cost and net realizable value.

Quoted investments

Value at market price.

Monetary assets and liabilities

The fair value of monetary assets and liabilities, including accruals and provisions, should take into account the amounts expected to be received or paid and their timing. Fair value should be determined by reference to market prices, where available or by reference to the current price at which the business could acquire similar assets or enter into similar obligations.

Contingencies

Contingent liabilities should be measured at the amount a third party would charge to assume them. For this purpose reasonable estimates of the expected outcome may be used, but these must reflect all possible outcomes, not just the most likely outcome or the minimum or maximum cash flow.

Finally, it should be noted that the fair value adjustments actually need to be put through only in the consolidated accounts. It is acceptable, although unusual, for the subsidiary not to recognize the fair values in its own accounts. The reason why it is unusual is that it makes the consolidation process in later years more complicated – at each year end the fair value adjustments as calculated at the date of acquisition need to be incorporated again, insofar as the assets or liabilities to which they relate still exist.

Fair value one year later

Let us continue our example above and see the situation one year later, assuming that the subsidiary has not incorporated the fair value adjustments in its own accounts.

Remember that on 31 December 20X0 Talbot plc purchased 90% of the share capital in Gloucester Limited for consideration of £100m. The two company's balance sheets at that date were as follows:

	Talbot £m	Gloucester £m
Fixed assets – tangible	400	20
Investment in Gloucester Ltd.	100	
	500	20
Current assets	210	30
Current liabilities	(120)	(10)
	590	40
Creditors due > one year	(100)	(10)
	490	30
Financed by:		
Share capital (£1 shares)	400	10
Revenue reserves	70	20
Revaluation reserve	20	
	490	30

On 31 December 20X0 the fair value of the fixed assets should have been £50m; inventory was overvalued by £5m and there was an additional provision required of £2m.

The balance sheets on 31 December 20X1 are as follows:

	Talbot £m	Gloucester £m
Fixed assets – tangible	500	39
Investment in Gloucester Ltd.	100	
	600	39
Current assets	240	50
Current liabilities	(140)	(20)
	700	69
Creditors due > one year	(120)	(10)
	580	59
Financed by:		
Share capital (£1 shares)	400	10
Revenue reserves	110	49
Revaluation reserve	70	
	580	59

During the year, Gloucester has purchased £20m of new fixed assets (not yet depreciated) and depreciated the old fixed assets by £1m.

Assuming that the fair value adjustments have not been incorporated, we now need to adjust Gloucester's accounts at the end of 20X1. Consider the fair value adjustments one at a time.

Revaluation of fixed assets

On 31 December 20X0, the fair value of the assets was £50m as opposed to book value of £20m. Thus we needed to revalue by £30m. Remember that if an asset is revalued, depreciation needs to be charged on the revalued amount. As well as incorporating the £30m revaluation, we need to take off the extra depreciation on the revalued amount.

The depreciation in Gloucester's books is £1m, so we can assume that the useful life of the asset is 20 years (£20m/£1m). Therefore we need to ensure that one twentieth of the fair value is written off in 20X1. That is, depreciation of £2.5m (£50m/20) needs to be charged, instead of the original £1m.

Fair value of fixed assets

	£m
Book value	39.0
Revaluation to fair value (£50m − £20m)	30.0
Extra depreciation on revalued amount	(1.5)
Fair value at 31 December 20X1	67.5

This can be proved as follows:

	£m
Original assets at 31 December 20X0	20.0
Revaluation	30.0
Fair value at 31 December 20X0	50.0
Depreciation (over 20 years)	(2.5)
Adjusted fair value at 31 December 20X1	47.5
New assets purchased in 20X1 (assume at fair value)	20.0
Fair value at 31 December 20X1	67.5

Inventory write-down and provision

At the end of 20X0 we needed to write down inventory by £5m and make a provision of £2m. Assume that that inventory is still held and the requirement for the provision still exists.

Gloucester's balance sheet at 31st December 20X1

	Before £m	Adjustments £m	After £m
Fixed assets – tangible	39.0	30.0	
		(1.5)	67.5
Current assets	50.0	(5)	45.0
Current liabilities	(20.0)		(20.0)
	69.0		92.5
Creditors due > one year	(10.0)		(10.0)
Provision	0.0	(2)	(2.0)
	59.0		80.5
Financed by:			
Share capital (£1 shares)	10.0		10.0
Revenue reserves	49.0	(5.0)	
		(2.0)	42.0
Revaluation reserve		30.0	
		(1.5)	28.5
	59.0		80.5

Having made the fair value adjustments we can now prepare the consolidated balance sheet.

Goodwill will remain unchanged at £52.3m because it is fixed at the moment of acquisition.

Minority interest will change every year; it will reflect the underlying balance sheet of the subsidiary:

MI% x net assets of Gloucester

10% x 80.5 = 8.05

Reserves

Revenue reserves

	£m	£m
Holding company		110.0
Plus holding company's share of subsidiary's		
post-acquisition reserves		
Reserves now	42	
Reserves at acquisition	(13)	
Post-acquisition reserves	29	
Holding company's share	90%	26.1
Group reserves		136.1

Revaluation reserve

	£m	£m
Holding company		70.00
Plus Holding company's share of subsidiary's		
post-acquisition reserves		
Reserves now	28.5	
Reserves at acquisition	(30.0)	
Post-acquisition decrease	(1.5)	
Holding company's share	90%	(1.35)
Group reserves		68.65

Consolidated balance sheet as at 31 December 20X1

	Group £m
Fixed assets – intangible – goodwill	52.30
Fixed assets – tangible (500 + 67.5)	567.50
	619.80
Current assets (240 + 45)	285.00
Current liabilities (140 + 20)	(160.00)
	744.80
Creditors due > one year (120 + 10)	(130.00)
Provision	(2.00)
	612.80
Financed by:	
Share capital (£1 shares) (Talbot only)	400.00
Revenue reserves (see working above)	136.10
Revaluation reserve (see working above)	68.65
	604.75
Minority interest (see working above)	8.05
	612.80

That is quite enough information for you to take in for one chapter. In the next chapter we will look at some more of the complications that can arise when preparing group accounts and consider what accounting treatment to adopt in the case of a merger.

Summary

Now that you have completed this chapter you should be able to:

♦ explain how companies should account for associated companies;
♦ outline the accounting implications of taking part in a joint venture;
♦ explain how companies should account for subsidiary companies;
♦ explain the issues surrounding fair value accounting in the case of a business combination; and
♦ demonstrate knowledge and understanding of the following accounting standards:
  IFRS 3 *Business Combinations*
  IAS 27 *Consolidated and Separate Financial Statements*
  IAS 28 *Investments in Associates.*

Eleven

Investments: group accounts 2

Syllabus

This chapter is the second of two covering syllabus Section 6: Investments. This section of the syllabus looks at the types of investment undertaken by (typically) business enterprises and the accounting treatment of such investments. Particular attention is to investment in other business enterprises and how the financial performance and position of 'groups' of enterprises should be reported.

Objectives

After studying this chapter you should be able to:

♦ recognize and account for some of the complications that arise when preparing consolidated accounts;
♦ explain the main exemptions from the need to prepare consolidated accounts;
♦ understand that some regimes allow merger accounting in certain circumstances, and how this method differs from the acquisition method (consolidation); and
♦ demonstrate knowledge and understanding of the following accounting standards:
  IFRS 3 *Business Combinations*
  IAS 27 *Consolidated and Separate Financial Statements.*

11.1 Subsidiary accounts: some complications

Inter-company balances and transactions

Group accounts are prepared on the basis of the principle of 'substance over form'; legally each company is a separate legal entity, the 'form' part, but the group accounts are trying to reflect the fact that those under common control operate as one commercial entity, the 'substance' part. As it is one commercial entity, showing balances arising on transactions between group companies makes little sense and these inter-company balances should be excluded from the group accounts. Likewise, where goods have been sold between group companies, the turnover and cost of sales figures should be reduced by the amount of the turnover so that only genuine sales to third parties are recognized in the group accounts.

For example, suppose that during 20X0 Gower Limited purchased 51% of the shares in one of its suppliers Orleans Limited. During the year Orleans sold goods costing £200,000 for £300,000 to Gower. At the year-end Gower owed £20,000 to Orleans.

In the group income statement we remove £300,000 from the aggregated turnover and the same amount from the aggregated cost of sales, so that what remains is the cost of the goods, £200,000, and the sale will be recognized only when sold to someone outside the group.

In the group balance sheet we need to exclude:

♦ £20,000 from group trade debtors (representing the balance in Orleans' books due from Gower); and
♦ £20,000 from group trade creditors (representing the balance in Gower's books due to Orleans).

Note we exclude the entire inter-company amount, not just 51% because we consolidate all turnover, cost of sales, debtors and creditors, not just the group share.

Inter-company inventory

When group companies trade with each other, they are likely to do so at a profit. Any inventory left in the balance sheet of the purchasing company will reflect the profit element charged by the selling company. This profit has not yet been realized outside the group however. The scope for profit manipulation would be great if the 'profit' element were not eliminated on consolidation. The group could easily boost profits by selling inventory to a fellow group company at an inflated value. The gross profit would show in the accounts and the inflated closing inventory value in the balance sheet.

Suppose that Williams plc sold £120,000 worth of inventory to its 80% subsidiary Ely Limited at a mark-up of 50%. At the year-end a quarter of the inventory had not been sold. Ely still owed Williams £30,000 for purchases at the year-end.

Initially, eliminate the inter-company balances.

Exclude:

♦ £30,000 from group trade debtors (Cr debtors)(representing the balance in Williams' books due from Ely); and

♦ £30,000 from group trade creditors (Dr creditors)(representing the balance in Ely's books due to Williams).

Secondly, we need to exclude the profit element in the year end inventory.

The inventory was sold at a mark-up of 50%, therefore the profit element was £40,000 (50/150 x £120,000). Three-quarters of this has been realized, ie sold outside the group. Therefore only a quarter needs to be excluded. Note, however, that the full £120,000 has to be eliminated from turnover and cost of sales, otherwise the transaction will have been recognized twice in the income statement.

We need to deduct £10,000 (£40,000 x 1/4) from the balance sheet value of closing inventory (Cr closing inventory). The other side of the entry will be to reduce reserves (Dr retained reserves). Minority interest is calculated after this adjustment is made so that the effect of it is shared between the holding company shareholders and the minority pro-rata.

Dividends

When a subsidiary pays a dividend, its share of it will be income for the holding company. If it is a proposed dividend, it will be a liability of the subsidiary and an asset of the holding company. Such balances would need to be eliminated on consolidation (as for other inter-company balances – see above). There are a number of other issues when a dividend is made from subsidiary to parent.

Pre-acquisition dividends

When a newly acquired subsidiary pays a dividend out of pre-acquisition profits the receiving company should record it in the same way it would record any other dividend receivable. It would record the dividend as income in the income statement (Dr Bank and Cr dividends receivable in the income statement of the holding company). It is theoretically possible, although in practice unlikely, that the payment of the dividend would reduce the net assets of the paying company sufficiently to represent an impairment of the investment. If this were the case, the dividend deemed to be pre-acquisition would be deducted from the cost of the investment and thereby reduce goodwill.

Dividends after acquisition

These are normally quite straightforward. You need to be sure about whether the dividend has yet been put through in the books of the subsidiary and the holding company. Although it will not appear in the consolidated income statement, the payment and receipt of the dividend will have to be recorded to get the balance sheet reserves figures correct. Also note any minority share in the dividend.

For example, let us say that on 1 January 20X0 Charles Limited purchased 60% of the share capital in Suffolk Limited for £22m. At the time of purchase Suffolk had net assets at fair value of £30m with share capital of £20m and reserves of £10m. At the year ended 31 December 20X3 the two companies' balance sheets are as follows.

	Charles £m	Suffolk £m
Fixed assets – tangible	110	60
Investment in Suffolk Ltd.	22	–
	132	60
Current assets	80	65
Current liabilities	(20)	(35)
	192	90
Creditors due > one year	(32)	(20)
	160	70
Financed by:		
Share capital (£1 shares)	100	20
Reserves	60	50
	160	70

Suffolk declared a dividend for the year ended 31 December 20X3 of £5m. This has not yet been incorporated into the accounts above. Prepare the consolidated balance sheet of the Charles Group as at 31 December 20X3.

Treatment

The first stage is to account for the proposed dividend.

The holding company is accountable only for 60% – £3m of the dividend. If we were to represent the two balance sheets after accounting for the dividend they would look like this:

	Charles		Suffolk
	£m		£m
Fixed assets – tangible	110		60
Investment in Suffolk Ltd.	22		–
	132		60
Current assets (£80m plus div. receivable of £3m)	83		65
		(£35m plus div.	
Current liabilities	(20)	payable of £5m)	(40)
	195		85
Creditors due > one year	(32)		(20)
	163		65
Financed by:			
Share capital (£1 shares)	100		20
Reserves (£60m plus div.		(£50m less div.	
receivable of £3m)	63	payable of £5m)	45
	163		65

We can now proceed with our usual workings. You should attempt the calculations for goodwill, minority and reserves before checking your answer below.

Goodwill

	£m
Cost of investment	22
Net assets acquired – adjusted for dividend (60% x £30m)	18
Goodwill	4

Minority interest

	£m
MI% x net assets at date of balance sheet	
40% x £65m (adjusted for dividend)	26

Consolidated reserves

Charles reserves plus group share of post acquisition reserves of Suffolk

	£m		£m
Charles (including dividend)			63
Suffolk – reserves now	45		
– reserves at acquisition	10		
Post-acquisition reserves	35	x 60%	21
Group reserves			84

Consolidated balance sheet as at 31 December 20X3

	Group £m
Fixed assets – intangible – goodwill	4
Fixed assets – tangible (110 + 60)	170
	174
Current assets (83 + 65 – 3div)	145
Current liabilities (20 + 40 – 3div)	(57)
	262
Creditors due > one year (32 + 20)	(52)
	210
Financed by:	
Share capital (£1 shares) (Charles only)	100
Reserves (see working above)	84
	184
Minority interest (see working above)	26
	210

Note that for simplicity the goodwill has not been amortized and the inter-company dividend balances have been eliminated.

Mid-year acquisitions

The difficulty presented by an acquisition taking place in the middle of an accounting year is that we need to identify the profit, reserves and net assets of the business at the date of acquisition. In practice, accounts would be made up to the appropriate date, in the exam it is usual to assume that profits arise evenly throughout the year and that the profit for the year can be apportioned. In a consolidated income statement, too, it is only the post acquisition results that are consolidated.

11.2   Exemptions from consolidation

Although the general trend of the accounting and legal requirements is to ensure that all companies that meet the definition of a subsidiary are consolidated, there are certain specific circumstances that are identified in either accounting standards or the Companies Act which mean that a subsidiary undertaking should not be consolidated:

♦ where there are severe long-term restrictions over the parent's right to control (for example, a subsidiary undertaking operating in a war-torn area);

♦ where an undertaking is held exclusively for subsequent resale and has not previously been consolidated in group accounts prepared by the parent undertaking; and

♦ where the activities of the parent and the subsidiary undertaking are dissimilar. This would be in the exceptional situation where consolidating the enterprises' results would give a misleading view. FRS2 gives strict criteria as to when this exemption may apply. It stresses this should only be in very exceptional circumstances. For example, a bank and a manufacturing company would not, in themselves, be sufficiently dissimilar. Nor would the combination of a profit making and a non-profit-making enterprise, in itself, be sufficient grounds for non-consolidation.

The Companies Act permits exclusion from consolidation in all the circumstances mentioned above, except for dissimilar activities where exclusion is a requirement. It is worth noting that although 'dissimilar activities' seems more easily met in the Companies Act version, the more rigorous definition of the FRS must be followed. In addition to the above, the Companies Act also permits exclusion for two other reasons:

(a)   where the subsidiary undertaking's inclusion would be immaterial, and

(b)   where the information needed to prepare consolidated accounts cannot be obtained without disproportionate expense or delay.

These two criteria are not grounds for exclusion under accounting standards, and the second should not therefore be used. As regards the first, no accounting standard applies to immaterial figures, but, where there is more than one subsidiary excluded on the grounds of immateriality, they can ultimately be excluded only if they remain immaterial in aggregate.

11.3   Merger accounting

So far we have only dealt with combinations of businesses that are acquisitions, which are characterized by one business taking control of the other, the subsidiary. You might also be familiar with the term 'merger'. In business parlance this is widely used in the context of two businesses combining their operations or assets in some formal or informal arrangement, and often the combination will be accounted for as an acquisition.

Pooling of interests

Under IAS 22 it was possible to account for a business combination using either the acquisition method, which we have covered in detail already, or a method called the 'pooling of interests method'. IAS 22 has now been withdrawn however, and its replacement, IFRS 3 *Business Combinations*, requires all business combinations to be accounted for using the acquisition (or 'purchase' method).

'Merger accounting' has a fairly prominent place in this section of the syllabus however, so rather than telling you about a withdrawn international standard we will look at a UK standard which is still in force at the time of publication of this book. This is FRS 6 *Mergers and Acquisitions*.

FRS 6 sets out a strict definition of a merger, together with a series of demanding criteria which must be met before merger accounting can be used.

The reason for attempting to limit the use of use of merger accounting is that it tends to give a more flattering picture of the combined entity than acquisition accounting. It is also much easier; there is no goodwill calculation, no revaluation to fair value and all reserves are combined, not just post acquisition reserves. These issues are all dealt with later in this section.

The criteria for merger accounting

Role of the parties

No party to the combination should be portrayed as either acquirer or acquired. In some ways this is a fairly nebulous test and would depend on things like the tone of press releases as well as, for example, the corporate name after the combination. If one party has paid over the market price for the shares in another company, for example, it is an indication that a control premium has been paid. The onus is on the 'acquirer' to rebut this implication.

Dominance of management

All parties to the combination should participate in establishing the management structure and personnel for the combined entity. The decisions should be based upon consensus rather than an exercise of voting rights. It does not mean that the final appointments have to be split pro-rata.

Relative size of the parties

Where one party to the combination is substantially larger than the other parties it is presumed that the larger party can or will dominate the combined undertaking.

The presumption is that if one party is more than 50% larger than each of the others, judged by reference to the ownership interest, then the combination is an acquisition not a merger.

Again the onus is on the parties, if they are substantially different in size, to rebut the notion that this is an acquisition not a merger.

Non-equity consideration

All but an immaterial amount of the consideration paid must be in the form of equity shares. Immaterial is not defined – although SSAP 23, the previous standard covering this subject, used 10% of the consideration as a benchmark.

Thus the consideration must be (virtually wholly) in the form of shares. The reason for this is that the process of the combination should have as little effect on the resources of the companies as possible. The ideal would be a share for share exchange. If cash changes hands, being paid by one of the companies to the shareholders in another, cash is leaving the new merged entity, resources are changing. In effect what happens in a true merger is that the shareholders in the old parties now become shareholders in the new combined enterprise – a 'pooling of interests'. 'Pooling of interests' is the name given to merger accounting in the USA.

Interests in the performance of the combined entity

No equity shareholders after the combination should have an interest in the post combination performance of a part of the enterprise. All of the parties involved should be interested in the whole of the new business, not just one part of it.

The requirement is that all five criteria must be met for merger accounting to be used. If the combination meets the criteria, merger accounting must be used.

Accounting for mergers

The idea behind the accounting for mergers is to combine the businesses involved with as few changes to either of them as possible. The easiest way to achieve this is not to revalue either company to fair value and to account for shares issued at par value rather than fair value. This means that no goodwill is valued. In addition no distinction is made between pre- and post-acquisition profits. Once the merger has arisen, the combination is accounted for as if the combining parties have always been combined. The following table summarizes the differences in accounting under the two methods. We will then look at an example that compares the two methods.

	Acquisition accounting	**Merger accounting**
Valuation of assets/liabilities	Use fair values	Use book values
Value of consideration	Use fair values	Use nominal values
Criteria	None	Very strict criteria
Reserves	Distinct split between pre-acquisition and post-acquisition	No split between pre- and post-merger
Goodwill calculation	Difference between fair value of consideration and fair value of separable net assets acquired	The concept of goodwill does not exist in merger accounting but a 'difference on consolidation' is calculated as the difference between nominal value of consideration and nominal value of shares acquired

For example, let us say that on 31 December 20X0 York plc purchases 90% of the share capital in Lewis plc. The consideration is 10 million York £1 ordinary shares. At the time of the combination the shares of York are valued at £10 each. The balance sheets of the two companies at 31 December 20X0 are as follows.

	York £m	**Lewis £m**
Fixed assets – tangible	100	50
Current assets	60	30
Current liabilities	(40)	(20)
	120	60
Creditors due > one year	(40)	(20)
	80	40
Financed by:		
Share capital (£1 shares)	20	8
Revenue reserves	60	32
	80	40

York has not accounted for the share issue for the purchase of Lewis' shares. The fair values of Lewis's assets are as follows:

	£m
Fixed assets – tangible	90
Current assets	28
Current liabilities	23
Creditors due > one year	20

We will prepare the consolidated balance sheets, using (i) acquisition accounting and then (ii) merger accounting.

Note that in this example York has issued shares to the shareholders of Lewis in order to acquire the shares in Lewis. This kind of arrangement can exist in merger accounting but it does look as if York is taking a dominant role. It is also possible in a merger situation for a new company to be set up which buys both companies' shares from the existing shareholders in exchange for shares in the new company.

Acquisition accounting

Although not strictly necessary in an exam question, unless included in the requirements, as a first stage we will recalculate the balance sheets of the two companies incorporating the share issue and the fair value adjustments.

		York £m		Lewis £m
Fixed assets – tangible		100		90
Investment in Lewis plc	(10m x £10)	100		
Current assets		60		28
Current liabilities		(40)		(23)
		220		95
Creditors due > one year		(40)		(20)
		180		75
Financed by:				
Share capital (£1 shares)	(20m + 10m)	30		8
Share premium account	(10m x £9 premium)	90		
Revenue reserves		60	(£32m – 2m – 3m)	27
Revaluation reserve			(£90m – 50m)	40
		180		75

We can now prepare our consolidation workings.

Goodwill

	£m
Cost of Investment	100.0
Net assets acquired (90% x £75m)	(67.5)
Goodwill	32.5

Minority interest

	£m
MI% x net assets at balance sheet date	
10% x £75m	7.5

Consolidated income statement

	£m		£m
Holding company – York			60
Group share of post-acq. reserves of Lewis			
Reserves now	27		
At acquisition	27		
Post-acquisition	0	x 90%	0
Group reserves			60

Since we are preparing the accounts at the date of acquisition, it will always be the case the there will be no post-acquisition reserves of the subsidiary, therefore the group reserves will comprise only those of the holding company.

Consolidated revaluation reserve

	£m
Holding company	0
Subsidiary	0
Group revaluation reserve	0

The consolidated balance sheet as at 31 December 20X0 will look as follows:

	Group £m
Fixed assets – intangible – positive goodwill	32.5
Fixed assets – tangible (100+90)	190.0
	222.5
Current assets (60+28)	88.0
Current liabilities (40+23)	(63.0)
	247.5
Creditors due > one year (40+20)	(60.0)
	187.5

Financed by:

Share capital (£1 shares) York only	30.0
Share premium account	90.0
Revenue reserves see working above	60.0
	180.0
Minority interest see working above	7.5
	187.5

Merger accounting

Using the merger method we do not have to account for either the fair value of the consideration or the fair value of the net assets acquired. Thus we start with the original balance sheets; the only adjustment is to include the investment in the subsidiary at nominal value:

	York £m	Lewis £m
Fixed assets – tangible	100	50
Investment in Lewis plc	10	
Current assets	60	30
Current liabilities	(40)	(20)
	130	60
Creditors due > one year	(40)	(20)
	90	40
Financed by:		
Share capital (£1 shares) (£20m + 10m)	30	8
Revenue reserves	60	32
	90	40

Instead of calculating goodwill, which is appropriate only where one business acquires control of another, we simply need to eliminate the cost of investment in York's balance sheet with the shares acquired in Lewis' balance sheet. If the two figures are equal then no further entries are required. This would happen where there had been a straightforward share for share exchange with shares of equal par value. It is not all that common for it to be as straightforward as this, but the accounting is still very straightforward. The working is as follows:

	£m
Cost of investment	x
Less share capital acquired	(x)
Merger difference	x/(x)
In our example:	
	£m
Cost of investment	10.0
Share capital acquired (90% x 8)	(7.2)
Merger difference	2.8

Where, as here, the cost of investment is higher than the share capital acquired, the amount is written off against reserves, usually the profit and loss reserve. If the nominal value of the share capital acquired is higher, ie a negative figure results from the above working, then a new reserve will be created, usually called a merger reserve.

As regards other workings to complete the consolidation, the only one required is the minority interest because it is still possible for there to be a minority of up to 10%. The calculation is still the minority percentage of the net assets, the only difference is that, in this case, there has been no revaluation to fair value.

Minority interest
10% x £40m = £4m

Notice, in the balance sheet that follows, that the reserves of the two companies are simply added together and then adjusted for the merger difference. Remember, in merger accounting, we make no distinction between pre- and post-acquisition reserves; we combine the two companies' reserves as if they have been combined since incorporation.

Consolidated balance sheet as at 31 December 20X0

	Group £m
Fixed assets – tangible (100+50)	150
Current assets (60+30)	90
Current liabilities (40+20)	(60)
	180
Creditors due > one year (40+20)	(60)
	120
Financed by:	
Share capital (£1 shares)	30
Revenue reserves	86
	116
Minority interest	4
	120

Comparison of merger accounting and acquisition accounting

♦ We can see that the balance sheets under the two methods are different. The asset base is higher under the acquisition method, mainly due to the revaluation of fixed assets but also because in acquisition accounting we recognize goodwill. This results from using the fair value for the consideration as opposed to the nominal value.

◆ Group reserves are different. The profit and loss reserve is higher under the merger method: £86m versus £60m. This is because we have pooled the reserves since incorporation not since the combination of the entities.

◆ It is much simpler to account for a merger than an acquisition because of the above.

As already mentioned, however, merger accounting is no longer allowed under international standards, and FRS 9 is under review.

Summary

Now that you have completed this chapter you should be able to:

◆ **recognize and account for some of the complications that arise when preparing consolidated accounts;**

◆ **explain the main exemptions from the need to prepare consolidated accounts;**

◆ **understand that some regimes allow merger accounting in certain circumstances, and how this method differs from the acquisition method (consolidation); and**

◆ **demonstrate knowledge and understanding of the following accounting standards:**
   IFRS 3   *Business Combinations*
   IAS 27   *Consolidated and Separate Financial Statements.*

Twelve

Interpretation of financial statements

Syllabus

This chapter covers the whole of syllabus Section 7: Interpretation of Financial Statements. It examines the interpretation of the information contained in financial statements. It commences with a reflection of the context within which such statements are produced and then reviews the use of traditional financial ratio analysis and that of more recent techniques based on the analysis of cash flow statements. The section incorporates learning relating to the following objectives.

Objectives

After studying this chapter you should be able to:

♦ explain the value of the information in corporate reports when interpreting an entity's financial position;

♦ calculate and interpret traditional ratios relating to profitability, profit, liquidity, working capital, gearing, and investors' interests;

♦ analyse cash flows for the purpose of risk assessment and in terms of cash performance, operating cash flows and free cash flows; and

♦ explain the limitations of ratio analysis.

12.1   Interpreting financial statements

If you are a banker, one of your key tasks will be to interpret financial information; to explain what the information means, and what it tells you about the position of the company; and what it tells you about its prospects in profitability and cash flow terms, its stability, its ability to repay debts and so on. These factors can be assessed both in absolute terms and more usefully in comparative terms. Comparisons are most helpful when made with previous years' results and with similar companies. Thus the relative performance of the company can be assessed.

Interpretation of accounts is done using some or all of the following techniques:

- a review of all relevant information in the company's annual report;
- ratio analysis of the financial statements; and
- comparison with industry trends.

It is unlikely that only one of the above methods would be necessary to come to a judgement about a company's performance and position. The skill in interpreting accounts is in the employment of the right methods of analysis and recognition of the limitations of the analysis performed.

For example, one could undertake a full financial analysis of a company utilizing all the above techniques and comparing with previous years and industry standards. The analysis would probably not be complete without an examination of what might be called the human aspects of the company.

Imagine, for instance, we were interpreting the position and future prospects of a company engaged in scientific research. Such factors as staff abilities, training, morale, length of service contracts, relationships between employees and management and links to local centres of excellence would all be relevant in our analysis. Such information may not be included in the financial statements, but these factors would affect the financial statements and future prospects of the company.

12.2   Corporate reports

When tackling an accounts interpretation problem consider the following questions:

- what is the purpose of the analysis?
- who is requiring me to do this exercise?
- what exactly am I being asked to do?

Financial statements

Once these questions have been answered satisfactorily, look at the company's financial statements. In general terms, the following questions should be asked:

♦ how well is the company performing?
♦ are profits increasing or decreasing?
♦ is the company liquid (that is, is there cash in the bank or a large overdraft)?
♦ what major changes have there been in the year (for example, major increases in fixed assets/borrowings repaid/working capital changes/share capital raised etc)?
♦ who is financing this company – mainly shareholders or loan creditors?

Finally, try to get an initial 'gut feel' judgement by asking the following questions:

♦ would I lend money to this company?
♦ would I invest in this company?
♦ will this company be here in three years time?
♦ is this company growing or contracting?
♦ is this company a winner or a loser?
♦ is there anything in the figures that stands out as inconsistent or strange?

The above analysis may sound simplistic, but it will give you a few pointers in the subsequent selection of appropriate ratios.

Other information

The second stage is to consider any other information you have.

In real life a banker would be likely to be able to ask the management for business plans, internal management accounts, cash flow projections and so on (provision of such information is often a condition of a loan or overdraft). A banker would be able to have meetings with the management to discuss the issues.

In an exam the examiner is asking you, in a limited amount of time, to report on the prospects of a company. In order to help you in such an exercise, the examiner will often give clues as to the performance of the company in question. For instance, debtor and/or inventory levels may be unusually high or have risen by more than expected. There may have been a substantial investment in fixed assets – how was that financed? Has it resulted in increased sales? A major loan might have been raised. How have the proceeds been utilized? What is the effect on borrowing costs in the income statement?

Complete information is never available, either in practice or exams. In reaching your conclusions, in an exam as well as in practice, you should use all the information available, whether narrative or numerical, and identify the limitations in your analysis and extra information that you need but have not been given.

Here are some examples of the kinds of information that might be available to you:

♦ comparative information is always useful, and periods of longer than one year are often necessary to see if any trends are apparent;

♦ information about competitors' performance or industry standards is valuable;

♦ non-financial information will add to the overall picture. Information about off-balance sheet assets, eg intellectual property, off-balance sheet liabilities, contingencies;

♦ in practice (although probably not in an exam) narrative information such as the directors' report and chairman's statement will give a wide range of information about current and future developments in the business, its industry and its markets;

♦ the notes to the financial statements can be analysed to discover a wide range of information about matters such as the nature and age of the company's assets, significant events after the balance sheet date, discontinued activities, and so on.

In summary, when faced with a question think about what information you would like but have not been given. It is not difficult to come up with a lengthy list. Construct the best analysis you can within the scope of the available data and, if required by the question, note down the key items of additional information you would want to see.

Trends

One year's figures in isolation are not particularly useful. Previous years' figures are of assistance, because we can then examine whether any trends have been established. A long-term trend is likely to be more significant than a one-off 'blip'. The Companies Act 1985 requires only one year's figures with comparatives to be shown, but many listed companies include a historical five-year summary of accounts so there may be plenty of information to compare.

Horizontal analysis

Horizontal analysis is the comparison of each item in a company's financial statements in the current period with the same item from a previous accounting period. The result is expressed as a percentage increase or decrease over the base year. In the following brief illustration, for example, this percentage is (400 − 350)/350 = approximately 14%.

	20X6	20X5	Percentage change
	$	$	%
Turnover	1,200	1,000	+ 20
Cost of sales	(800)	(650)	+ 23
Gross profit etc	400	350	+ 14

Vertical analysis

Vertical analysis is a type of financial analysis that reveals the relationship of each financial statement item to a specified financial statement item during the same reporting period. Each item is divided by the specified item (typically turnover) and the result is expressed as a percentage.

This type of analysis is most likely to be used when comparing the performance of different companies. For example:

	Company A	Percentage compared with turnover	Company B	Percentage compared with turnover
	$	%	$	%
Turnover	1,000		350,000	
Cost of sales	(650)	65	(280,000)	80
Gross profit etc	350	35	70,000	20

12.3   Ratio analysis – overview

Ratio analysis is a tool of interpretation. It is a very useful tool, but it is not an end in itself. Time and again, a common failing noted by examiners is that students faithfully prepare accounting ratios and then neglect to interpret them meaningfully. You are unlikely to pass an interpretation question by merely calculating the appropriate ratios, however accurate your calculations are. Of equal importance is the initial selection of the appropriate ratios and subsequent interpretation of what the ratios mean, and what they show about the company's position, performance and adaptability.

Simply put, an accounting ratio is the relationship of one figure in the accounts to another, for example, the ratio of profits to assets, or inventory levels to turnover. The biggest single benefit they give is that they allow comparisons of relationships where volumes have changed. For example if a company has a turnover of £1.3m and a gross profit of £0.4m one year and a turnover of £2.4 the next with a gross profit of £0.7m it is not obvious whether their profitability is static, up or down.

Ratios allow us to eliminate the effect of volume. This also helps if we are trying to compare companies of different sizes.

On its own a ratio is largely meaningless. It needs to be judged in the context of the industry involved and in comparison with something else, either the same ratio from other years or from other companies in the same industry.

We have seen throughout this book that the Companies Act and accounting standards set specified formats and methods for calculating and displaying accounts items. This standardization of presentation and calculation gives us confidence in preparing ratio analysis using these accounts items.

Businesses are not required to include ratios in their accounts, although increasingly PLCs do include a selection. It is largely left to outside analysts to do the calculations. Care needs to be taken, even when a company publishes some ratios, because they may well calculate them slightly differently from the way you would. Ratios are not set in stone and there is a large degree of flexibility about how the components are selected. Banks, as lending institutions, may have the advantage of access to more detailed and regular information than other accounts users, so they may be able to carry out a more thorough analysis.

Ratios are simply expressions of the relationship between two variables. In considering the wide number of different figures in a set of accounts, you can appreciate that the number of potential ratios is enormous. In order to produce a meaningful analysis, the ratios calculated should be based on figures that have a logical connection in that industry. For example, linking net profit to sales makes sense because higher levels of sales are expected to generate higher levels of profits; a connection between share capital and inventory levels would be pointless because there is no identifiable relationship between the figures.

Form of ratios

Ratios are usually presented in one of four different forms, as follows:

- ♦ as a simple ratio, for example a ratio of 3 to 1, current assets to current liabilities;
- ♦ as a percentage, for example gross margin at 25% percent of sales;
- ♦ as a number of 'times', for example the profits may be five times the level of interest payable;
- ♦ as a function of time, for example inventory could be turned over (sold) every 35 days.

It is not the presentation of the ratio that is important, it is the interpretation of what the ratios mean and show about the company. Simple comments that the ratio has 'gone up' or is 'good' or 'bad' will of themselves be of little use.

Interrelationships between ratios

A point to consider is any interrelationship between ratios. An unfavourable change in a ratio may be mitigated by a favourable change in another ratio. For instance, a company may embark on a strategic repositioning of its product line and image, perhaps taking the company 'up-market' as it were. The company might then refocus on higher margin, luxury products and delete cheaper, poorer quality products from its sales portfolio. As a result overall sales may fall.

This could lead to a fall in the asset turnover ratio, the relationship between sales and net assets. In isolation, this could be seen to be a 'bad' thing. The company's net assets are generating fewer sales. When considering the gross profitability of the firm, the relationship between gross profit and turnover, this should show an increase. Thus the overall effect of the policy should be looked at.

On the other hand, ratios may be complementary. The results of one ratio may herald problems shown by another ratio. One example could be where a slowdown in the rate of debtor collection, highlighted by ratio analysis, could explain the apparent liquidity problems indicated by a fall in the ratio of current assets compared with current liabilities.

Interpreting ratios

We have already noted that ratios are of little use on their own. For instance, you may be told that a company earns a profit of 10% on its net assets. Your initial judgement may be that that seems a reasonable return. Other factors you would need to consider include:

- last year's return;
- the return of other similar companies; and
- alternative returns (for example the return available on a building society deposit).

Other factors, such as the riskiness of the company, the volatility of the returns over recent years and the company's liquidity are all relevant.

In addition you would need to look behind the figure of 10%. It is composed of two main elements: profits and assets. Consider each of these in turn.

- **Profits**
  - How have the profits been earned?
  - What are the individual components of profit: gross profit, operating profit, etc? (As a general rule, it is bad practice to refer simply to 'profit' or even 'net profit'. Both of these terms can be interpreted in many different ways. In the published income statement there could be eight or nine different subtotals containing the word 'profit', to avoid misunderstandings you should always be precise: operating profit, pre-tax profit etc.

- What were the profits last year?
- Is there an identifiable trend in profitability?
- Did any one-off factors affect profit?
- What is the relationship between profits and sales?
- What change has there been in the industry's profitability?
- How have the new operations/deleted operations affected profits?

♦ **Assets**
- What is the composition of the net assets?
- How are the assets valued?
- Have any asset revaluations taken place in the year?
- Which accounting policies have been adopted?
- When did the asset additions/disposals take place?
- How does the asset base compare with previous years/comparative companies?

Groups of ratios

Traditionally ratios have been grouped into the following categories:

♦ profitability and return on capital;
♦ liquidity and solvency;
♦ working capital;
♦ gearing;
♦ investor performance (or shareholder) ratios.

In an exam question, the examiner will often ask you to report on particular aspects of a business; for instance, its profitability and liquidity. Thus the classification of ratios is useful in identifying which ratios to select.

Sometimes the question will specify which ratios to calculate. More often, the examiner will leave it to your judgement to select appropriate ratios.

Do not fall into the trap of calculating too many ratios. Two or three per section will usually be sufficient. The mere calculation of the ratios is not enough, it is the interpretation of the results, especially the overall impression that the ratios give. Even if you are not asked to report on a particular area of the business, a ratio from within that classification can be calculated to help you to form an overall impression of the business's performance. Consider the interrelationships between ratios, 'good' performance in one area masking 'poor' performance in another.

Occasionally, the examiner will set a very general question asking you to comment on the standing of a company. Little or no direction may be given as to which areas of the business you should focus on. In these circumstances it is best to concentrate on the company's profitability, borrowings and cash flow.

12.4   Profitability and return on capital

Profit is generally seen as the most important indicator of a company's performance but a profit figure in absolute terms is of limited value. A profit of £1m may represent a great success for a sole trader, but for an international conglomerate it could be a disastrous performance.

Return on capital employed (ROCE)

The traditional primary indicator of financial performance is usually calculated with reference to the size of the company, its net assets. Basically expressed, return on capital employed is calculated by dividing profits by assets.

The next question is how to define 'profit' and 'assets'.

The standard ratio is calculated as follows:

$$\frac{\text{Profit before interest and tax}}{\text{Capital, reserves and long-term liabilities}} \times 100$$

(We say x 100 because this ratio is expressed as a percentage.)

The key point is to make sure that the numerator and the denominator are consistent (that like is compared with like). In the above version, capital employed includes both equity and debt, therefore the numerator must include the part of profit that each to these is entitled to. Debt providers are entitled to interest, shareholders are entitled to profit after tax. Conventionally, if we are looking at the profit before interest is deducted, we look at the pre-tax profit, so we end up with profit before interest and tax (often referred to as PBIT or EBIT; earnings before interest and tax).

Return on equity

Another version of this ratio uses shareholders' funds as capital employed. This is known as return on equity because we are considering only equity funding. To be consistent, our measure of profit in this case should be the profit available to the shareholders, ie profit after tax:

$$\frac{\text{Profit after tax}}{\text{Capital and reserves}} \times 100$$

Either method is appropriate as a measure of return on capital employed in the correct circumstances. Unless you are told otherwise, it is probably best to use the first method because this is the more comprehensive version of capital employed.

Return on gross assets

Other variations on the ROCE theme include return on total or gross assets. This is calculated as follows:

$$\frac{\text{Profit after tax (or profit before interest and tax)}}{\text{Fixed and current assets}} \times 100$$

Return on average capital employed

Alternatively, you may be asked to calculate return on average capital employed. This is calculated as follows:

$$\frac{\text{Profit before interest and tax}}{\text{Average capital, reserves and long-term liabilities}} \times 100$$

The denominator (Average capital, reserves and long-term liabilities) is usually worked out by taking the capital employed at the start of the year added to the capital employed at the end of the year and dividing by two.

The exact method you employ is not overly important. It is vital though to be consistent, from year to year and from company to company, so that comparisons remain valid.

The ROCE ratio is often referred to as the primary accounting ratio because it looks at the most basic measure of success. In open-ended questions that ask you to assess a business this is often a good starting point. Bear in the mind that this ratio is not the end of the story: what makes up this ratio, the components of profit and assets, their valuation and accounting treatment, are of critical importance.

Analysing ROCE

Following on from the primary ratio are two secondary ratios that can be used to analyse the information provided by the return on capital employed. These are the net profit ratio and the asset turnover ratio. The relationship between the three ratios is as follows.

ROCE   =   Net profit ratio x   Asset turnover

$$\frac{\text{Net profit}}{\text{Assets}} = \frac{\text{Net profit}}{\text{Turnover}} \quad x \quad \frac{\text{Turnover}}{\text{Assets}}$$

Net profit ratio

This shows the relationship between profit and sales.

In general, you would expect there to be a relationship between these two figures. As turnover increases you would anticipate higher profits but the rate of increase may well not be the same. Take care to define your terms: in the context of ROCE, net profit would be profit after tax.

Remember the example given above where a company decided to reposition itself in the market. Conversely, a company could decide to boost market share by cutting prices. The effect on the net profit percentage ratio would be likely to be downwards as gross profit fell but asset turnover could be increased, extra sales being generated from the same assets. Thus the overall effect on ROCE could be balanced out.

Asset turnover

In simple terms this is the level of sales that the company's (net) assets generate.

It is sometimes referred to as asset utilization. This figure will differ from industry to industry as well as being affected by whether assets are revalued or not. Capital intensive industries, such as heavy manufacturing businesses, are likely to have a much lower asset turnover than service industries, eg travel agents, which have a smaller asset base. Again the company's policies and strategies will affect this ratio. The example above of a company going down market, cutting prices to boost sales will, as a by-product, show increased asset turnover.

Variations on the basic ratio include the following:

$$\text{Fixed asset turnover} \quad = \quad \frac{\text{Turnover}}{\text{Fixed assets}}$$

$$\text{Current asset turnover} \quad = \quad \frac{\text{Turnover}}{\text{Fixed assets}}$$

All the above ratios attempt to examine how efficiently the company is utilizing the assets at its disposal, or how effective are the fixed, current or total assets in generating turnover.

This can be a difficult ratio to interpret. Always state the exact formula you have used and look out for major changes in assets that might have affected the ratio. For example, a significant investment in fixed assets, say a new factory, may not immediately lead to an increase in turnover. There may be a time lag until production reaches full capacity and marketing and distribution functions are undertaken.

Take care also when looking at the company's level of turnover: changes may be due to one-off factors, seasonal or cyclical variations.

Usefulness of ROCE

Overall the ROCE is seen as an indicator of the return the owner is generating from his or her investment. The ROCE can be compared to returns the investor may generate from alternative investments. There are a number of points to bear in mind.

- ◆ It may not be easy to withdraw from the business in question and reinvest somewhere else.
- ◆ The balance sheet values are generally expressed at historic cost, which may not be the same as realizable values.
- ◆ In the case of owner-managed companies the business often represents the entire employment and livelihood of the investor.
- ◆ Finally, there may be a difficulty in finding an alternative investment with which to compare the current return. If the return on an investment in, say, a money market deposit, is used as a comparison, we are not comparing like with like. One is risk free, while the business investment carries an element of risk. It is likely that the business investor will require a higher return from the business to compensate for the extra risk involved.

12.5   Detailed profitability ratios

We have already considered the net profit ratio, which compared net profit to sales. The net profit is the end result after taking:

- ◆ profit from trading, ie gross profit

and deducting

- ◆ overheads;
- ◆ financing costs; and
- ◆ taxation.

Thus we can break down our analysis of profitability into subsections.

Gross profit margin

$$\frac{\text{Gross profit}}{\text{Sales}} \times 100$$

This ratio indicates the profit margin earned on each £ of sales. The percentage is called the gross profit percentage or gross (profit) margin.

Note that if you are asked to calculate the 'Mark up' this refers to the Gross profit as a percentage of Cost of sales. Thus, for instance, a gross margin of 20% is the same as a mark up, on cost, of 25%.

	£	Gross profit margin	Mark up
Sales	100	100%	125%
Cost of sales	(80)	80%	100%
Gross profit	20	20%	25%

Interpretation

Once again we have difficulty in interpreting this ratio in absolute terms. For example, a gross margin of 30% may represent a reasonable return for a newsagent; however a jeweller may expect a much higher gross margin. The reason is usually the volume of products sold. A newsagent, selling small items quickly may be satisfied with a lower gross margin; in comparison, a jeweller will sell higher-priced products more slowly but at higher margins.

Once again it is important to look at changes in ratios rather than at the absolute figure. There are many possible reasons for a change in gross margin:

♦ company policy to boost margins;
♦ company policy to increase market share by cutting margins;
♦ repositioning in the market;
♦ increased costs not passed on to customers;
♦ fall in input costs not passed on to customers;
♦ increased turnover leading to more buying power, and hence lower purchase prices; and
♦ increased competition leading to falls in selling prices.

Fundamentally, changes in gross margin happen because of changes to either costs or selling prices and the points indicated above will have a bearing on one or other of these. The movement in this ratio cannot be explained by changes in volume because this affects both elements equally.

Net profit margin

Following on from the gross margin, we take away administration and distribution overheads to give operating profit. The operating margin, commonly called the net (profit) margin then becomes:

$$\frac{\text{Profit before interest and tax}}{\text{Turnover}} \times 100$$

This is a component of ROCE, as we saw earlier.

Some of these costs (and indeed some of the costs of sales) will be fixed, ie they will not alter with changes in volume of activity. Generally one would expect overheads to change in line with activity, ie turnover. So more ratios can be prepared:

$$\frac{\text{Overheads}}{\text{Turnover}} \times 100$$

This can be further broken down into:

$$\frac{\text{Administration expenses}}{\text{Turnover}} \times 100$$

and

$$\frac{\text{Distribution costs}}{\text{Turnover}} \times 100$$

Interpretation

Again look for any clues as to why the ratio of expenses to sales has changed. For example, more fixed assets might have been purchased which would lead to higher depreciation charges. A pay increase might have been granted. The directors might have reduced their remuneration but increased their dividends (this last point is particularly relevant to owner managed businesses). Overall activity may have decreased, therefore the proportion of fixed costs would have increased, leading to higher expense/sales ratios.

Interest cover

Next in line in the income statement is 'interest payable and similar charges'. Normally these are not compared to sales because there is no direct relationship.

Instead the usual calculation is to look at the interest cover; the relationship between profit before interest and interest itself.

This is calculated as follows:

$$\frac{\text{Profit befor interest and tax}}{\text{Interest payable}}$$

and is expressed as the number of times the profit covers the interest.

This gives a margin of safety, indicating how many times the current level of operating profits can cover the current level of interest payable. It is therefore as valid as a measure of the risk associated with borrowings as it is in assessing profit. Note that the figure for interest payable should not be reduced by either interest capitalized or interest receivable

Remember we are dealing here with profits. Even if we have the profits to cover the interest, it does not follow that we necessarily have the cash to pay the interest and any repayments of capital due. Interest cover is therefore also relevant to liquidity and solvency.

In general, the higher the ratio the greater the margin of safety. Interest payable is a charge on profits, payable whether the company makes a profit or not. Thus a lower or negative interest cover spells potential future problems for a company.

Again, look for any explanations resulting in the change in interest cover. A change in overall profitability would obviously be one explanation, but the company may have raised or repaid finance in the year or interest rates may have changed.

In summary, after considering the overall position and changes in profitability look behind the scenes to examine in detail why the company's profitability has changed. There may be compensating factors, for instance improved gross margins countered by increased interest charges, or increased overheads in absolute terms mitigated by a proportionally greater increase in turnover.

12.6   Liquidity ratios

A company may be profitable, but it may not be liquid. This can occur in a fast-growing business that is expanding so rapidly that it does not have sufficient cash to pay its debts as they fall due. This situation is referred to as overtrading. Using ratio analysis we can review a company's position in a number of ways. One way is to look at the company's cash operating cycle (see below). The other way is to look at the company's liquid assets in absolute and relative terms.

Two common ratios are normally calculated.

Current ratio

$$\frac{\text{Current assets}}{\text{Current liabilities}}$$

The rationale behind calculating this ratio is that the current assets will be used to finance the payment of the current liabilities. The current assets, inventory and debtors will be converted into cash and used to settle the liabilities due.

Interpretation

A broad rule of thumb often quoted is that the ratio should be 2 to 1. That is, current assets should exceed current liabilities by a factor of 2. Treat this rule of thumb with caution. A 'high' ratio is good ostensibly but it could be because inventory levels are too high (perhaps old/obsolete inventory is held) or it could indicate a debtor collection problem.

Remember that any assets held need to be financed: think back to the accounting equation, Net assets = Capital. The capital financing the business has an associated cost, either dividends for equity finance or interest for loan finance. Therefore businesses will, in general, try to minimize inventory and debtor levels to reduce the level of net assets and hence financing costs.

Another point to consider is the type of business the company is in. A supermarket chain, for example, is likely to have few or no debtors because it does not sell on credit. Also, because of its buying power, it is likely to be able to demand extended credit terms from its suppliers. In addition, supermarkets employ sophisticated inventory management schemes to minimize the levels of inventory held. All these factors mean that the current ratio, for a supermarket, will be in the order of 0.2 or 0.3.

Quick ratio (acid test ratio)

A more stringent test is the acid test or quick ratio.

$$\frac{\text{Current assets less inventory}}{\text{Current liabilities}}$$

The reason behind the modification is that inventory is less liquid than other current assets, therefore it should not be included when assessing the current assets available to pay current liabilities.

A rule of thumb is again often quoted that this ratio should not be less than 1. The caveats noted above apply equally to interpretation of this ratio.

Once again the absolute level of the ratio is not as important as the change or trend in the ratio. A sudden deterioration in the ratio could mean that the company has cash flow problems. A ratio significantly higher than the industry average could imply, for example, that the company has problems in collecting its debts. It is important, as with all ratios, but especially with these ratios, that they are examined in conjunction with other accounting ratios and cash flow data.

12.7   Working capital

Current assets are sometimes referred to as operating assets, used in the day-to-day operations of the business, changing identity on a regular basis. The movement in these current assets (and liabilities) can be expressed as a diagram.

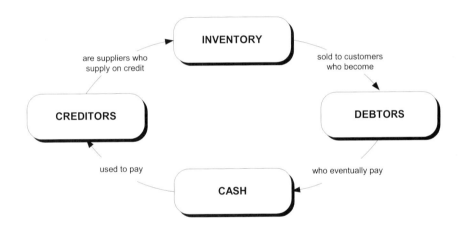

This is referred to as the working capital cycle. Time is involved from the original order to the supplier, to the delivery of the inventory, to the sale of the inventory, to the receipt of the cash from the debtor. These delays are not in the business's favour. The only delay in the company's favour is the delay between receiving the goods and paying the supplier.

As a general rule, the company will want to keep its levels of working capital as low as possible, chiefly to reduce the funding costs associated with holding such current assets. Ratios can be computed for each of the three main current assets and liabilities above. They are extremely useful for developing the initial results of the current or quick ratios because they will identify the component(s) of net current assets that have caused any changes.

Inventory turnover period

This is calculated as follows:

$$\frac{\text{Average inventory}^*}{\text{Turnover}} \ \text{x} \ 365$$

* Note: if average inventory is not available for both years, use closing inventory.

This ratio expresses, in numbers of days, how long on average the company holds its inventory. Note the consistency in the ratio – average inventory (at cost price) compared with cost of sales (at cost price).

Interpretation

There is no ideal period of time that a company should hold its inventory. The relative performance of the company, in comparison to other similar companies and previous periods should be examined. In general, the quicker the company can sell its inventory the better. The just-in-time philosophy promotes very low inventory levels. The drawback in holding low levels of inventory is the risk of stock-outs, where customer or production requests cannot be met.

As with all ratios, the type of industry in which the business operates will determine what the likely/desired inventory turnover ratio should be. A construction firm is likely to have a much longer inventory turnover than an ice-cream vendor.

There may be a linkage to the gross profit percentage. A company might have increased its inventory selling prices to boost gross margins but the inventory turnover might have suffered.

Debtor collection period

This is calculated as follows:

$$\frac{\text{Average trade debtors}^*}{\text{Credit sales}^\#} \ \text{x} \ 365$$

Note:

*If average debtors are not available for both years – use closing debtors.

#If credit sales are not available – use total sales.

This ratio expresses, in days, how long on average a company takes to collect its debts.

Interpretation

In general, the quicker a company can collect its debts the better. The credit taken by its customers is usually a free source of finance for them and the tendency is for customers to delay as long as possible before settling trade debts. Once again, to interpret the effectiveness of the company's debt-collection policy, compare the period with other companies, previous years and the company's stated credit period. Again, different industries traditionally may have different credit periods.

In attempting to explain why a collection period has changed, consider if the company has recently changed its policies if that information is available. It may not previously have offered credit, or it may have started offering discounts to customers to encourage early payment, or it may have employed a debt collection agency, or it may have decided to factor its debts.

Creditor payment period

This is calculated as follows:

$$\frac{\text{Average trade debtors}^*}{\text{Credit purchases}^{\#}} \times 365$$

Note:

*If average creditors are not available for both years, use closing creditors.

#If the purchases figure is not available, use cost of sales as a surrogate.

This ratio calculates, on average, how many days the company takes to pay its trade creditors.

Interpretation

In general, the longer a company takes to settle its current liabilities the better from its cash flow point of view. It is usually a free source of finance and helps to reduce the overall level of working capital. Once again, comparison needs to be made with previous periods, comparable companies and the official credit period granted by the suppliers.

There are a few caveats when interpreting this ratio. On the surface, an increase in this period is a good thing: the company has increased its usage of this free source of finance. It may not have been a conscious policy to extend the average period of credit taken, it may be a necessity due to a cash flow problem. Perhaps the company does not have the available funds to settle its debts on time. The company's cash flow statement should be analysed in conjunction with this ratio.

In addition, deliberately extending the credit period may not be without cost. The company may have to forgo discounts for early settlement; if the credit period is extended too far, the supplier may refuse to supply; or the supplier may impose penalties such as demanding that the company pay a deposit up front before any supplies are made, or insisting on cash-on-delivery. There are also statutory provisions on late payment that suppliers can invoke, requiring late-payers to pay interest on overdue debts.

Cash operating cycle

If we add the inventory turnover period to the debtors collection period and take away the creditors payment period it will give us the cash operating cycle: the amount of time that elapses between the company paying its suppliers and receiving payment from debtors for the same goods. Obviously, from a cash flow point of view, the shorter the period the better.

It is possible for a business, especially a retail businesses, to have a negative cash operating cycle.

As before, it is the relative performance in terms of previous periods and similar businesses that is the important point of comparison.

12.8   Gearing

As we have seen, all of the net assets of a business have to be financed. We commented that businesses often attempt to reduce their holdings of non-earning assets, such as debtors, to reduce their financing costs.

A business can be financed in two ways – either by shareholders (represented by share capital and reserves) or by loan creditors, and you should be aware of the advantages and disadvantages of the two main types of finance.

We will now go on to look at the impact that financing a business through debt has.

General comparison of equity and loan finance

Equity finance (share capital and retained profits) is perceived as being less risky than loan finance, mainly because the company is under no obligation to repay the capital.

This does not mean that the equity providers can be ignored or that the finance is at no cost. The company is obliged to look after its shareholders' interests. First, the directors are appointed and can be removed by the shareholders. Secondly, the company is under pressure to pay a reasonable level of dividends to satisfy the shareholders. If inadequate levels of dividends are paid, the shareholders may divest and the company's share price may fall. This could make it more difficult for the company to raise equity finance in the future. In addition, a low share price could make the company vulnerable to take-over.

Loan finance is different. The company is contractually obliged to pay interest and repay capital at the due dates. While a company will pay a dividend only if it has the retained profits and cash available to do so, the company must pay its interest and capital when due. The loan creditors have sanctions to force the company to do so. Quite often the loan will be secured on the company's assets. This could take the form of a fixed charge on the company's fixed assets or a floating charge on its other assets. In the event of a default in payment of interest or capital the creditors can exercise their right to sell the secured assets and force the company to repay outstanding interest and capital.

Interest is a charge on profits whereas dividends are an appropriation of profits.

In interpreting the position of a business, one of the key indicators is the relationship between equity and loan finance. In general, the higher the debt element, the more risky it is for the company, because of the priority rights of loan creditors.

With the inherent increased risk, why do companies utilize loan finance in preference to equity capital? There are several reasons:

♦ it may be easier to raise loan finance;
♦ the existing company shareholders may not want their existing level of control diluted by introducing more shareholders;
♦ there are lower transaction charges and it is generally less complex to raise loan finance;
♦ loan interest may be cheaper than equity finance. This is because loan interest, as a charge against profits, is allowable against corporation tax, whereas dividends are not.

Gearing (or leverage) ratio

To calculate the relationship between equity and loan finance we use the following formula:

$$\frac{\text{Long term debt}}{\text{Shareholders' funds}} \times 100$$

You may find variations on the above formula – sometimes long-term debt is added to the denominator to give a gearing percentage always less than 100%. Consistency is the most important consideration.

Interpretation

No hard and fast rules can be given as to an ideal level of gearing. As mentioned earlier, higher gearing normally implies higher risk. The trend of gearing should be considered as well as the relative gearing in comparison to other similar companies. The industry in which the business operates is significant. Capital-intensive industries tend to have higher gearing levels because of the high amount and long-term nature of their asset base. Cash-generative, stable businesses, such as utilities, also often have high gearing levels. Service companies may appear to have very high gearing levels, when really it is the fact that they do not have large amounts of assets which means that the shareholders' funds figure is relatively low.

Gearing levels should be relatively stable, but some of the following factors could mean a noticeable movement in the gearing ratio:

♦ equity capital raised;
♦ loan capital raised;
♦ redemption of share capital;
♦ repayment of loan capital;
♦ high levels of retained profits; or
♦ low levels of profit, or losses incurred.

Look again for the explanation behind the change in the gearing ratio. Major loan finance might have been raised – why? Share capital might have been redeemed – why? Raising more share capital will improve the gearing ratio but does not in itself mean the company is any more able to service its existing debt.

To complete our assessment of the company's ability to sustain a given level of debt we should also look at interest cover, which we looked at earlier in this chapter, and cash flow, covered later.

12.9   Investor performance ratios

All the above categories of ratio are of interest to investors, but there are certain ratios that are of particular concern to investors, both current and potential, when assessing the performance of a company.

Earnings per share (EPS)

EPS is a key indicator of the financial performance of the company. It expresses, in an amount per share, how much profit the company has earned in the last financial year. It is not necessarily the amount of dividend that is paid, nor is it the maximum dividend that could be paid, because the company can pay out a dividend from previous years' profits. The EPS is, however, is a good indicator of the performance of the company in profit terms. It has the advantage of allowing comparisons between companies of different sizes. The key price/earnings (P/E) ratio is derived by dividing the share price by the EPS.

The P/E ratio is an indication of the value the market places on a company's shares relative to its profitability.

EPS is the subject of IAS 33 *Earnings per Share*, but this is not in your syllabus. Basically earnings per share is calculated as you might expect:

$$\frac{\text{Earnings}}{\text{Number of ordinary shares}}$$

'Earnings' means the profit or loss attributable to ordinary equity holders, in other words profits after:

♦ tax; and
♦ preference dividends.

'Ordinary shares' means the number of equity shares in issue.

Price/earnings ratio

The market uses the EPS to work out the important price/earnings (P/E) ratio. This is calculated as follows:

$$\frac{\text{Market price per share}}{\text{Earnings per share}}$$

The P/E ratio is an indication of the value the market places on a company's shares relative to its profitability. The higher the P/E ratio the more confidence the market has in the company's future.

Dividend cover

Another useful shareholder ratio is the relationship between dividends and profits. This is calculated as follows:

$$\frac{\text{Profit available for distribution}}{\text{Dividends}}$$

The profit available for distribution is the profit after tax and after preference dividends. 'Dividends' include ordinary dividends only, both those paid and proposed.

Interpretation

The dividend cover is an indication of how 'safe' the dividend is. Generally, the higher the level of cover, the 'safer' the dividend. Once again, there are a number of factors to take into account, in particular the company's dividend policy (if it has one).

A company may have a progressive dividend policy, ie it is committed to increase its dividend every year. Alternatively, it could have a policy of paying out a set percentage of available profits every year. This would mean a constant dividend cover. A company's dividend is seen by some as a sign of company virility – such a company may pay a dividend out of retained profits if it does not have the current profits to pay a dividend.

Another possible constraint is the company's cash availability. The company may have available profits but no cash to pay a dividend.

The level of dividend cover may indicate how prudent the company is. A low dividend cover may indicate that the company is perhaps paying out too high a dividend, possibly concerned more about short-term share price rather than long-term stability. Companies, particularly listed companies, are under great pressure from investors to maintain or increase the level of dividends.

Remember that the level of profits can fluctuate due to many factors, as discussed previously. If you are given a historic summary of company results, say over five years, you may be able to identify a dividend policy.

Dividend yield

Dividend yield shows the return that can currently be expected on a share:

$$\frac{\text{Dividend per share}}{\text{Current market value of the share}}$$

This is useful because it enables investors to compare an investment in shares with other forms of investment, for example with bank or building society interest rates. Short-term investors and those who depend on dividends for income will be particularly interested in this. Longer-term investors will also be interested in growth in the market value (capital growth).

Earnings yield

Earnings yield is calculated as Dividend yield x Dividend cover:

$$\frac{\text{Dividend per share}}{\text{Current market value of the share}} \quad \text{x} \quad \frac{\text{Profit available for distribution}}{\text{Dividends}}$$

The purpose of this is to indicate what the dividend yield could be if the company paid out all its profits as dividends, retaining nothing. The earnings yield can therefore be used to compare the performance of companies that have significantly different earnings retention policies.

12.10   Cash flow analysis

We saw how to prepare a cash flow statement in Chapter 3 and we have mentioned the importance of considering the cash position a number of times already in this chapter.

Cash flow information is critical to a full analysis of a company for the simple reason that cash is vital to the ultimate survival of a business. It is also more reliable than profit inasmuch as it is possible to manipulate profit by careful selection of accounting policies, whereas cash is either received or it is not. Cash flow ratios are generally less well known than the 'traditional' ratios we have dealt with so far in this chapter but this is simply because the cash flow statement is a relatively recent addition to the financial statements.

In practice the cash flow information works best if used in conjunction with the other elements of the accounts because it helps provide a different perspective on the business' position.

Let us look at an example.

THOMAS LTD
CASH FLOW STATEMENT FOR THE YEAR ENDED 30 JUNE 20X1

	€000	€000
Cash flows from operating activities		
Cash receipts from customers	280	
Cash paid to suppliers and employees	(242)	
Cash generated from operations	38	
Interest paid	(10)	
Income taxes paid	(5)	
Net cash from operating activities		23
Cash flows from investing activities		
Purchase of property, plant and equipment	(80)	
Proceeds from sale of equipment	12	
Dividends received	5	
Net cash used in investing activities		(63)
Cash flows from financing activities		
Proceeds from issue of share capital	50	
Proceeds from long-term borrowings	10	
Dividends paid	(10)	
Net cash used in financing activities		50
Net increase in cash and cash equivalents		10
Cash and cash equivalents at beginning of period		70
Cash and cash equivalents at end of period		80

THOMAS LTD
INCOME STATEMENT FOR THE YEAR ENDED 30 JUNE 20X1

	€000
Revenue	300
Cost of sales	(160)
Gross profit	140
Distribution costs	(20)
Administration costs	(60)
Operating profit	60
Dividends received	5
Interest paid	(10)
Profit before tax	55
Taxation	(10)
Profit for the financial year	45
Dividends	(25)
Retained profit for year	20

THOMAS LTD
BALANCE SHEET

	20X1 €000	20X0 €000
Fixed assets	150	100
Current assets		
Inventories	60	50
Debtors	120	100
Cash	80	70
	260	220
Current liabilities		
Creditors	70	80
Taxation	10	5
Dividend	25	10
	105	95
Net current assets	155	125
Total assets less current liabilities	305	225
Less long-term loan	(60)	(50)
	245	175
Financed by:		
Share capital (a)	150	100
Profit and loss	95	75
	245	175

It is useful to analyse how the cash generated has been used. For example, the interest paid may be compared with both profit and the loan interest cover seems acceptable and the rate of interest paid is again reasonable. The fixed asset acquisition is quite significant and has been funded largely by the increase in debt and issue of share capital. Maintaining and improving the fixed assets of a business is important for its long-term success.

The following analysis shows the inflows and outflows in both money (in absolute form) and as percentages (in relative form). It is useful to make comparisons on a percentage basis because this may highlight matters that are not apparent from looking at the financial statements. For example, the following analysis highlights the significance of the fixed-asset purchase and the fact that over half the funds for this came from the issue of shares and debt.

Outflows	€000	%	Funded by:	€000	%
Interest paid	10	8.5	Cash from operations	38	33.0
Tax	5	4.5	Sale of equipment	12	10.0
Purchase of equipment	80	70.0	Dividends received	5	4.0
Dividends	10	8.5	Issue of share capital	50	44.0
Increase in cash	10	8.5	Loan	10	9.0
	115	100.0		115	100.0

This is not an analysis that is 'prescribed' in any standards, it simply illustrates that you can rearrange the figures however you like to yield useful information.

Operating cash flow

The most basic test of health in a company must be that it is generating positive operating cash flow (OCF). Thomas passes this test as you can see form the top part of the cash flow statement.

If a company does not generate adequate cash flow from its operations the funds will have to be raised elsewhere, from lenders, shareholders or through selling assets. Operating cash flow must provide a substantial part of a business's cash flow for success in the long term. Operating cash flow is the lifeblood of a business. Its absence can spell the end of a business.

Negative operating cash flow and overtrading

A negative operating cash flow for one year can be condoned if the answers to the two following questions are in the affirmative:

♦ is there real sales growth?

♦ are accounting profits plus depreciation positive?

If the answers to both questions are yes, then we can condone a negative OCF for a single year, because OCF is only negative due to working capital requirements (ie increased inventories). If OCF is negative for two successive years, the business is possibly 'overtrading'. If OCF is negative for three years then, without a shadow of doubt, the firm is overtrading.

A business is said to be overtrading when it accepts orders and tries to fulfil them at a level that it cannot support by its working capital – in other words it does not have enough cash and cannot obtain enough cash quickly.

Free cash flow

Analysts use this ratio for various purposes and it is a useful way of getting an impression of a company's performance. The calculation of free cash flow varies but the following, based on Thomas Ltd, is commonly used:

	€000
Operating cash flow	38
Less:	
Interest	(10)
Tax	(5)
Net cash flow from operating activities	23
Less: maintenance capital expenditure	
(using depreciation as an approximation)	(20)
Free cash flow	3

The purpose of this calculation is to identify how much cash is left after the unavoidable charges have been paid for. There is some debate about whether it is appropriate to deduct an amount for a maintenance level of capital expenditure. What is agreed is that any capital expenditure that will lead to expansion of the business should not be included in the calculation, because expansion is one of the things that free cash flow can be used for. As we have no way of determining exactly how much capital expenditure was incurred on maintaining the current level of fixed assets, an approximation can be made by using the depreciation figure. This is used because the depreciation figure represents the amount of the fixed assets that has been 'used up' in the current year.

The fact that Thomas Ltd has free cash flow is a positive indicator. The company can then choose what to do with the free cash: typically it might repay some debt or by re-investing.

Principal repayment ratio

We can go further with the analysis by calculating a principal repayment ratio, comparing the free cash flow to the outstanding loans figure from the balance sheet and comparing the result with the term of the loans. It would be unreasonable to expect the result to be too precise but it will give an indication of whether the company will be in a position to repay its loans on time, assuming that the current cash flow is representative.

$$\frac{\text{Long-term loans}}{\text{Free cash flow}} = \frac{60}{3} = 20$$

To complete the analysis we need to know the term of the loans. If it is a five-year term loan then we know the company is going to have to improve its cash flow dramatically or possibly refinance; if the term is, say 15 to 20 years, it looks as if the company is on the right track.

Interest cover (cash flow based)

Can interest payments be covered out of operational cash flow (OCF)? Calculate OCF/interest paid and compare with the traditional measurement of interest cover, which is operating profit/interest payable.

Cash flow ratio

A cash flow ratio may be calculated, comparing a business's net cash inflow from operating activities with its total liabilities. In the case of Thomas Ltd this would be:

$$\frac{€38,000}{€(70,000 + 60,000)} = 29\%$$

This ratio needs to be compared with previous years and with industry averages to decide whether it is acceptable or needs improving. It is designed to show whether a business is earning enough cash flow from its operations to be able to meet its debts. To get a full picture, analysis also needs to be made of the other financial statements, particularly with respect to liquidity and gearing. These terms will all become clear to you later in this book when we deal with ratio analysis.

Cash margin on sales

This ratio uses operating cash flow in comparison to sales. It is expressed as:

$$\frac{\text{Operating cash flow}}{\text{Sales}} = 100\%$$

In the case of Thomas this is 38/300 = 12.7%

The result should be compared to

$$\frac{\text{Profit before interest and tax (PBIT)}}{\text{Turnover}} \times 100\%$$

to confirm whether due profit is being converted into cash. In the case of Thomas the latter ratio is 20%, so the answer is that not all due profit is being converted.

Cash flow from operations/current liabilities

We have regularly discussed the fact that cash is the only real source of liquidity. This ratio allows us to see how able a company is to pay its immediate obligations. A figure of less than 1 would mean that the company was going to have to raise finance from alternative sources to pay short-term liabilities. This is not a good sign.

Cash flow per share

A variation on EPS is cash flow per share. The ratio is trying to achieve the same as earnings per share but this time uses pure cash information. To be directly comparable, we would use operating cash flow less interest, tax and non-equity dividends and divide that by the number of equity shares in issue.

12.11   Limitations of ratio analysis

Ratios can be no more accurate than the information on which they are based. In terms of accounting ratios, the information we are using is taken from the accounts and many transactions a company is reporting are capable of alternative treatments. In particular, consider how the choice of the accounting policies and the effect of the numerous estimates contained within the accounts may affect the end result. For example, consider the following items and the possible effect on profit and asset levels:

- ◆ fixed asset revaluations;

- depreciation: method, estimates of residual value and useful lives;
- leased assets: operating or finance leases;
- research and development: write off or capitalize;
- inventory valuation: LIFO, FIFO etc, estimates of NRV;
- construction contracts: calculation of stage of completion;
- debtors: estimates of bad debt provisions;
- contingencies: estimates; and
- intangibles: recognized or not, period of amortization.

In addition to all of the above variables, remember, when comparing different companies, to consider if both companies adopt similar or different accounting policies. Think about, for example, the effect on ROCE when a company exercises the option to revalue its fixed assets: profits fall (because of higher depreciation charges) and asset values increase. Thus the ROCE will automatically be less than it would have been had the company chosen not to revalue.

Another factor that may need to be taken into account is the effect of any one-off, non-recurring or unusual items, which periodically affect the accounts. For example, a company may be hit by an exceptionally large bad debt, loss of a major order or other similar one-off event. It may be necessary to adjust the company's or comparative company's accounts for such items. One of the things you will be trying to ascertain is the company's maintainable earnings.

Other factors may be important. For example, when comparing two owner-run businesses, one may pay its directors a salary as remuneration while the other may decide to reward its directors through dividends. The former will show lower profits than the latter but the underlying earnings may be identical.

Summary

Now that you have completed this chapter you should be able to:

- **explain the value of the information in corporate reports when interpreting an entity's financial position;**
- **calculate and interpret traditional ratios relating to profitability, profit, working capital, gearing, and investors' interests;**
- **analyse cash flows for the purpose of risk assessment and in terms of cash performance, operating cash flows and free cash flows; and**
- **explain the limitations of ratio analysis.**

Thirteen

Valuing businesses

Syllabus

This chapter is the first of two covering syllabus Section 8: Valuing Businesses, which builds on the previous section by extending the analysis into that of approaches to the valuation of businesses, based (in part) on their financial statements. In doing this, it recognizes the deficiencies of traditional financial statements for business valuations and explores other approaches.

Objectives

After studying this chapter you should be able to:

♦ explain the matters of concern to buyers and sellers when valuing a business;

♦ discuss the characteristics of asset-based valuations, in particular going-concern basis, book value, break-up value and replacement cost; and

♦ discuss the characteristics of flow-based valuations, in particular earnings yield, the price-earnings method and dividend-based approaches.

13.1   Buyers and sellers

A share price rises when there are more buyers than sellers and falls when the opposite is true. This chapter will attempt to explain why different parties place a different value on a business and will examine some of the methods most commonly used to arrive at a valuation.

In the negotiations between a buyer and a seller both parties will be attempting to achieve a price most favourable to them. They will both have a price that they realistically hope to achieve. In addition the buyer will have a maximum price after which the purchase would be uneconomic and the seller will have a minimum below which the sale would not be worthwhile.

The seller would hope to achieve a price that fully reflects the business's earnings and the scope to improve those earnings in the future but his determination to wait until that price can be achieved may be undermined by various factors:

- the business's borrowings; if loan covenants have been broken or the interest and capital repayments requirements are proving difficult to meet a quick sale would be the main priority;
- the interest expressed in the business; if several parties appear interested it would be logical to wait and see who is prepared to make the best offer;
- the general economic climate; if the economic outlook is poor the owners may feel that it is important to sell the business before the climate worsens. Alternatively if the outlook is expected to improve they may feel that it is better to wait in the hope that they will achieve a better price as business picks up;
- the personal circumstances of the owners; this can vary from the need for money due to debt, divorce, etc; or a wish to retire or to move on to other things.

Buyers adjust their negotiating position to take into account the factors given above, if they are aware of them. The maximum price they would be prepared to offer would be where the additional profits earned only just exceed the cost of the capital used to fund the purchase.

The buyer is therefore concerned with forecast profits and the net gain from the acquisition. If the buyer is already operating a similar business there may be some synergy and economies of scale that would enhance their profits which must be taken into account.

The buyer's initial offer will be based on current prospects, taking into account any future trading difficulties. This opening offer will be as low as the buyer thinks he or she can get away with but may be higher if the buyer is eager to purchase the business and there are other interested parties.

The final price will depend on how desperate either party is to complete the sale. If the seller is under heavy pressure due to large amounts of debt he or she may be forced to accept the buyer's initial offer. Conversely, if the seller has no particular need to sell and there are several other interested parties the buyer will be forced to pay the maximum price.

Valuation methods

There are many different ways in which a business can be valued based on the size of holding involved, the nature of the business and the purpose of the sale. They will potentially give rise to very different valuations and ultimately the figure that becomes the basis for a deal will be arrived at by negotiation and will be a compromise. In assessing a company's value it is always wise to attempt a value on as wide a range of bases as possible because this will identify the negotiating range available.

13.2   Asset-based valuations

A business's balance sheet shows its assets and liabilities. The assets less the liabilities equal the owner's capital in the business. It is therefore tempting to state that this is what it is worth, particularly as more traditional balance sheet analysis refers to the balance sheet total as 'net worth'. In most cases this would be unwise.

Imagine that you have been offered £500,000 for the house that you live in which you bought ten years ago for £100,000. The original cost of the house would be irrelevant. The original cost has no bearing on what the house is worth to the potential buyer, and when you consider whether or not you should accept the offer the original cost is only relevant to you in the sense that is probably the value that your mortgage is based on. You would be more concerned with:

- whether you were likely to receive a better offer;
- what it would cost to buy another property for yourself to live in;
- other options, such as dividing the house into flats before selling; and
- whether you wanted to move in the first place.

A business valuation based on the balance sheet must also take into account similar considerations, namely:

- book value;
- net realizable value;
- replacement cost;
- break-up value; and
- going-concern value.

Book value

Book value depends upon the nature of the business's activities and its accounting policies. If its fixed assets were purchased several years ago it is highly likely that their book value no longer fairly represents their value to the business. Even where a company has a policy of revaluing some of its assets, it is unlikely these valuations will be fully up to date. It is also worth bearing in mind that when a business is acquired, the acquiring company is required to record the acquired assets at fair value as at the date of the acquisition. There is no need to keep these values up to date every day, however. The net result of all of these points is that the book values of fixed assets are highly unlikely to give a good approximation of commercial value of the business.

Its current assets, which are near to being turned into cash, are usually stated at close to their true value, assuming the business does not possess a large amount of obsolete stock and has provided for all of its potential bad debts. Thus by deducting all of a business's liabilities from its current assets a minimum valuation can usually be obtained, although if the object of the exercise is the sale of the business this value is unlikely to be anywhere near the commercial value.

Net realizable value and replacement cost

The lowest amount that a seller should accept is the amount that its assets could be disposed of for, in piecemeal sales at fair value, after settling any liabilities. This is its net realizable value (NRV).

If the business is making regular losses and there is no foreseeable upturn in its fortunes it is likely that the NRV of net assets is greater than the value of the business as a going concern. In that case there is no economic argument for continuing in business and the owners should get as much as they can for the assets and put the money to a different use.

Remember, however, that problems can arise when it comes to obtaining the necessary values, particularly where technological change means that the particular asset is no longer being produced, as we saw back in Chapter 3.

A replacement cost valuation is similar in concept to NRV but not identical. Replacement cost is best seen as the amount that would be required by somebody else to set up an identical business from scratch. In principal this is the greatest amount that a buyer should offer. We say in principal because creating an identical business may well involve considerably more time and effort than the buyer is willing to expend. Intangible factors such as staff skills or relationships with customers may be impossible to replace.

Break-up value

In the 1960s one of the main motivations for hostile take-over bids was to acquire the target company in order to break it up and sell off its assets for a higher price than was paid for the company. This was known as 'asset stripping', and was possible at that time because many companies had large numbers of tangible assets that were underutilized.

Asset stripping is successful when valuing companies at their net realizable value gives a higher value than a going-concern basis. In the 1980s the take-over boom included the operations of corporate raiders whose motivation was similar to the asset strippers of the 1960s. This time they used more sophisticated valuation techniques to identify the segments of the target business that were undervalued and to sell them off at a profit. This did not usually involve the liquidation of the target company's assets in total. Possibly as a response to this, businesses now are much more likely to focus on a few core activities rather than being widely diversified. It is felt that the stock market is more likely to rate the company accurately if it is clear what the company does.

An illustration might help.

Suppose that a company called Legion plc consists of four subsidiaries. The recent financial results are detailed below:

	Matt Ltd	Mark Ltd	Luke Ltd	John Ltd	Legion plc Total
	£m	£m	£m	£m	£m
Profit after tax	25	10	35	30	100
Net assets	42	78	300	200	620

The subsidiaries operated the following businesses which are typically given the following P/E ratios (we will look at this valuation method in a moment: just accept it for now).

	P/E ratio of similar quoted companies
Matt Ltd – Pharmaceuticals	30
Mark Ltd – Cigarette manufacturer	11
Luke Ltd – Computer software	33
John Ltd – Financial services	23

Assume that at the time conglomerates were typically valued using a P/E ratio of 15. Legion plc would therefore have a stock market valuation of:

$$£100m \times 15 = \underline{£1,500m}$$

If the different businesses were sold off their combined value would amount to:

			£m
Matt Ltd	£25m x 30	=	750
Mark Ltd	£10m x 11	=	110
Luke Ltd	£35m x 33	=	1,155
John Ltd	£30m x 23	=	690
			2,705

The break-up value of Legion plc is thus much greater than its apparent value if it continues as a group.

Intangibles and goodwill

It is also worth remembering that there are aspects of a business that contribute to value but which may not be recognized on the balance sheet, in particular the intangibles which a successful business will also have accumulated, such as a loyal customer base, staff experienced in the particular product and market. As you know, such things are excluded from the valuation unless they have a well-established market value.

Conventionally the more nebulous aspects of this intellectual capital is referred to as goodwill and because it will earn a return in the same way that the company's other assets do it needs to be included in the calculations.

Valuing non-purchased goodwill

Some companies involved in valuing companies have attempted to devise a formula for calculating the value of goodwill. None is entirely accurate, because of the nature of goodwill. We will attempt to deal with some of these below.

The various parties involved in the valuation of a business will often agree on a multiple of recent profits. Another commonly used method is the 'dual capitalization method.'

The dual capitalization method assumes that the excess profits earned over and above those expected from the tangible capital employed are earned by the goodwill. These excess profits can therefore be used to calculate the value of goodwill by dividing them by the rate of return expected on goodwill.

Exercise 13.1

Think about the following activity before looking at the answer that follows.

Z Ltd has been trading for many years and a summary of its balance sheet as at 31 December 20X0 was as follows:

	£000
Fixed Assets	1,000
Net Current Assets	500
	1,500

In each of the last few years the company made a profit of £400,000, all of which was paid out in dividends.

Companies in Z Ltd's trade usually earn a return on capital employed of 12% per annum. Z plc earns a higher return due to its geographical location, which is close to its customers, but where the market is too small for a competitor to become established. Technological change means that it might be possible for a competitor to emerge at some time in the future.

For this reason industry experts have concluded that the discount rate to be applied to the excess profits earned by the goodwill should be higher than usual at 20%.

What value would the industry experts place on Z Ltd?

A – £1,500,000

B – £2,000,000

C – £2,600,000

D – £3,333,333

Solution

The company would be valued as follows:

	£000	**£000**
Net tangible assets		1,500
Goodwill:		
Total profit	400	
Return on tangible assets 12% x £1,500,000 =	180	
Excess profits	220	
£220,000/0.20 =		1,100
		2,600

The correct answer is therefore C.

Going concern

For a business that is profitable and earning a reasonable return on its capital employed, selling the assets is likely to generate less cash than continuing to operate the business as a going concern. In this case some method of valuation is needed that takes into account future cash flows.

The general rule regarding the value of anything is that its value equals the discounted future cash flows likely to arise from it. (See Appendix 1 if you do not know what discounted future cash flows are.)

This is equally true of business valuations. It therefore follows that asset-based valuation methods are relevant only where selling the assets is seen as the best source of cash flows.

13.3   Flow-based valuations

Earnings yield

A business that is a going concern has a value to its owner equal to the net present value of its future earnings.

It is quite simple to arrive at a valuation if we use using the most recent earnings and discount them at the owner's adjusted cost of capital. For example, if the owner of Z Ltd in the exercise above had a 15% cost of capital the present value of the business would be the profit available for distribution discounted in perpetuity at this rate.

£400,000/0.15 = £2,666,667.

(See Appendix 1 if you are not sure about discounting, present values, cost of capital and so on.)

We are concerned not with the most recent results but with the company's future earnings stream. Ideally we should forecast the company's earnings for each year for several years ahead and then calculate their net present value. Unfortunately the further ahead we look the more uncertain it becomes and such a forecast is arbitrary at best.

Let us suppose that the Brown family has owned Straw Ltd for many years and has been approached by the company's management who wish to purchase the company from them. The company's profit after tax for each of the last three years has been as follows:

	£000
20X3	460
20X4	520
20X5	600

Usually when an examination question provides three or more years' earnings you will be expected to calculate the average earnings to produce an earnings-based valuation, with greater weight being given to the profits of the more recent years. For example if you had been required to value Straw Ltd using a 10% average earnings yield, the calculation would have been as follows:

Average profits	Weighting	£000
20X3 – £460,000	1	460
20X4 – £520,000	2	1,040
20X5 – £600,000	3	1,800
	6	3,300

The weighted average is £3,300,000/6 = £550,000.

The company valuation is therefore £550,000/0.10 = £5,500,000.

P/E ratio

A simpler approach is to adjust the discount rate to reflect future growth and the risk that this growth might not be attained. This can often be achieved by examining the price earnings (P/E) ratio of similar quoted companies.

The price earnings ratio represents the number of years profits a company must earn to equal its current quoted value. For example a company whose shares are currently £1.60 each with earnings per share of 20p would have a P/E ratio of 8 (160/20).

The P/E ratio reflects all that is known about a company and its future profits. Once we have identified a quoted company (or group of companies) comparable to the company we wish to value, the only additional adjustment needed relates to the marketability of the company's shares. It is quite simple to sell shares in companies quoted on the Stock Exchange but a discount of at least 25% needs to be made to reflect the difficulties in selling unquoted securities.

To remind you, the Brown family has owned Straw Ltd for many years and has been approached by the company's management who wish to purchase the company from them. The company's profit after tax for each of the last three years has been as follows:

	£000
20X3	460
20X4	520
20X5	600

There are two similar quoted companies:

	Share price	**Earnings per share**
Barn plc	£2.70	18p
Hay plc	£5.20	40p

What is the highest price the family could reasonably expect to receive for the company?

To answer this we begin by calculating the P/E ratios for the two quoted companies.

Barn plc	270/18 = 15
Hay plc	520/40 = 13

Neither company would be exactly the same as Straw Ltd and in the absence of any further information an average of the two P/E ratios could be used to value Straw Ltd, ie 14. You can see, even from this simplified example, that there is a lot of imprecision in this approach, simply because finding a similar quoted company is by no means easy.

The P/E ratios are based on the companies' most recent earnings and recent profit growth or fluctuations in profits are adjusted for in the P/E ratio through reactions in the share price. Straw Ltd's earnings for 20X5, the most recent year, should therefore be used.

The highest price that could be reasonably expected for the company is therefore:

	£000
14 x £600,000 =	8,400
Less 25% for lack of marketability	2,100
	6,300

Dividend-based valuation

The above methods are relevant to valuing the business as a whole, which in turn means they are really relevant only when control over the company is at stake. In many cases the valuation will be needed for a minority shareholder. We have already established that the value of anything is the discounted future cash flows arising from the investment. In the case of a minority shareholding the relevant cash flows are dividends, unless the company elects to buy back shares.

The simplest approach is to divide the gross dividend by the purchaser's cost of capital. For example, if a company is paying 9 pence in dividends each year and the purchaser's cost of capital is 10% the value of a share to that purchaser would be:

$$\frac{9p + 10\% \text{ tax credit} = 10p}{0.10}$$

$$= £1.00.$$

It is probable that the dividend will increase over time and this needs to be built into the valuation model. For shares where the dividend is growing at a modest rate it is possible to use Gordon's Growth Model.

$$P = \frac{d \times (1 + g)}{(i - g)}$$

where:

P = the share price

d = the current dividend payment

i = the required rate of return

g = the dividend growth rate

Thus in the previous example, if the dividend was expected to grow by 5% per annum the value of one share would be:

$$\frac{10p \times 1.05}{(0.10 - 0.05)} = £2.10$$

The model does not work when the dividend growth rate exceeds the required rate of return. When this occurs it is necessary to discount each future estimated dividend payment to the current date.

Cash flow valuation

The above valuations are all based on accounting profits. At times these can be an arbitrary measure of a business's performance, being entirely dependent on the accounting policies selected and, as a result, subjective. Many analysts who are responsible for calculating and assessing quoted share prices believe that cash flow, a more objective figure, provides a better measure of how well a company has performed. The same reasoning applies to valuing businesses.

Some people base valuations on free cash flow derived from the cash flow statement (see the previous chapter). The essence of free cash flow is that it represents the cash available after all non-avoidable expenditure has been dealt with, and therefore it should be sustainable in the future. This figure is discounted using the required rate of return to calculate the value of the business overall.

If free cash flow were £800,000 and the required rate of return were 10%, the value of the company would be:

£800,000/0.10 = £8,000,000

13.4 The valuation of majority and minority interests

By now you will have discovered that there are numerous methods for valuing a business and that they can produce widely differing results. We will now discuss when each method may be appropriate.

You have already seen that an investment is worth the net present value of the cash flows that accrue to that investment. The only return a minority shareholder in a company will receive will be in the form of the dividends the company pays.

A minority shareholder has little or no influence over the company's dividend policy and the company's earnings and cash flow provide assurance only as to whether or not the company can afford the dividend each year. It is therefore appropriate to value a minority shareholding using a dividend valuation model.

A majority shareholder can control a company's dividend policy and in effect has access to the company's earnings/cash flow. The majority shareholder also has control over the company's assets and is able to arrange for their sale if this is felt to be advantageous.

It is therefore usually appropriate to value a majority holding on an earnings basis, but the NRV of the company's assets exceeds the earnings valuation this would represent the value of the holding to the majority shareholder.

Exercise 13.2

Beta Ltd produced the following income statements for the five years ending 31 December 20X5:

Income statement for Beta Ltd

	20X1 £000	20X2 £000	20X3 £000	20X4 £000	20X5 £000
Profit after tax	220	240	180	290	320
Dividends	110	115	121	127	134
Retained for year	110	125	59	163	186

The company had 1,000,000 ordinary shares in issue throughout the five years. Its balance sheet as at 31 December 20X5 was as follows.

Beta Ltd Balance Sheet

	£000	£000
Fixed assets		
Land and buildings		1,250
Plant and machinery		750
		2,000
Current assets		
Inventory	300	
Debtors	480	
Cash at bank	500	
	1,280	
Creditors due within 1 year	730	
Net current assets		550
		2,550
Creditors due in more than 1 year		400
		2,150
Financed by:		
£1 Ordinary shares		1,000
Share premium account		200
Retained earnings		950
		2,150

The Cornwall family owns all the shares in the company. Sidney Cornwall inherited 15% of the shares and wishes to cash in his inheritance. He has made enquiries and the following parties have expressed some interest.

Highfield Estates plc, which is interested in purchasing the land and buildings for £1,800,000.

Wellrusted Ltd, which buys and sells second-hand machinery and would pay £400,000 for the plant and machinery.

Bill Squires, an acquaintance of Sidney, who would be interested in purchasing Sidney's shares from him. Bill currently has all his funds invested in government stock yielding 9% per annum. He feels that Beta Ltd's growth prospects outweigh the extra risk he would be taking.

Consolidated Conglomerates plc, which is prepared to make an offer for the company provided that it can achieve a return of 20% per annum on its investment.

Sidney has discussed this with the other members of the family. Their best alternative investment is in government stock yielding 9%. Sidney's Uncle Cyril, who owns 51% of the shares is prepared to sell his shares, if he receives a 'reasonable offer'.

Required

(a) Calculate the amount Sidney can expect to receive under each of the alternatives available.

(b) Advise Sidney's Uncle Cyril on whether liquidation or the sale to Consolidated Conglomerates plc is reasonable.

(c) Advise Sidney on what action he should take.

Solution

You should have obtained the following answer.

(a) Sidney would receive the following amounts from the available alternatives.

(i) *Net realizable value*

	£000
Sale proceeds:	
Land and buildings	1,800
Plant and machinery	400
Net current assets	550
	2,750
Less creditors due in more than 1 year	400
Net proceeds	2,350
15% of the net proceeds amounts to	£352,500

(ii) *Sale to Bill Squires*

The dividend has grown by 5% per annum over the last four years. It is well covered by earnings and it can be assumed that this growth will continue in the future. Using the dividend growth model we obtain the following valuation:

$$\frac{(134 + 10\% \text{ tax credit}) \times 1.05}{0.09 - 0.05} = £3,908,333$$

15% of this amounts to £586,250

(iii) *Sale to Consolidated Conglomerates plc*

The major difficulty here is in deciding which earnings figure to use. Any reasonable choice would probably be acceptable, but because several years' profits are given a weighted average figure might be most appropriate.

The three year weighted average profits are:

	Weighting	£000
20X3 – £180,000	1	180
20X4 – £290,000	2	580
20X5 – £320,000	3	960
	6	1,720

£1,720,000/6 = £286,667

The required return is 20% per annum, valuing the company at £286,667/0.20 = £1,433,333.

15% of this amounts to £215,000

(b) Sidney's Uncle Cyril owns a majority holding and an earnings or break-up valuation are relevant to him. His next best alternative investment is to invest in government stock yielding 9%.

The only 'reasonable' offer is from Bill Squires, but unless he is also prepared to buy Cyril's shares, Cyril should retain them.

(c) It is clear from the above calculations that Sidney will receive the highest offer from Bill Squires and should therefore sell his shares to him.

Summary

Now that you have completed this chapter you should be able to:

- ◆ **explain the matters of concern to buyers and sellers when valuing a business;**
- ◆ **discuss the characteristics of asset-based valuations, in particular going concern basis, book value, break-up value and replacement cost; and**
- ◆ **discuss the characteristics of flow-based valuations, in particular earnings yield, the price-earnings method and dividend-based approaches.**

Fourteen

The capital asset pricing model

Syllabus

This chapter is the second of two covering syllabus Section 8: Valuing Businesses. It recognizes the deficiencies of traditional methods of business valuation and explores other approaches.

Objectives

After studying this chapter you should be able to:

♦ explain the concepts underlying the capital asset pricing model and use the model to value a business.

14.1   The capital asset pricing model (CAPM)

We have devoted a short separate chapter to the capital asset pricing model (CAPM), partly because it has a separate line to itself in Section 8 of the syllabus but mainly because it can appear to be difficult and we did not wish to distract you from the main issues in the previous chapter.

CAPM involves polysyllabic terminology such as 'unsystematic risk', 'beta coefficients', and the like, but we hope to show that it is not nearly as scary as it may appear. The maths is very simple. Nevertheless, it would be wise to make sure you have absorbed all the ideas in Chapters 12 and 13 before you continue.

It is unusual for the CAPM to be included in a 'financial reporting' syllabus, although it is not an inappropriate topic and the illustrations in this chapter are typical of events that you read about in the financial press every day.

What is CAPM?

The capital asset pricing model (CAPM) is a method of calculating the cost of shareholders' capital. CAPM may be seen as an alternative to the dividend growth model, covered in the previous chapter.

The uses of the capital asset pricing model in financial management include:

- ◆ establishing the 'correct' market value of a company's shares;
- ◆ establishing the cost of a company's equity (and the company's average cost of capital), taking account of both the business and financial risk characteristics of a company's investments; and
- ◆ establishing the value of a business.

We will cover what we think are the most important matters, beginning by explaining the underlying concepts behind CAPM. These are, in any case, of general relevance to the valuation of a business from the point of view of an investor.

14.2   Risk and diversification

CAPM approaches matters from the point of view of someone who may be considering buying shares in a company.

Your personal interest may be from the point of view of someone who is considering lending money to the company, on a banking basis, say, but if shareholders are not willing to invest then that is obviously relevant to your lending decision: you would want to understand why. In particular if there is any risk involved you would want to know about it.

Unsystematic risk

'Buyers' cannot know in advance whether their spending will result in a better return than hoped for or a worse return. Some risk will be involved whenever an investor invests in some shares, or when a company makes an investment in another company, or invests in some new venture. Risk like this cannot be avoided unless the investor chooses only risk-free investments such as government gilts.

Provided, however, that investors put their money into a suitably wide 'portfolio' of different investments, the investments that perform well and those that perform badly should cancel each other out.

In other words, this kind of risk can be diversified away and a risk that can be diversified away is called an 'unsystematic risk'.

Systematic risk

Unfortunately not all risk can be diversified away. All investments will be affected to a greater or lesser extent by risks of the 'system' as a whole. This means the environmental factors that individual companies cannot control – economic changes, political developments, wars, natural disasters, and so on.

This is called systematic risk and it cannot be diversified away because it affects all investments other than risk-free ones such as government gilts. In return for accepting a company's systematic risk investors expect to earn a higher return than the return available on risk-free investments.

The amount of systematic risk varies between different companies; some shares will be less risky and some will be more risky than the stock market average.

14.3   The model

The capital asset pricing model compares the systematic risk of shares in a particular company with the risk of all shares in the market as a whole.

The model makes the major assumption that there is a linear relationship between the return obtained from an individual company and the average return from all shares in the market. The return that investors will require from an individual company will be higher or lower than the average market return, depending on whether the company's systematic risk is greater or less than the market average.

Returns

For example, suppose that the following information is available about the performance of an individual company's shares and the stock market as a whole.

	Individual company	Stock market average
Price at start of period	240	525
Price at end of period	260	550
Dividend during period	13	38

The return on the company's shares – r_j – and the return on the 'market portfolio' of shares – r_m – may be calculated as:

$$\frac{\text{Capital gain (or loss)} + \text{dividend}}{\text{Price at start of period}}$$

Individual company

$$r_j = \frac{(260 - 240) + 13}{240}$$

Stock market average

$$r_m = \frac{(550 - 525) + 38}{525}$$

Beta factors

A statistical method called linear regression (we need not go into this any further) suggests that a linear relationship exists between returns from an individual company and from the average market.

The measure of this relationship is known as a 'beta factor' or beta coefficient. Beta measures a company's share price volatility relative to the market. A share with a beta of 1 precisely mirrors the market. If a share's beta is below 1, it is less volatile than the market and offers a lower return because it is less risky than average. A beta of more than 1 means the share is more volatile than the market and offers a higher-than-average return.

For example if returns on shares in SFI plc tend to vary twice as much as average returns from the market as a whole, then if market returns went up by 2%, say, returns on SFI plc shares would be expected to go up by 4%. The beta factor of SFI plc shares would be 2.0.

The *actual* return from SFI shares might rise by, say, 5%, or even fall by, say, 3%, but the difference between the actual change and a change of 4% due to factors that affect everybody would be due to unsystematic risk – matters specific to the company and/or the industry it is in.

Risk-free returns

The capital asset pricing model also has reference to the difference between market returns and risk-free returns. This is known as the 'excess return' or 'market risk premium'. For example, if the return on British Government stocks is 2% and market returns are 5%, the excess return on the market's shares as a whole is 3%.

In CAPM, the difference between the risk-free return and the expected return on an individual share can be measured as the excess return for the market as a whole multiplied by the share's beta factor.

In other words if shares in FIS plc have a beta of 2.3 when the risk-free return is 2% and the expected market return is 5%, the expected return on FIS plc shares would exceed the risk- free return by $(5 - 2) \times 2.3\% = 6.9\%$ and the total expected return on FIS shares would be $(5 + 6.9)\% = 11.9\%$.

The CAPM formula

The capital asset pricing model makes use of all the principles explained above. It can be stated as follows.

The expected return from an individual security equals the sum of:

♦ the risk-free rate of return;

and

♦ the beta factor multiplied by the difference between the expected return from the market as a whole and the risk-free rate of return.

The annotation typically used for this is as follows:

$E(r_j) = r_f + \beta_j \times (E(r_m) - r_f)$

where $E(r_j)$ is the expected return from an individual security

  r_f is the risk-free rate of return

  β_j is the beta factor of the individual security

  $E(r_m)$ is the expected return from the market as a whole.

Applying this, suppose that IFS plc's shares have a beta value of 0.7. The market return is 8% and the risk-free rate of return is 3%.

Under CAPM the expected return on IFS's shares is:

$3\% + 0.7 \times (8 - 3) \% = 6.5\%$.

14.4   Using CAPM

Predicting share prices

The CAPM can be used to predict the values of shares, not just find out the expected return on a share.

Suppose that A plc and B plc both provide an annual return to shareholders of 25p per share in perpetuity. The current average market rate of return is 10%. The risk-free rate of return is 4%. Company A's * factor is 1.2 and Company B's is 0.6.

We start by using this information to calculate the expected return from A and B.

- ◆ The expected return for A is 4% + 1.2 × (10% − 4%) = 11.2%
- ◆ The expected return for B is 4% + 0.6 × (10% − 4%) = 7.6%

The valuation model that we introduced in the last chapter can now be used to derive expected share prices.

- ◆ The predicted value of a share in A is $\dfrac{25p}{0.112}$ = 223p

- ◆ The predicted value of a share in B is $\dfrac{25p}{0.076}$ = 329p

In practice the actual share prices of A and B might be higher or lower than 223p and 329p. If so, CAPM analysis indicates that the shares are currently either overpriced or underpriced.

Finding the beta value

Betas are clearly a useful tool in the context of business valuation and you'll be glad to know that you do not need to collect large amounts of share price data or be an expert in statistics to find out the beta factor of a company you are interested in.

If business valuation is a significant part of your job it is likely that your organization will subscribe to an on-line information service such as those provided by Reuters, LexisNexis, Merrill Lynch, Save and Prosper, and similar companies. These give up-to-the-minute information about betas, based on the latest movements in the individual and overall stock market prices.

Failing that, there are more accessible (though less complete and up-to-date) free sources for information about betas, such as Yahoo!Finance, as illustrated below.

Judging from this illustration do you think the shares of the company in question were more or less volatile than the market as a whole, at the time when the information was captured? Why might this be?

Business valuations and CAPM

CAPM might typically be used to value a business when a company is obtaining a stock market listing. We will look at a final example that pulls together many of the ideas and techniques that you have learned about in Chapters 12 and 13 as well as this one.

Suppose that Plato plc is going to obtain admission to the London Stock Exchange by offering 40% of its 10 million existing shares to the public. No new shares will be issued. Its most recent results are as follows.

	£m
Turnover	350.00
Earnings	4.35

The company has low gearing.

It regularly pays out 60% of its earnings as dividends. It is expected to achieve 2% dividend growth each year.

Two listed companies have been identified that are in the same industry as Plato plc, and the following information is available.

	Aristotle plc	**Diogenes plc**
Gearing (total debt/total equity)	40%	12%
Equity beta	1.40	0.82

The current yield on Treasury bills is 5% a year. The average market return is 9%.

To increase the chances of a successful take-up the new shares will be issued at a discount of 20%.

What will the issue price be?

Solution

Using the CAPM, we must first estimate a suitable β value for Plato. In the absence of other information we will assume that since Plato's gearing is low its systematic risk is most similar to that of Diogenes plc. Therefore a β of 0.82 is appropriate.

The cost of Plato's equity is 5% + (0.82 x (9 − 5))% = 8.28%

This can now be used in the dividend growth model. The dividend this year is 60% of £4,350,000 = £2,610,000. This is expected to grow by 2% per year.

The total value of Plato's equity is $\dfrac{£2,610,000\ (1.02)}{(0.0828 - 0.02)} = £42,391,720$

There are 10,000,000 shares and so the market value per share is £4.24 but the shares will be offered at a discount of 20% to this value, so the share price for the market launch should be 80% of £4.24 = £3.39.

Summary

Now that you have completed this chapter you should be able to:

♦ **explain the concepts underlying the capital asset pricing model and use the model to value a business.**

Appendix 1

Discounted cash flows

Discounting and compounding

This appendix is included for the benefit of those readers who are not familiar with the concepts of discounted cash flows and present values, which are relevant in a variety of contexts in this book.

The time value of money

If you give it a moment's thought you will see that £100 received in one year's time is worth less than £100 received today. The value of money reduces over time, and the further into the future we go the lower the value of any given sum.

The reasons why we prefer money now rather than later are threefold:

♦ risk;
♦ investment return forgone; and
♦ inflation.

Risk is important because we can be certain of the spending power of money received today, but not of that received in the future. Even worse, we cannot be certain of getting the cash in the future, and so having it now is much less risky.

Cash invested today will earn interest, but that interest will be less if there is a delay in receiving the cash in the first place. The value of the forfeited interest means that we value future receipts less than current receipts.

Inflation erodes spending power and so, if we have to wait to receive cash, we will find that any given sum of money will buy less for us in the future.

Adjusting for changes in the value of money over time can be done via either discounting or compounding. Discounting converts future amounts into present values, and so it is the exact reverse of compounding, a procedure that most of us remember from school. We will start by looking at compounding, before moving on to present-value calculations.

Compounding

If £1,000 is placed on deposit in a bank and the annual interest payable is compounded at a rate of 5%, the value of the deposit increase over time as follows.

End of Year 1: Value = (£1,000 × 1.05)

= £1,050.00

End of Year 2: Value = (£1,050 × 1.05)

= £1,102.50

End of Year 3: Value = (£1,102.5 × 1.05)

= £1,157.625

and so on.

It is possible to work out the value of the sum on deposit at the end of any future year by using this long-hand approach to the calculation. The disadvantage of the approach is that it is increasingly time-consuming the further into the future we wish to go.

An alternative way of computing the future value is to use the formula for compound interest that is shown below.

Sum receivable in year n = Sum deposited in Year 1 × $(1 + r)^n$

Here, r denotes the interest rate expressed as a decimal (eg 5% is 0.05), and n denotes the future year for which the value is sought.

For example, suppose you make bank deposit of £1,000 now (this is frequently referred to as Time 0 or t0) and interest is receivable at 5% per annum.

Value in year 10 (t10)   = £1,000 × $(1.05)^{10}$

= £1,000 × 1.629

= £1,629

Using a calculator

If you have never used power functions on a calculator before except for squaring a number, the process is quite simple.

♦ On a scientific calculator *bought recently* you are likely to have a function button marked ^ and to raise one number to the power of another you simply enter the first number, then the ^ button, then the power, then the equals button. So, if you want to know the value of $(1.05)^5$, then you enter 1.05 ^ 5 =. As you may know, the ^ symbol is also used for powers in spreadsheet formulas.

♦ On an older scientific calculator you are more likely to have a function button marked x^y. The 'y' denotes the power level to which you wish the number to be raised, so if you want to know the value of $(1.05)^5$, then the 'y' value is 5.

Discounting

You can perhaps now see that if the formula for the future value using compounding is re-arranged, the value of the present sum placed on deposit can be calculated, provided we know the future value and the interest rate. As with any equation, if we know the value of two out of three of the components, it is possible to derive the value of the third, unknown element.

Re-arranging the formula gives the following:

$$\text{Sum deposited in Year } 1 = \frac{\text{Sum receivable in Year } n}{(1 + r)^n}$$

Using the figures from the example above,

$$\frac{£1,629}{(1 + 0.05)^{10}} = \frac{£1,629}{1.629} = £1,000$$

If the net cash flows from an asset or investment – the 'future economic benefits', to use the jargon of accounting standards – are known or can be estimated, the discounting formula can be used to revalue them in terms of present-day prices. The present value can then be directly compared with other present-day amounts.

Perpetuities

A simpler formula exists where the same future economic benefits will be receivable every year for as long as can be foreseen. This is known as a perpetuity.

$$\frac{\text{Annual sum receivable}}{r}$$

For example if you and your descendants expect to save £10,000 per year for ever more and can invest it at 5% the present value is £10,000/0.05 = £200,000. This is because the larger the value of n, the smaller the present value becomes until it becomes infinitesimally small (eg the present value of £10,000 invested at 5% 285 years from now is less than a penny).

Cost of capital (r)

A value for r, the interest rate, or discount rate, or cost of capital is the hardest figure to obtain in practice. If we are compounding a present value forward, we can simply use the interest rate received on the investment, to obtain a future value. In the case of discounting it is not quite so simple. Instead of the interest rate received, r (the discount rate), represents the cost of the capital which has been used to fund the investment.

The cost of capital is not easy to calculate as it involves consideration of all the sources of funding used by a business. The various mechanisms for deriving a cost of capital/discount rate is outside the scope of this syllabus, although there is some discussion in Chapter 14. For the purposes of this course, you can assume that the figure for cost of capital will be given in the exam question.

In many cases in practice, firms choose to simplify their own decision making process by using what is termed a hurdle rate for investment decisions. The hurdle rate is the discount rate that is applied to all investment decisions in the business, and represents the rate of return sought by the company. As indicated earlier in this chapter, the rate of return must be at least equal to the cost of capital if the company is not to lose money on an investment.

Appendix 2

Draft Regulations on the Operating and Financial Review 2004

Objective and contents of the operating and financial review

The following schedule is included in the DTI's draft Regulations on the Operating and Financial Review (2004). At the time of publication these regulations were still subject to public consultation. It is possible that they have passed into law by the time you are reading this, but bear in mind that there may have been changes to the requirements set out below.

Review objective

An operating and financial review shall be a balanced and comprehensive analysis of:

(a) the development and performance of the business of the company and its subsidiary undertakings during the financial year;

(b) the position of the company and its subsidiary undertakings at the end of the year;

(c)   the main trends and factors underlying the development, performance and position of the business of the company and its subsidiary undertakings during the financial year; and

(d)   the main trends and factors that are likely to affect their future development, performance and position, prepared so as to enable the members of the company to assess the strategies adopted by the company and its subsidiary undertakings and the potential for those strategies to succeed.

Other general requirements

The review shall include:

(a)   a statement of the business, objectives and strategies of the company and its subsidiary undertakings;

(b)   a description of the resources available to the company and its subsidiary undertakings;

(c)   a description of the principal risks and uncertainties facing the company and its subsidiary undertakings; and

(d)   a description of the capital structure, treasury policies and objectives and liquidity of the company and its subsidiary undertakings.

Details of particular matters

The following paragraphs apply to an operating and financial review to the extent necessary to comply with the general requirements above.

The review shall include information about:

(a)   the employees of the company and its subsidiary undertakings;

(b)   environmental matters; and

(c)   social and community issues.

The review shall also include information about:

(a)   the persons with whom the company or its subsidiary undertakings have relations (whether contractual or otherwise) that are essential to the business of the company and its subsidiary undertakings; and

(b)   receipts from, and returns to, members of the company and its subsidiary undertakings in relation to shares held by them.

The review shall include analysis using financial and other key performance indicators, including information relating to environmental matters and employee matters.

The term 'key performance indicators' means the factors by reference to which the development, performance or position of the business of the company and its subsidiary undertakings can be measured most effectively.

The review shall, where appropriate, include references to, and additional explanations of, amounts included in the company's annual accounts.

Parent companies

If the company is a parent company, the review may, where appropriate, give greater emphasis to those matters that are significant to the company and its subsidiary undertakings taken as a whole.

Compliance with standards

The review must:

(a)   state whether it has been prepared in accordance with relevant reporting standards; and

(b)   contain particulars of, and reasons for, any departure from such standards.

Auditors' reports on operating and financial reviews

If an operating and financial review is prepared for the financial year for which the annual accounts are prepared, the auditors shall state in their report:

(a)   whether in their opinion the directors have prepared the review after due and careful enquiry;

(b)   whether in their opinion the information given in the operating and financial review is consistent with those accounts; and

(c)   whether any matters have come to their attention, in the performance of their functions as auditors of the company, which in their opinion are inconsistent with the information given in the operating and financial review.

Appendix 3

Current issues

The purpose of this appendix

The world of financial reporting is highly dynamic and unfortunately any book on the subject is likely to be out of date very quickly after publication.

In this appendix therefore we draw your attention to a number of known issues (as at mid-August 2004) where there are likely to be developments within the shelf-life of this book. We restrict our comments to matters that could possibly be relevant to your syllabus.

You can be fairly confident that nothing in this appendix will be examined in detail – unless, that is, you are advised otherwise by the IFS. If an exam question gives you the opportunity to show that you are aware of recent developments in a relevant context then mentioning them *briefly* in your answers cannot do you any harm.

For more information about current issues see the suggestions at the end of the syllabus for further reading: this lists various periodicals and websites that you may wish to consult.

IASB activities

Problems with IAS 39

IAS 39 *Financial Instruments: Recognition and Measurement* is highly complex and we only scratched the surface of it in Chapter 9 – hopefully we gave you enough information to understand the spirit of the standard, if not its very detailed provisions.

At the time of publication there is some doubt over whether IAS 39 on Financial Instruments will be among the set of standards that are fully accepted by the European Union as generally accepted accounting practice to be implemented by all EU listed companies from January 2005.

Some commentators and organizations – notably banks, securities companies and insurers – have expressed concerns that the 'fair value option' might be used inappropriately.

♦ Entities might apply the fair value option to financial assets or financial liabilities whose fair value is not verifiable. If so, because the valuation of these financial assets and financial liabilities is subjective, entities might determine their fair value in a way that inappropriately affects profit or loss.

♦ Use of the option might increase, rather than decrease, volatility in profit or loss, for example if an entity applied the option to only one part of a matched position.

♦ If an entity applied the fair value option to financial liabilities, it might result in the entity recognizing gains or losses in profit or loss for changes in its own creditworthiness.

The IASB has issued an exposure draft proposing changes to IAS 39 intended to address these concerns, but those proposals have not gained the approval of the European Financial Reporting Advisory Group (EFRAG) which advises the EU on accounting standards.

At the time of publication of this book it is impossible to draw any conclusions on how this debate will be resolved – if, indeed it is resolved at all.

The IASB has also recently issued proposed amendments to a number of other aspects of IAS 39; we consider these to be somewhat beyond the scope of your syllabus.

Exposure Draft ED 7 *Financial Instruments: Disclosures*

In late July 2004 the IASB issued an exposure draft that would add some new disclosures about financial instruments to those currently required by IAS 32, would replace the disclosures now required by IAS 30 (which deals with disclosure by banks, but is not in your syllabus), and would put all of these financial instruments disclosures together in a new standard.

IAS 32 would then deal only with financial instruments presentation matters.

Again this is relevant to Chapter 9 of this book.

Accounting standards for small and medium-sized entities

The IASB is currently consulting interested parties on whether it should develop accounting standards for small and medium-sized entities (SMEs).

Remember that as far as international standards are concerned it is only listed companies that will be required by the EU to adopt such standards from January 2005. The UK government has stated that it is considering allowing unlisted companies the option of using either UK or international standards.

The aims of the IASB project are that financial reporting standards for SMEs should:

(a) provide high quality, understandable and enforceable accounting standards suitable for SMEs globally;

(b) focus on meeting the needs of users of SME financial statements;

(c) be built on the same conceptual framework as IFRSs;

(d) reduce the financial reporting burden on SMEs that want to use global standards; and

(e) allow easy transition to full IFRSs for those SMEs that become publicly accountable or choose to switch to full IFRSs.

In the UK there is already a single *Financial Reporting Standard for Smaller Entities.* This includes all the accounting requirements and disclosures that apply to smaller companies and simplifies some of the disclosure requirements; smaller companies can follow the full UK standards if they wish.

At the time of publication of this book views on whether to proceed with this project are still being sought. Further developments are not likely until 2005. Given that many bankers are not involved with large public companies at all, but have many smaller clients that would potentially be affected by this, it is well worth keeping an eye out for any news.

Other projects

At any time the IASB is likely to have a considerable number of other projects in progress or under consideration. Currently these include the following matters that could be of particular relevance to items in your syllabus:

♦ issues surrounding recognition of revenue, liabilities and equity (relevant to most chapters);

♦ tightening up on the approach to recognition and measurement of intangible assets (relevant to Chapter 5);

♦ improving accounting for leasing, possibly requiring all leases to be treated as finance leases (relevant to Chapter 8); and

♦ various issues related to IFRS 3 *Business Combinations*, and IAS 27 *Consolidated Financial Statement* (relevant to Chapters 10 and 11).

Index